Safe Hands

• • • • • • • • • • • •

Safe Hands

My Autobiography

DAVID SEAMAN

ORION

First published in Great Britain in 2000 by Orion Media,
an imprint of the Orion Publishing Group Ltd,
Orion House, 5 Upper Saint Martin's Lane
London, WC2H 9EA

A CIP catalogue record for this book is available
from the British Library.

ISBN 0–75283–1836

Typeset by Deltatype Ltd, Birkenhead, Merseyside

Printed in Great Britain by
Clays Ltd, St Ives plc

My thanks to the following people for use of pictures:
Sheffield Newspapers Limited, Popperfoto, Associated Sports Photography,
Bob Thomas,
The Carlton Television Picture Desk, Action Images, PA Photo Library,
Ross-Parry Picture Agency, All Sport UK Ltd., OK magazine.

Contents

To my wife Debbie, my two sons Daniel and Thomas
and our baby daughter Georgina.

Acknowledgements

My thanks to:

Bob and Megs Wilson for all their encouragement and support during the last 12 years and especially to Bob for being the oldest Best Man ever.

Tony Peisley for the long hours he spent listening to my story and then unravelling it all for this book.

All my team-mates, past and present – with special thanks to the Arsenal back four.

All the fans who have supported us. Please keep it up because I haven't finished yet.

And finally . . .

Special thanks to my wife Debbie for putting my life in order . . . to Mum and Dad for being, well, Mum and Dad . . . and to my father-in-law Robbie and my late and much-missed mother-in-law Georgina.

Illustrations

Section One

1. Aged nine months.
2. With my younger brother Colin.
3. Aged seven.
4. As a teenager.
5. My mum and dad, Pam and Roger.
6. Attending the premiere of *Judge Dredd*, with Debbie.
7. Winning the *Elle* style award in 1998.
8. Fishing.
9. Golf.
10. With Debbie during Euro 96.
11. With Debbie on *Wish You Were Here . . . ?*
12. With Debbie, Colin and Mum and Dad.
13. Debbie and her mum, Georgina.
14. Debbie's dad, Robbie.
15. With Ian Wright, Paul Gascoigne and Paul Ince.
16. With Debbie on our wedding day.
17. With our daughter, Georgina.

Section Two

18. Playing for Birmingham against Sheffield Wednesday in 1986.
19. Joining Arsenal in 1990.
20. Enjoying our victory over Parma to win the European Cup-Winners Cup in 1994.

Section Three

I

· · · · · ·

Euro 2000 – Under Attack

Kevin Keegan's question was straight to the point – it had to be. 'Can you give a hundred per cent out there?'

I knew I would be left out of the side if I told him I couldn't, but I had to be honest. 'No,' I admitted – and promptly burst into tears.

Crying's not something grown men from Rotherham make a habit of doing in public and it surprised even me just how upset I felt but this was no ordinary game. It was England's final game in the qualifying round at Euro 2000, and we needed just a draw against Romania at Charleroi in Belgium to go through to face Italy in the quarter-finals.

What made it worse for me was that, 15 minutes before kick-off, I was fit and as 'up' as I have been for any game in my career. I was just finishing my warm-up out on the pitch when I stooped to pick up a shot and felt a tweak in my hamstring. I tested it on another couple of shots and could feel it pulling.

I came off straightaway and told our goalkeeping coach Ray Clemence what had happened. He sent me off to see the medical team. They did a few tests on my leg and agreed with me that I had a problem.

By then, it was only a few minutes before the team was due to go out on to the pitch for the kick-off. My name was on the team sheet that Kevin had already given to the officials and the media.

It was tempting to give the injury a try in the game but, if I couldn't shake it off and had to come off, it would mean Kevin having to use up one of his three substitutions. These days, particularly at international level, managers usually need every one of these for tactical reasons just as much as for injuries.

So I was honest and suddenly Leeds United's Nigel Martyn found himself in the team. And, through my tears of disappointment, it crossed my mind that all my critics had, thanks to a freak injury, finally got their way.

I had been England's undisputed number one goalie for most of the Nineties, but the tabloid press had decided I was past it and had been rooting for Nigel to take over at Euro 2000. As the tournament began, I had never felt under so much pressure since I started playing for England, but then neither, I suspect, had the rest of the team.

This was roughly the same group of players who had played well and been unlucky not to have gone further at the 1998 World Cup in France, and some of us had even become national heroes during Euro 96. But some people have short memories.

Just about as short as the careers of modern England managers, in fact. Immediately after Euro 96, Terry Venables was out and Glenn Hoddle was in. Then, after the World Cup, Hoddle was out and Kevin Keegan was in.

If you want a team to develop and progress, this is hardly the way to go about it. What made it worse was that, with Terry and Glenn, the main reasons for their departures had nothing to do with what had happened on the pitch. In both tournaments preceding their exits, England had played well – certainly better than most of the critics had expected.

Kevin had taken over part-way through our qualifying games to make the Euro 2000 finals, so it was hardly surprising that our form had been in and out, to say the least. We only qualified through the play-offs, where we squeezed past Scotland over two games.

We were still delighted to have made it, but the press seemed almost to resent the fact and spent most of the run-up to Euro 2000 rubbishing Kevin and the team, with Alan Shearer and myself singled out for particular attention.

Alan took a lot more stick than I did and, knowing how much I was hurt by the criticism, I can only imagine what it did to Alan. He handled it brilliantly and never let it affect him out on the pitch, although it was obviously a factor in his decision to retire from international football after the tournament.

For my part, I could not understand why I was suddenly under attack. The 1999–2000 season had not started well for me because I had a recurring injury which kept me out of the Arsenal side for two long spells. A goalie is just like any outfield player, he needs games to become match fit, so it took me until the second half of the season to be right back on my game.

Arsenal had the same kind of season: a slow and inconsistent first half which saw us off the pace in the Premiership and failing to get through our qualifying group in the Champions League; then a great run at the end of the season, going 12 games unbeaten before losing the very last game at Newcastle with a weakened side as we prepared for the UEFA Cup Final.

We finished second in the Premiership and qualified for the Champions League. But we were a long way behind Manchester United and we would not have argued with those who suggested that, with the quality in our squad, we had under-achieved. But finishing second in the Premiership and reaching a European cup final is hardly a bad season.

The games included a clean sheet in the UEFA Cup Final against Turkish side Galatasaray in Copenhagen. However, it was not enough to win the cup, as – not for the first time in my career – I was involved in a penalty shoot-out. More often than not I have been able to play my part in winning these, but not this time.

But it should not have come down to penalties. Copenhagen had been a lucky place for us once before, when we beat Parma there to win the European Cup-Winners Cup, and could well have been again.

We knew Galatasaray were a good side. In the semi-final, they had beaten Leeds United, the club I supported as a boy and joined as a young player. But we felt we had a better squad and our good run at the end of the season had given us extra confidence. Maybe too much, in fact, as we never really imposed ourselves on the game.

Some of our best players did not perform to their ability, while the whole Galatasaray team worked very hard throughout. They swamped the midfield, had more possession and probably edged the game, although we had more shots on target and the best chances.

In normal time, Martin Keown made a great tackle to save a goal, but almost immediately scooped over an open goal at the other end.

Kanu also came on as substitute and had a good shot well saved. But the best chance for either side came in the 'Golden Goal' extra-time period when Thierry Henry's far post header from Ray Parlour's cross was brilliantly saved by their goalie Taffarel.

But the Turks had to play with ten men for most of extra time after their star player, the Romanian Hagi, was sent off after a tussle with Tony Adams. Hagi pulled Tony back, Tony flung his arm back to push him off and the Romanian raised his arm to half punch and half push Tony.

The sending-off was a bit harsh, but it did not cost them in the end because we could not make our advantage count.

I can't really put my finger on why we didn't play our best. It may have just been the pressure there always is in the run-up to a major game. It affects players in different ways. Sometimes even top players freeze and have stinkers, and that is certainly one reason why so many cup finals are disappointing games.

When it came to the penalty shoot-out, Galatasaray had a definite advantage because they were shooting at the end filled by the Turkish fans. It did not affect me, as I was not facing them and, in any case, they kept quiet when their players were taking them, but our players were looking straight at the Turkish fans, who were making a hell of a noise to put them off.

It isn't easy to take a pressure kick under those circumstances. What made it worse was that the referee chose where the penalties were taken rather than having a coin-toss for ends. I did hear afterwards that it was because Tony had won the toss for ends in extra time but, if that's true, it is a complete nonsense. There is no real advantage to which way you play in extra time but a clear one when it comes to the shoot-out.

When someone as experienced and as good a striker of the ball as Davor Suker misses, as he did when he hit the post with our first spot-kick, you know you're in trouble. Ray Parlour scored, but he was the only one for us and we went down 4–1.

There had been a great atmosphere at the game. Both sets of fans were very noisy and I can remember this Turkish drum going non-stop throughout the game. But the violence before the game was some of the worst I had seen. We were in the hotel but we watched it

4

on Sky and also on the local Danish TV, where we saw a lot worse incidents than were shown on Sky or back in the UK.

It was all a hangover from the murder of the two Leeds fans in Istanbul and I heard that there were a lot of English hooligans in Copenhagen who weren't Arsenal fans. It's impossible to say whether Arsenal fans were involved or not, but until then our fans had behaved well in Europe. We certainly hadn't had any problems like that in previous matches.

But, sadly, what happened in Copenhagen was to set the tone for the summer: more trouble with fans, more penalties and more disappointing results.

Yet it all started pretty well. England had three friendlies lined up before Euro 2000, and the first, at Wembley, was against the team still rated as the world's best: Brazil.

We started well and Michael Owen scored a good goal, which he really needed as there had been so much speculation about his fitness after his recurring hamstring problems during the season. Although Brazil equalised before half-time, we more than held our own for the rest of the game and fully deserved the draw.

But I couldn't believe it when I read the papers the following day. For most of the season, there had been a lot of press comment suggesting Nigel Martyn should replace me as England's Number One, but I thought my displays in the two Scotland games had been good enough to keep them quiet.

The Brazil goal had come from a Rivaldo corner. Our marking was poor as I came for the cross but it was hit with so much pace that I couldn't reach it. Sol Campbell misjudged it as well and it went over his head straight to the Brazilian striker Franca, who was completely unmarked as he headed it past Gary Neville on the line.

I had made a small error of judgement coming for the cross, but I still managed to readjust my body to cover the header and, if Gary hadn't moved a yard off his post, he would have cleared it. I did make a mistake but it wasn't a terrible one. But, if you believed the reports, I had thrown the ball in the net myself. If not before, it became clear to me then that some reporters had their own agenda.

Kevin's attitude was brilliant, though. He took me aside and told me I was his Number One whatever the press said, and that he would play me in our opening Euro 2000 game against Portugal. That was all I needed to know.

I didn't play in the other two friendlies, though. Kevin had already told me Nigel would play in one of them, and so I was not surprised when he was picked for the second, again at Wembley, against the Ukraine.

Kevin tried playing with three centre-backs instead of 4–4–2 for that one and, although we looked a bit exposed defensively at times and Nigel had to make a few good saves, it was another fine performance overall, even if the 2–0 win flattered us slightly.

But, with the two other injury doubts Robbie Fowler and Tony Adams both scoring, it was another good day at the office for Kevin.

We then flew out to Malta for the final friendly. We were always going to be on a hiding to nothing in this one. Because of the quality of the opposition, we were expected to win easily, yet it was in all the players' minds that they didn't want to pick up a knock with the tournament starting in just a week.

Predictably we struggled to win 2–1 and the third-string goalie, Richard Wright, had an eventful first game for England. He gave away a penalty which had to be taken twice, with the second kick rebounding off him and going in for an own-goal.

Almost exactly the same thing had happened to him in the First Division play-off final a week earlier, but his club, Ipswich, had recovered to win, and so did we with goals from Martin Keown and Emile Heskey and a penalty save from Richard in the last minute.

But, although we won, the press conveniently forgot the Brazil and Ukraine performances and rubbished the team, Kevin and our chances in the tournament.

We flew back to England and had a few days at home before flying out to Belgium and settling into our base, the Hotel Balmoral in the small town of Spa.

It was unusual to be in the middle of town and not tucked away in the countryside, as we have been for other tournaments, but it really didn't make much difference because we were pretty much confined to barracks.

The hotel had a decent games room and Kevin, who likes the horses himself, had made sure there was a big-screen TV to show some horseracing. The lads got into that quite seriously, with Dennis Wise making a fair few calls to his bookie.

Wisey was great fun to have around and the spirit was good between the players, although there was no holding back in training. The squad had been cut back to the final 22, but everybody knew there were places still up for grabs in the first XI.

There was one tackle between Gareth Southgate and Steven Gerrard that could have been heard back at Villa Park and on the Kop. They met either side of the ball simultaneously – it was fair but very, very hard.

What I didn't think was fair was the stick I was now getting in the press from former goalies Gordon Banks, Peter Shilton and John Burridge.

Banks had already had a go at me during the season, suggesting I was past my best, and I had half a mind to take it up with him when some of the 1966 World Cup-winning team visited us in Spa. But I decided to pay him the respect he deserves.

I was friendly and did not mention what he had said, but then the next day in the paper there he was, having another go at me.

Shilts was then quoted as saying I was in the worst form of my life. Excuse me, but I'd just played for a team that had come second in the Premiership and reached the final of the UEFA Cup. Maybe I'm kidding myself, but it does not seem very likely that a team would achieve that with their goalie playing badly.

I am old enough and experienced enough to take most criticism in my stride, but this was beginning to get to me. Maybe Banks and Shilts had been misquoted but, if they were, they never rang to put things right with me. If they really said those things, they should have known better.

And it wasn't just me. The criticism of Kevin and of other individual players in the squad was not helping our confidence at a critical stage.

We all knew it was vital not to lose the first game, because of the pressure it would put on us for the next one. As the second game was against Germany, there was going to be enough pressure on that result already.

With all this in his mind, I was not surprised when Kevin opted to stick with 4–4–2, as this is what most of us were used to playing week in, week out in the Premiership.

As I will explain later in the book, I have played behind three centre-backs from time to time at Arsenal and know it can work as well as the usual four across the back, but some of our squad had rarely played in that system.

Playing 4–4–2 can be a problem when the other team has just one striker, but I am a great believer in imposing the system we want to play on the other side.

Unfortunately, that is exactly what we did *not* do against Portugal.

Even though we made a great start going forward, scoring two goals through Paul Scholes and Steve McManaman from superb David Beckham crosses, we were constantly under pressure in midfield and at the back. In fact, I can't remember having a busier half in an international. They were running through us, having shots on goal and getting dangerous crosses in from both sides.

If I'm honest, Portugal did take us slightly by surprise. We knew they had good players and what style they would play, but they did surprise us in just how well they played. After all, Portuguese sides have always had good technical players but they have rarely gelled into a real force in a tournament.

At 1–0 up, I had to make a flying save from Rui Costa and deal with a series of crosses. I couldn't reach one fierce centre and they should have scored, but Joao Pinto's downward header bounced over the bar. We then went 2–0 up, but they didn't change the way they were playing at all and it paid off.

Luis Figo ran straight at us, we backed off and he hit a screamer. It looked bad for me because I didn't move for it as it went high into the corner of the net on my left side.

When I watched it on the video, I saw that my weight was all on my right side because, from Figo's body shape as he hit it, I thought it was coming more or less straight at me. But it took an immediate deflection off Tony's heel and, as it was moving so fast, I had no chance to readjust.

The second goal came because we did not close down their players when they had the ball out wide. It was far too easy for them to cross the ball. Joao Pinto got in front of Sol and I had no chance with his flying header but, when it went in off the post, I can remember thinking why was it happening to me again? There seemed to have been more deflected and in-off goals against me than I can remember in any season I'd played.

We were lucky to go in all-square at half-time, so completely were we over-run in midfield, so Kevin's team talk was all about being more compact and defending better throughout the side. Part of the plan was to cut out playing the ball about in our own half. Instead, the onus was on me to kick it long. We wanted to be scrapping for the ball in their half and not ours.

We had a bit of joy with this tactic in the second half, but then they scored and from then on they could just sit back and protect their lead. We had a few half-chances but, by the end, we were chasing the game and just couldn't get hold of the ball. Frankly, they looked more like scoring than we did.

That killer third goal had been so frustrating because the ball had gone across Tony, leaving their lone striker Nuno Gomes clear on goal. I couldn't be sure whether Tony was going to get back to him so I had to come out. Tony reckoned he was just half an inch away from getting a block in, but Gomes just got his shot away – an excellent one across me, giving me no chance.

And 'no chance' was exactly what the press thought we had of qualifying after that result. I was even being criticised in the Spanish press. One report described me as 'a piece of meat with eyes' and suggested that England would be better off without me – but, then, the Spanish have never forgiven me for the penalty saves which knocked them out of Euro 96. And, given the mistakes the Spanish goalie made during Euro 2000, they were hardly in a position to criticise.

I could laugh off the Spanish stick, but the British press were becoming beyond a joke. Every competition I have played in for England, there has been the same relentless criticism. It is always the same reporters and they seem to be getting worse.

The fact is that Portugal were a very good side. Even so we scored twice against them and they had to play some excellent football to beat us, but our press just preferred to say we were crap.

It is no wonder that England squads have begun to build up a siege mentality. Gareth Southgate was reported as saying that some players were beginning to wonder whether playing for England was worth all the stick that came with it, and I can well believe it.

I will always want to play for England, but I can't pretend that it is always a pleasant experience any more. Mind you, I heard during the tournament that at least 13 of the French squad were refusing to speak to any journalists at all, so it is obviously not just an English problem.

Kevin has always been good with the media, but even he went ballistic with them in the run-up to the Germany game. Sky had edited an interview with Les Reed, whose job for Kevin was to prepare detailed reports on the sides we were due to play. The way Sky cut and used it, they had him just saying that Lothar Matthaus was old and very slow.

In fact, Les had said that Matthaus was still a great player but was obviously slower now and maybe we could exploit that. However, by highlighting just half a sentence, they had made it look as though the England team were deliberately rubbishing a German player. It was the sort of comment that could easily have wound up a side like Germany and made them play even harder against us.

Keegan told Sky that he had thought the TV people were the only ones left he and his team could trust, because they didn't distort interviews the way the newspapers did, and now here were Sky starting to do exactly the same thing.

I don't think it is a coincidence that the only half-decent performance we put on at Euro 2000 was for the German game, when the press did make some attempt to get behind us. They were really forced into this by the nation as a whole, which was desperate for us to beat the Germans for the first time in a competitive game since 1966.

This really came through to us and it did give us a lift to feel that, for once, everyone was behind us. We were also wound up by seeing that a German TV station, which we could pick up at our hotel, was replaying the Euro 96 semi-final. We had lost that game despite outplaying them, so seeing it again gave us an extra incentive.

We were disappointed by the way we had played against Portugal and it did knock our confidence, which had not been that high anyway going into Euro 2000, but we did believe that, if we could beat the Germans and then go on to qualify from the group, we could still go a long way in the competition.

Our confidence would be boosted by qualifying and some of the pressure would be lifted because we would have achieved the minimum expected of us. Also, whatever the press says, we do have good players who have played in Europe and won tournaments with their club sides.

Since the first game, most of our training talk had been about defending and making our team shape more compact. Playing well was not about everyone pushing forward; we had to remember we all had a duty to defend as well.

There was no question, though, of changing our overall tactics for Germany and we did receive a boost when their main striker, Oliver Bierhoff, was ruled out with an injury. On the other hand, we were missing Tony and Macca, who had both picked up injuries against Portugal.

We had travelled to Eindhoven in the Netherlands for the Portugal game, but we were playing Germany at Charleroi, in a stadium which had been criticised for being too small, old and ramshackle for such a big game.

If it had been as bad as some papers suggested, it would not have survived that evening because it was one of the noisiest crowds I have ever played in front of, with the England fans outnumbering, outsinging and outshouting the Germans throughout.

Watching the TV film afterwards, we could see that they had literally made the stands shudder. The shadows on the pitch proved that the noise had even shaken the floodlights.

The fans had made an impressive noise during the Portugal game but that had been marred by some idiots by the tunnel who poured abuse on some of the players at the end of the match.

Afterwards it was reported that it was all aimed at Becks, who had given them the finger back, but I walked off with Phil Neville behind me and they gave him some terrible stick, too. As they had ignored me and most of the other players, I can only imagine they were targeting Man Utd players.

But we had one hundred per cent support against Germany and we needed it. We were so determined to stay tight that for half an hour we hardly created a chance, but then Michael Owen had a great header well saved by Oliver Kahn and it lifted the whole team. Paul Scholes had two great shots and we were well on top as we went in at half-time.

Kevin just told us to keep the momentum going but still to stay tight and hold our shape. After the interval, neither side looked like scoring at first, but then Alan found some space at the far post to score with a clever header from Becks's free-kick.

It was then a question of hanging on for the last half an hour or so. It wasn't pretty, and we took more stick for that, but I thought it was inevitable. Our confidence wasn't high and then there was the history of our games with Germany.

Before the game I thought we could win, but in the back of my mind was their record against us and the thought that they might get their usual little bit of luck and destroy our chances once again. And you can bet I was not the only one in our side thinking that.

They created few chances from open play and it was their corners that gave us our main problem throughout. From one in the second half, they had their best chance of the game. It was poor marking again and the ball was flicked to one side of me. I just thought, 'Get something, anything, in the way' and stuck out my standing leg, the left one. I blocked it, but it rebounded straight to Carsten Jancker, the huge forward who had replaced Bierhoff.

There was no challenge, so he had a free shot from just a few yards out but, when he hit it, I knew I had my part of the goal covered so that it would hit either me or Phil Neville on the line or else go wide. Unlike the rest of the country, I was not too worried as I watched it go past the post.

We did put pressure on ourselves by giving the ball away, but still managed to hang on, and everyone watching could see just how much winning the game meant to us by the way we reacted at the end. It felt like winning a cup, and the three points did mean we could still qualify from our group. Most of all, though, it meant we had at last beaten Germany in a game that really mattered.

It might not have been the best German team of all time but they had made their reputation by winning tournaments with 'poor' teams. Few reporters mentioned the fact that Germany had only lost one game in a whole year before we beat them.

After the game, it was fantastic to put on the TV and see people in the fountains at Trafalgar Square – just like at Euro 96 (of which much more later). It was a great feeling to know that we had delivered what the nation had wanted and it was only a pity that some of the English who had come to Belgium did not know how to celebrate.

I was appalled at the behaviour of some of these so-called fans, but I can't pretend that I know the solution to the kind of hooliganism that follows us around. I was not surprised when it came out that most of those arrested and deported were not known to our police. After all, every year new, younger hooligans start following the example of their older brothers and friends.

I do think our governments – past and present – could have done more. I think what Germany did in removing passports from potential trouble-makers was sending out the right kind of message. But it is not an answer in itself. Most of those causing the trouble were not even going to the games, they were just there to cause trouble, much as they would be doing outside pubs and clubs on a Friday or Saturday night back in England.

But it is so shaming to the country when they export their violence. At Euro 2000, it led to UEFA threatening to throw England out of the tournament. Before our final group game against Romania, the Football Association's Chief Executive Adam Crozier came and spoke to us.

He assured us that there was no way UEFA would carry out its threat and that the only way we would be going home would be if the FA itself decided to withdraw England from the tournament – or if we lost to Romania.

So, our minds put at rest on one issue, we were left to focus on the game and our return to Charleroi.

Looking back, there is no doubt the tension was getting to all of us. I can remember that Nigel, Richard and I were all feeling unusually tired on the day before the game. We had not been doing more than we would usually do, but the ups and downs of the

Portugal and Germany games and all the media attention had used up a lot of our nervous energy, I think.

At Charleroi, Nigel and Richard went out on to the pitch earlier than me and did a fair bit of diving about. As I was playing in the match, I went out later and just did my usual warm-up.

But it was at the end of this that I did my hamstring, not the beginning when I might have been cold. I have never done anything like it in a warm-up before a game and have never had to pull out of the side at such a late stage in all my long career.

It was the shock of this, and the realisation that I was going to miss such a big match and maybe – you never know in this game – my last chance of helping England win something, that brought on the tears.

Paul Ince, my closest friend in the squad, came up and said it would be OK because they were going to get the result we needed and I would have more chances to play in the tournament.

I tried to wish Nigel luck, but wasn't at my best, and I'm not sure how much help I was to him when he suddenly found himself playing just a few minutes before kick-off.

I missed the great save he made from an early Romanian free-kick because I was in the shower and I was still there when they scored through Christian Chivu. When I saw the TV replay, I couldn't believe it when it was suggested the goal was somehow Nigel's fault.

Chivu's chip was definitely meant as a cross, but it went in off the woodwork at the far post and there was no way in the world Nigel could either have positioned himself for a fluke like that or got across to it when it happened. Maybe our defenders could have closed players down better when the original corner went beyond the far post, but no one who knew anything about goalkeeping would point the finger at Nigel.

I watched the rest of the first half on TV with one of the Belgian groundstaff and our physio in a small room below the stand. When Incey went through and won a penalty and then Michael sprinted through for our second goal, that room exploded.

When the team came in at half-time, Incey and Kevin both asked me if I was OK and I just said: 'I am now.'

The team talk was obviously easier than it might have been

because of the way we had played right at the end of the half, turning 0–1 into 2–1 up.

As we only needed a draw, we just had to play sensibly and we were through, but we seemed to panic. To be fair, we conceded a goal just a couple of minutes into the second half. If we had kept it at 2–1 for 20 minutes, I am sure we would have gone on to win or at least draw the game.

The goal was a strange one because Nigel came for a cross and, having got both hands to it, chose to punch rather than catch it.

I can only imagine he was expecting a challenge but, whatever he was thinking, he was unlucky that the punch went straight to a Romanian player. In the German game, I had to punch a cross away one-handed and didn't get too much distance on it, but fortunately it landed in a group of players and in the scramble the German shot wide.

Unfortunately for Nigel (and the rest of us) the Romanian Munteanu controlled it and volleyed a great shot just past his dive. After that, we just defended too deep and the team was stretched again. Just as happened against Portugal, we didn't defend as a team. I know some of the players, particularly Wisey, were suffering badly from blistered feet, but we still should have kept the ball much better.

Even so, we looked as though we were going to hang on. With a couple of minutes to go, I can remember sitting next to Ray Clemence on the bench and seeing that the former Coventry striker Moldovan was getting past Phil Neville on the byline. I was just shouting: 'Stand up, Phil, stand up.' Then his tackle went in and it was 'Oh shit' – I just knew that a penalty would be given.

Somehow penalties seem to follow England, Arsenal and me around. I have won some, lost some with spot-kicks, but this was the first time I had been involved when I had absolutely no chance of influencing the outcome.

From the bench, it was impossible to judge which way the penalty was going to go. Later, having watched it on the TV replay, I reckoned I would have guessed right from Ganea's run-up and dived to my left, but who knows whether I would have saved it?

I can't deny that, as I watched the drama take place, a very tiny part of me was thinking that, if Nigel did save it, he would be the hero and I might not get back in the team, but obviously I wanted him to save it. If he didn't, we were all going home.

He dived right, the ball went left and the rest is history.

After the game, Kevin just told us that he was proud of the commitment and effort we showed. There was no shortage of either, but he didn't have to tell us that we hadn't played anywhere near as well as we could in any of the games – although it was the result, not the performance, that mattered against Germany.

It was hard to escape the feeling that most of the press were happy we were out – it made a better story and proved them all right, after all. But I wonder if they realise just how much their constant criticism can affect the confidence of individual players and of the team as a whole. I can't believe that this is what they want to achieve, but maybe it is.

When I was ringing my mum and dad from the tournament, I could tell that all the criticism of me in the papers back home was really getting to them, and that upset me even more.

But there is no way I will give my critics the satisfaction of letting them make my decisions for me. So long as I believe I am playing well for club and country, I want to keep on doing both. One of my proudest moments was captaining my country (against Moldavia in 1997), but I don't want or expect to be picked on sentiment. If I believe I am still worth my place, I shall be aiming to play in the next World Cup in 2002.

I just hope the organisers of that tournament do not make the same mistake of choosing the event to introduce a completely new rule. Replacing the four-step rule for goalies with a six-second rule was a recipe for disaster. I can remember, the first time I had the ball in my hands in the Portugal game, thinking, 'What do I do now?' I started to bounce the ball the way goalies used to years back before the steps rule, and then I realised that I didn't have to – I could just run with it.

Fortunately, Euro 2000 was generally well refereed and I think they made allowances for goalies trying to adjust to the new rule.

It was also daft to introduce the new, much lighter Adidas ball. I was lucky because I had a chance to get used to it in the UEFA Cup Final, adjusting to the way it moves a lot more and much faster in the air. It would make more sense if these major changes were introduced at the start of the season in club league games and not in such a high-profile tournament.

But England may not have to worry about new rules or new balls at the next World Cup – we have it all to do just to qualify after the disappointment of Euro 2000.

Changes will have to be made, but, not, I hope, to the manager. The FA chose Kevin, and they must give him a chance to see the job through. The last thing we need now is yet another upheaval.

But there is no doubt that the shape of the team was never right at Euro 2000. The lack of left-sided players gave us real problems defending and going forward. None of the players who played wide on the left for us – Wisey, Macca or even Nicky Barmby when he came on – is a natural left-footer.

For the World Cup qualifiers, we must play with one, whether it is a fit again Graeme Le Saux, Jason Wilcox, Steve Guppy or young Gareth Barry.

Looking longer term, I put the case later in this book for having a midwinter break in our game, as they do in so many other countries, and having a look at limiting the number of foreign players in Premiership teams.

But for now I think some of our problems are exaggerated. The big complaint from the press after Euro 2000 was that our players are way behind other countries in their individual skills and technique.

These, remember, are the same players who destroyed Holland and outplayed the Germans in Euro 96 and stood toe to toe with the Argentinians in the 1998 World Cup. And as recently as 1990 an England side was a hair's breadth away from making the World Cup Final.

I think it is fair to say that some teams – like Portugal – have made more progress than we have recently because their players are now playing for top clubs all over Europe, but the idea that we have fallen miles behind is a myth. It was only two seasons ago that Man Utd won the Champions League with a predominantly British squad including four of the current England side.

It might not seem probable or even possible that England could win in 2002, but look at the Dutch, a side we murdered in '96, and the way they played in Euro 2000 on their way to the semi-final. They started without much confidence in their first game after indifferent results in the run-up and a critical press. But they had a lucky break with a penalty two minutes from the end of a game in which they had been outplayed by the Czech Republic.

They improved in the second game and then, with the fans getting right behind them, they played out of their skins beating France and Yugoslavia and would have made the final and maybe won it if they hadn't missed two penalties against Italy in the semi-final.

If England can just get on that kind of a roll again, we do have the ability to win things.

And, when I look back on my life and career, it teaches me that you should never rule anything out. I have had an amazing journey so far – who's to say it won't end with England World Cup winners in 2002? Stranger things have already happened.

2

• • • • •

Playing It Safe

I don't think I was cut out for a life of crime.

It was hardly going to be the biggest or most original heist – even for Rotherham – but then we were just a gang of hard-up lads looking for a way to make a few bob. A mate suggested stealing lead off the youth hostel roof and selling it down the local scrapyard. At the time it seemed as good an idea as anything else. Except, when we all got up on the roof, I immediately got cold feet and left the others to it while I went down to the street to be look-out.

A rotten look-out, as it turned out. I was anxiously looking up at my two mates on the roof, paying absolutely no attention to the street, when three police cars suddenly appeared outside. It must have been a particularly quiet night for crime in my Yorkshire hometown. Before any of us knew what was happening, my two mates were nicked.

I froze where I was until one of the coppers finally spotted me. 'You anything to do with these lads?' he asked me. There was none of that 'honour among thieves' principle from me. 'No, never seen them before,' I said quickly. They let me go and I shot off home.

But an hour later there was a knock on the door and standing outside was a policeman. My mates had grassed me up. Who could blame them? To begin with my mum wasn't particularly bothered about having a policeman come to her door. My parents were running a sandwich shop at the time and the police were always in and out as customers. She even knew this particular officer and was completely taken aback when he said, 'It's about your lad David, Pam.'

She asked him if he was sure he meant me and not my brother

Colin, as he was the one who got up to more mischief, but the copper said, 'No, it's definitely David because the one we want has got dark hair.' Mum immediately said, 'But David's fair.'

At that moment, I came downstairs. I'd been in the bath and my hair was wet. Mum looked and realised all of a sudden how dark my hair had gone. Like all mothers, she still thought of me as a little boy (probably still does) and, because I'd been born blond, that's the way she still thought of me, even though by then I was a strapping teenager.

I owned up immediately, although I always told my parents that I had just been a passer-by when these lads had called me up to help them 'reach something'. I don't know whether they believed that story or not but they just couldn't believe I'd been so stupid as to get into that kind of trouble – and not just because we'd been caught trying to lift the lead from a roof in full view of a busy road. Their real worry was that I'd ruined my chances of making it as a professional footballer. I had just been invited to join Leeds United.

The police were told all this and, at the station, in front of my dad, which made it worse, the inspector gave me the biggest telling off I'd ever had in my life. I was let off with a caution and, although I was a big lad, I was still a young one and the whole business frightened me to death. I decided there and then that a career in crime was not for me.

Fortunately, I already had another career in mind. In fact, it had been in my mind ever since the day I 'crossed the line' in the playground at my first school. It was a combined primary and junior school, and there was an all-important line which divided the younger kids from where the older ones played. At that age, the line seemed a bigger barrier than any national border, and I used to look over at the older boys playing football, just wishing I could join in.

In fact, I can't remember a time when I didn't want to play football. My earliest memory is of my dad standing in one corner of the kitchen at home and getting me to stand in the other corner. He would then throw a ball at me as I ran towards him. Although I was only a toddler at the time, Dad says I never missed a kick. (Having said this he'd been working on me since I could walk and I was walking before I was a year old.) To start with, he virtually threw the ball on to my foot, but soon I got the hang of it and was giving it a real kick. So much so that Mum was always on at us to watch the kitchenware. Dad was proud of his first-born and was always getting his mates round to show off my skills, but he admits now that he never really knew where the ball was going to go when I kicked it. Some of the Arsenal strikers might say not much has changed since – but they probably wouldn't say it to my face. Being 6ft 4in definitely has its advantages.

I have always been tall, even as a boy. If I hadn't been, my life would have turned out quite differently. No championships or premierships, no cup-winner's medals, no MBE and, biggest loss of all, no fanzine named after me (a Spurs one, of course, called *One Flew Over Seaman's Head*). When I was finally old enough to cross that playground line, the other boys said to me straightaway, 'You're tall, you can go in goal.' I did as I was told – you do when you are the new boy – and found instantly that I enjoyed it. I made a few saves and thought I could make a go of this goalkeeping business. Best of all, some of the older boys clapped and told me how well I had done. It was only later that it occurred to me that, when boys play football, no one ever wants to go in goal so they might just have been overdoing the praise to ensure they had at least one mug to stand between the coats. Either way, I was hooked. I was a goalkeeper and that was all I wanted to do from then on.

The difference between me and most others who actually made it in professional football was that I didn't have any kind of family background in the game. My parents had never been involved in professional football (or any sport for that matter) and didn't know anyone among their family and friends who had. Nothing in their lives had prepared them for the responsibility of turning their little boy's dream of a football career into a reality.

My parents met at a local youth club and they started going out properly after a New Year's Eve dance. Dad's dad was strict with him and made him come in early if he went out and, as they lived four miles apart, Mum reckons that she used to have to walk herself home after a night out rather than have Dad getting into trouble for arriving home late, as he would if he took her home first. They were still teenagers when they were married at Rotherham Registry Office and although neither family was happy for them to be married so young, Mum's parents let the newly-weds live in the front room of their semi – along with her four brothers and sisters.

Dad was then working as an apprentice motor mechanic, earning about seven guineas (£7.35) a week, which in Rotherham in 1963 was a good wage for someone of his age. He had a great passion for motorbikes and would go to the youth club in a bikers' gang, Dad showing off with the rest of them. But when they were married and I came along, making money very tight, his bike was one of the first things to go.

Mum worked in an accountant's as a junior clerk although she still regrets putting 'junior' on her wedding certificate. But, then, as she admits, she *was* rather junior. When she had her hair done for the wedding, she didn't tell them it was her own wedding as she was embarrassed about being married so young. It was quite a scandal in those days. In the ambulance on the way to the hospital to give birth to me, she was asked her age. When she told them she was 16, they were shocked and it was all round the hospital by the time she arrived. Now no one would turn a hair.

I was born in Listerdale Maternity, Wyckersley, Rotherham, which is now an old people's home – entirely appropriate for a card-carrying member of what the press would have you believe is the world's oldest back five. But, in case some journalists and fans really believe I was born in the late Jurassic Age, let me put the record straight: I was born at 7.10 p.m. (just in time for an evening kick-off, in fact) on 19 September 1963 weighing in at nine pounds and two ounces. Or, as Mum puts it: 'Forceps delivery, made my eyes water.'

After this slightly rocky start, I was apparently quite a well-behaved baby and child but I was always something of a daredevil – fearless in the way that only kids (and some goalkeepers) seem to be. My brother, Colin, was two years younger than me and he was just as fearless. We'd climb or jump anywhere. Dad used to take us both to the swimming pool and, although we could barely swim at the time, we loved diving or jumping in from as high up as possible. Dad had to stop us going in from the top diving board as even he was frightened of that one – and he was a good swimmer.

When we had learned to swim properly, we still took some risks but drowning was not the main threat when we went to our favourite stretch of water: the local canal. Right alongside it were what we used to call the 'shit-beds', the place where all the local sewage was dumped. Over the years, this would turn into a powder and form a hard crusty surface. Trees and bushes would grow in it and rabbits would even live there, but if you walked or ran over it, your foot would, all of a sudden, go down a crack in the crust. It would all be soft underneath and you'd pull your foot out and it would be covered in muck. It didn't stop us having daft dares – who could run fastest and furthest across the beds. I like to think this experience made me quick off the line – but I don't know how I had the nerve to complain about training on mudheaps as I did later in my career. We used to dive or jump into the canal itself off the sewage pipe which really proved you were hard. The sewage was not supposed to get into the canal, but, when we jumped in and hit the bottom, all this sludge and muck would come to the top. The water must have been filthy and there were leeches on the canal walls which we'd dare each other to attach to ourselves. We would also take a Lilo out on the water and paddle out about 200 yards from the lock to the pipe and dive in. Afterwards, we'd pull the Lilo out and the bottom of it would be covered in horrible scum and slime.

One day down by the canal, we spotted a bird in the weed. It was flapping about and it was obviously a pigeon, not a swimming bird, so I swam across and rescued it. We saw it had been shot and that it had a ring on its leg. Beside the canal, there were huts where racing pigeons were kept in between flights so we took it to one of them and a woman said she would find its owner. The water wasn't that deep but I think any public health expert would agree that I certainly risked my life saving that pigeon.

We also risked our lives a few times indulging in something that is very non-PC these days – collecting birds' eggs. After a while, we could always spot the nests. We knew the seasons when the chicks would be about and which birds nested in certain trees and we climbed up some very dangerous places to collect them although we would only take one egg at a time. To stop the eggs going off, we would stick a pin in each end and empty it by blowing it, using a straw or just our lips. We did test them first, by putting them in water. If they sank, they had chicks inside; if they floated, you could blow them.

I used to go collecting on my own as well as with Colin and my friends, and I didn't have to go too far afield. At the end of our terrace was a church, and sparrows used to nest in its steeple walls. The brickwork had every other brick sticking out, which made it look temptingly easy to climb. It was very steep, though, and my parents can remember being appalled when our next-door neighbour, aged 70, came round and said, 'You better go get your David, he's halfway up the church steeple and he'll break his bloody neck.' I was seven at the time and I didn't even want to take the eggs. I just wanted to look at the nests and the chicks. I kept my collection in a big box in my room. The one I prized most was a kingfisher, because it was such a good-looking bird and such a hard one to get. But the hardest to get was a starling. There are thousands around, but they nest in awkward places up on roofs and eaves.

But, as much as I enjoyed this kind of Just William lifestyle, it was more conventional sports that really dominated my life – and Colin's too. Football, cricket, basketball – we played them all. And, whatever sport I was playing, I was lucky with injuries and the luck has continued through most of my career. My only major schoolboy injury happened when I was 11 and I broke my leg on a school outing to Primrose Valley at Filey. I was not even in goal or playing any sport; I did it jack-knifing off a swing and it was *my own head* which smashed into my leg and broke it. The trip was supposed to be for the week and I'd only been on it for two hours. I was taken to Scarborough Hospital – the same place my mother ended up in when she broke her leg 20 years later. Perhaps they'll reserve us a bed there now.

My accident could just have been down to over-excitement at the thought of going as far afield as Filey. In those days, we couldn't afford family holidays abroad – which is probably why I've enjoyed travelling around the world with England and Arsenal so much.

Not that I didn't enjoy the holidays we did have. Dad knew the landlord at The Woodman, the pub at the bottom of our road, and when money was tight in the first years of their marriage, Dad would collect the empties in return for a pint or two and service his cars and

Mum worked there as a barmaid. In return, the landlord let us all go on holiday to the caravan he kept on a site in Skipsey, near Bridlington and Scarborough. He even lent us his tiny van to drive down there.

The first time we went there I was about four and Colin was two. There was a nice flat beach, ideal for playing games on. It was also the only place Dad had a haircut – once a year whether he needed it or not. Mum would put her feet up for once and Dad would set about organising non-stop activities to keep us occupied all day and wear us out, so that hopefully they could have a few quiet evenings on their own.

We would spend all day playing football, cricket, swimming, cycling or fishing. It was a toss-up who was having more fun, us or Dad. In fact, he admits he did not know what to do with himself when some years later – I was 14 and Colin nearly 13 – we finally discovered an alternative holiday activity that definitely did not involve him. Dad was preparing for our usual game of football when he suddenly realised we weren't in the caravan. Mum, smiling broadly, told him that we'd found a better game. We'd gone off with a couple of girls we'd met.

It was about the same time that I'm supposed to have saved somebody's life. A lad whose parents ran the shop by the beach had borrowed an inflatable boat and paddled it out. But he drifted too far out and was going round in circles. He started calling for help. I swam out and brought him back in with Colin coming to help me as well. My parents and Colin remember all this well but I don't, which just goes to show up your priorities when you're that age: saving a pigeon you remember, saving another lad – forget it.

But I do remember being scared out of my wits at Skipsey one sunny day. We had rowed our own little boat a few hundred yards out and were quietly fishing with hand lines over the side for mackerel and flatties when we saw dark, triangular fins coming alongside the boat. We had recently seen *Jaws* and we were positive they were sharks. We screamed and pulled our lines in. It even gave Dad a turn, but it turned out they were porpoises.

There is a picture taken when Dad had been out sea fishing with his friends and had come back with a boatful of mackerel. They had all the fish on the floor by the boat and wanted me in the photograph as well. But in the frame, I'm crying my eyes out. I hated having my picture taken. I was only about eight then and wasn't so much embarrassed as just frightened of the camera. As far as I can remember, I thought something bad might come out of the camera and hurt me. Perhaps it was a premonition, as footballers (along with other celebrities) all know how the wrong photo published at the wrong time can damage careers and relationships.

Although Colin and I were good at most sports, our ambitions to become professional footballers must have given our parents plenty to think about. One wrong move by them and certainly the career I had set my heart on might have gone pear-shaped. It might just never have happened at all. It was some responsibility. But they rose to it and, in the event, the fact that it nearly did come to an untimely end was nothing to do with them.

3

......

Playing the Game
and Playing the Field

My dad's dad was good at football and Mum's family were sporty, but they weren't really interested in sport themselves. Dad always used to say riding motorbikes and chasing girls were his favourite sports. But they both supported Colin and me all the way in our sporting ambitions.

After his time working as a garage mechanic, Dad started at the local steelworks at the end of our street – he is still there, in fact, although he has had other jobs in between – and he started out with no more idea than I had of how you go about carving out a career as a professional footballer. But he made it his business to find out. I could not have made it without him, and later on he helped me negotiate better deals from my early clubs.

Before I came along, Dad's real passion was those motorbikes. He wore all the Rocker gear, had slicked-back hair with a genuine DA cut, and a Triumph Bonneville was his pride and joy. Although both my parents always worked, there still wasn't a lot of money about. But about the only way I remember this affecting our lives was that our two-up, two-down terrace only had an outside toilet. Right from the start, I have never had any fear of diving in where the boots are flying, but braving the creepy-crawlies in that toilet was another matter. I don't think I have ever moved quicker than when I had to go last thing at night.

We lived in the terrace until I was about 14, apart from the weeks when we moved into The Woodman, looking after it when the owners went on their own holidays. Then, when I was 14, my parents bought the sandwich shop and we moved out of the terraced house in Devonshire Street to live over the shop. This was definitely a step up – it had an inside, spider-free toilet, for a start. I think Mum was tired of barwork and, as the future of the steelworks looked fairly bleak at the time, she and Dad saw an opportunity and took it. They kept that shop for 11 years.

Dad carried on at the steelworks so Mum ran the shop mainly on her own with a bit of help from Colin and me. Though we weren't that helpful, now I think about it. Mum and Dad used to have a lie-in on Sundays so Colin and I were supposed to open up the shop at nine and deal with the early rush, mainly workmen. But just before nine, Colin and I would sneak a look out through our bedroom curtains and see how much of a queue had built up. As they started work early, the workmen were starving by nine so there were usually quite a few of them. And we knew they weren't going to be ordering just one sandwich each; they would be asking for a dozen at a time for the rest of their gang. There were just the two of us to make them, so, if we thought it was going to be too hectic, we would simply not open up until some of them had given up on us and gone away. We were the only shop round there that didn't have early closing days – we had late opening ones instead. But then some of the regulars started complaining that the shop wasn't opening on time and Mum quickly put an end to our skive.

When we weren't skiving it was hard work, but we still had a laugh and one thing it taught us was that adults had some very strange tastes. The workmen would come in asking for dripping sandwiches but 'no brown'. We were partial to dripping butties ourselves but without the 'brown' they were basically just eating lard with salt on – disgusting!

Mum gave us a couple of quid apiece for our 'help' but then I took a Saturday job as a baker's boy. It meant getting up at six o'clock to help the baker deliver from his van but the pay – £5 a go – was a fortune to me at the time.

Years ago there was a saying that, if any football club in the North of England was short of a decent player, it just had to shout down the nearest pit. As far as I knew, no club had ever found a player by shouting across the counter of a sandwich shop or into the back of a baker's delivery van. So, if I was going to make my dream of becoming a professional footballer come true, I was obviously going to have to do it the hard way. But at least my parents were always right on the case.

When it was time for me to leave junior school, it was well known round our way that Kimberworth Comprehensive was the school that took football seriously, but we lived just across some bureaucratic border which meant I was supposed to go to South Grove – a rugby-playing school and a bus-ride away. Kimberworth was only up the road and two teachers in charge of the football there, Bob Cox and Bob Earnshaw, had already spotted my potential. They advised Mum to write to the local Education Department.

Mum wrote – and laid it on with a trowel. She even warned them that they could be ruining my future, predicting that 'David could play for England one day' and that their decision could make the difference between that prediction coming true or not. I had already played for Rotherham Boys and South Yorkshire Boys and there had been some good write-ups about me in the local press, too. But she received a letter back saying that I couldn't go to Kimberworth. In the end, Mum went to see Mr Affleck, headmaster at Kimberworth, after the two Bobs (Cox and Earnshaw) wangled her an appointment. If he said there was a place for me there, I'd be able to go. When she walked in, aged just 27, she was very nervous. The Head made her go through everything again even though he had probably already decided to let me in. But if Mum hadn't put herself through the ordeal it could – who knows? – have made all the difference to me. No professional career, no back-passes from Martin Keown – how much less rich my life might have been. Flushed with success, Mum did exactly the same thing – with the same result – for Colin when they tried to send him to another school.

Not that either of us set the world alight academically at Kimberworth. All my school reports said I could do a lot better if I tried harder, but that all I was interested in was sport. Colin and I even used to sign our own school reports and take them back rather than show them to our parents. The only subject I did well in, apart from sport and PE, was Art. The teachers knew me well – if I did anything wrong, I wasn't put in detention. They just stopped me doing PE or football.

My parents were quietly confident that Colin and I would go on to sports careers. And, even if we didn't make it, that we would be able to find apprenticeships in engineering, which was what most people around our way did then if they were not academically-minded. In those days – the late 1970s – there were still plenty of those types of jobs around in the steelworks and coal mines. Even so, Mum and Dad still went on at me to get my homework done so I could pass some exams but in the end I left school without sitting even one.

I was always a Leeds fan because, when I was growing up in the 1970s, Leeds was *the* team – managed by Don Revie, and with the likes of Billy Bremner, Norman Hunter, Allan Clarke and Jack Charlton all playing. The first league game I ever saw was Rotherham v Leeds at Rotherham's Millmoor ground which was just a few minutes from where we lived. Dad took me down the front but I was only about ten and I couldn't see over the wall around the pitch. Dad asked this man if I could share the orange box he was standing on and he let me. I forget who won but I remember the fantastic atmosphere and watching both goalies, thinking, 'That's going to be me one day.'

I saw quite a few games at Rotherham (I still look out for their results), but Leeds were always the team for me although I never saw them play at Elland Road until I was 14 when I was down there for a trial.

After taking to goalkeeping from the start, I've never really played anywhere else out on the pitch. But Kimberworth had such a good team that, in some games, I'd only touch the ball a couple of times in the first half. Then, just to give me something to do, the coach would play me up front in the second half. In one game, I even equalled the school record, scoring nine goals. But, although most goalies are supposed to think they could play out on the park, I can now see that the players around me in the Arsenal team are miles away in ability from anything I could produce. But anyone who saw my penalty miss in the Charity Shield in 1993 will already have worked that out for themselves.

Not that I have always been successful even in goal. In the first game I played for my junior school, I managed to let in 14 goals – and I only played one half. We actually lost 26–0 – eight more goals than I let past in the whole of my first championship season (1990–91) with Arsenal. But I'm jumping ahead.

Those two Bobs at Kimberworth were a big help to me: Bob Earnshaw, the PE teacher, and the late Bob Cox, who was my football coach throughout my time at school. Bob Cox was a great guy although he didn't know that much about professional football. Bob Earnshaw did however and, although he was a winger in his time, he occasionally put me through some specialist goalkeeper coaching that he'd picked up while he was training at Barnsley. Mainly, though, I learned my trade simply through playing games. In fact, I've been self-taught for most of my career. It is only recently and at the very top level that English clubs have started to introduce specialist coaching for goalkeepers. Considering how important a good goalkeeper is to a team, it is amazing how undervalued and little understood the position has been.

Fortunately there were plenty of games to learn in when I was in my teens. At that stage I was playing football for the school, town and county during the week and on Saturdays. On Sundays, I played for a team called Red Scorpions. I don't know how they got the name but Sunday leagues are full of teams with daft names. My favourite is one called Norfolk Enchants (say it quickly and you'll see why). And when I wasn't playing organised games, I would always be up for a kickabout in the street – until the people living there told us to get off to the park and stop knocking the ball into their gardens.

Although he wasn't a big football nut, Dad had seen my enthusiasm and potential and he started taking me down the park at every opportunity to play football or cricket. When he was old enough, Colin came along too. He had more sense than to go in goal, though, and became a classy midfield player instead. Round our way, the usual Sunday routine for working men involved having a few pints, a big roast dinner and a snooze in the afternoon so Dad's mates were probably only half-joking when they told him he was showing them all up by being down the park in all weathers with us every Sunday afternoon.

It wasn't all football, though. I played cricket and basketball as well as football for Rotherham and Yorkshire schools. When I was 16, Yorkshire Cricket Club offered me a place on their books and the headmaster at Kimberworth, who was a great cricket – and Yorkshire – fan, was keen for me to take the offer, probably because Yorkshire were desperately short of fast bowlers, which was my speciality. I was tempted because I enjoyed cricket but even then I could see that, as a career, football had more potential. Football wasn't quite the huge, global business it has become now but it clearly offered more chance of fame and fortune than cricket. As things have turned out, it was obviously the right decision but I can't pretend I had any idea then just how great the rewards would turn out to be for top footballers in the Nineties.

I also played cricket for Dad's works team and, although I was a boy playing against men, I turned in some decent performances including taking eight wickets for one run with a hat-trick in the middle of it – Darren Gough, eat your heart out. And just to keep things in the family, Colin took the other two wickets.

The cricket games I remember best, though, were Kimberworth's annual visits to a posh private school, Worksop College. The place was like something out of a Billy Bunter book. It was by Columba Park and set in huge grounds with half a dozen football, rugby and cricket pitches. It was so smart that Yorkshire's Second XI even used to play some games there. It was a real case of scruffs against toffs, comprehensive kids against Hooray Henrys, and each time we played there we were in a 'let's stuff it up them' mood.

One year, Colin was also in the team. He was fielding at short leg to my mate Tony Crookes's bowling. Unfortunately he sent down a long-hop and their batsman caught hold of it and smashed it straight into the side of Colin's head, catching his ear quite badly. Colin was crying in pain and had to go off and the batsman seemed to think it was funny. I told Colin, 'Don't worry, I'll get him back for that.' Next over I sent down a wicked bouncer – so wicked it bounced straight off the batsman's ear. An ear for an ear ... Mind you, I wasn't too impressed when our captain sent me to silly mid-on to replace Colin next over.

There was no question of starting anything with the other team after the match. Every time we played there our teachers hammered it into us that we had to be on our best behaviour, which was strange as the College boys were ten times worse behaved than we were.

They stole things from our pockets and, when they went into their refectory (canteen, to you and me), they immediately started throwing food and plates around – showing off, I suppose. While all this mayhem was going on, we were all putting our hands up and asking, 'Can we leave the table, sir?' which wasn't quite our usual style.

We were more used to getting in a few scrapes. On one family holiday with my Uncle Steve, Colin and I hired bikes. I was riding round a bend only to meet a motor scooter coming straight at me. I swerved to the right just as he veered to the left. He hit me head-on and I went straight up in the air and landed on the road with a real whack. I was lucky again. I banged my elbow but wasn't badly hurt. I was so shocked, though, that the first thing I did was pull my trousers down and pee everywhere, which was a little unfortunate seeing that a young woman driving a Mini had stopped to see if she could help. Fortunately – at least for the fans and even more for the groundsmen – facing penalty shoot-outs in big Cup games doesn't frighten me half as much as falling off my bike did.

Another time, I borrowed my pal Christopher Spooner's brand-new bike and rode it straight into a pillar. The front wheel was bent at right angles, and I can remember desperately trying to bend it back straight – as though he might not notice the whole frame was mangled. Chris was one of six kids and his dad had died when he was young so there wasn't much money spare in his family but I knew I couldn't afford to buy him a new one, either. I didn't hear any more about it, though, so my parents must have seen him right with the money for a new bike – although I have a feeling it came out of my pocket money in the end.

I did the right thing myself for Chris another time. One of the school bullies – Pye, I think his name was – was showing off in front of the girls in the school dinner queue and made Chris kiss his shoes. He told the teacher so Pye was suspended for a week. I used to walk to school with Chris and, a few days later, Pye came running up and hit Chris. I stepped in and told him that was enough and to get lost. He turned straight round and smacked me in the face. I laid into him and saw him off. But the funniest part of the whole fight was this old lady in the bus shelter opposite. When she saw Pye hit Chris, she shouted, 'Stop it, you bully, leave him alone.' Next thing, when I'm hitting Pye, she's going, 'Go on, lad, hit him, hit him.'

Big as I was, I did not always win my schoolboy battles. I wasn't really a fighter but just being big made me a target. There was this guy, Russell, who was a real shit-stirrer and he decided there ought to be a fight between me and Gavin 'Guv' Senior, the other big lad in our year. It was the only time I let myself be pushed into something by someone else but Russell wound both of us up and we ended up having a fight after school in front of all the other kids at Bradgate Park.

It was all a bit like *High Noon* – except that I was a fair bit taller than Gary Cooper and didn't have a script that told me who was going to win. Our gang from Ferham Park Avenue arrived at the fight scene via the steep hill to the park, while Guv's gang, which had some real hard nuts, marched in from the opposite direction. I was giving Guv a fair hammering when, out of the blue, he landed one on my nose and knocked me sparko. I went down like a railway sleeper – at least that's how Colin described it from the safety of the sidelines.

I still reckon Guv had some help from something steely in his fist that isn't in the Marquess of Queensberry's rules, but at least he didn't put the boot in when I went down. Our gang must have looked a pretty pathetic sight as we left the battlefield defeated and went back down the hill to our homes. Dad certainly wasn't too impressed and told me to get back out there and hit him back. Geed up by stirrer Russell again, I offered a rematch but Guv wasn't interested – he had more sense.

Colin saw him recently, selling 99s from an ice cream van and he reckons he got a free cornet out of his memories of the Big Fight, which – if we re-enacted it – we could now call 'The Thriller in Vanilla'.

Because we were so close in age and were both good at sport, Colin and I spent a lot of time together. We got on very well – still do, in fact – but we did have one major falling-out when Colin really dropped me in it with the police.

My air rifle was my pride and joy. It had telescopic sights on it and I used to take it down to the canal to shoot rats. For some unknown reason, my brother decided to have a go with it – showing off to his mates, I suppose. The problem was his chosen target: the Zacharias Glass Factory which was over the wall from the yard of our shop. The wall was about six foot high on our side, but the drop their side was about 15 foot so the people working there used to climb up a ladder and shout across their sarnies order. Because of this, we were quite friendly with them and yet, that particular weekend, Colin decided to shoot the wing mirrors and other bits off their van parked outside the back. They came in Monday morning, saw the damage and it didn't need Inspector Morse to work out where the pellets had come from.

The police came round and, although Colin was let off with a caution and told he had to clean the factory vans for a week, it was me who really suffered. I was told to get rid of the gun and I was not even allowed to fire any parting shots into Colin's backside, which is what I felt like doing.

But the one time I nearly did kill Colin was entirely accidental. I was 12 and, at the time, it cost just 2p for children to go anywhere on a bus in Rotherham. One dinner-time, Colin pinched my 2p for the bus back to school. He now reckons it was the other way round and that I had spent my 2p on sweets, but I know that was wrong as we used to nick sweets from our own shop.

Anyway, I tried to get the 2p back and, as we were messing about, Colin put the 2p in his mouth. I knocked him, he accidentally swallowed it and it caught in his throat. For some reason – watching too many kung-fu films, I suppose – I decided that a karate chop across his neck would do the trick. All it did was make him throw up – but the 2p stayed wedged. Colin was panicking by now, choking and shouting out, 'I'm gonna die.' Mum came out to find out what all the fuss was about and found me holding Colin upside down by his ankles, trying to shake the coin out. She called an ambulance and went with him to hospital where an X-ray showed it lodged right in his windpipe. It was stood upright and they were worried that, if it fell sideways, it could block his air passage. They were preparing him for theatre, where they were going to open up his throat and retrieve it, when he had one last, nervous swallow – who can blame him? – and it went right down. Another X-ray showed it in his stomach and it was left to emerge in the normal way. Colin said he did look for it once but quickly decided that it was a mug's game and – to the eternal gratitude of local bus-drivers – that 2p piece was never seen again.

But one of the funniest memories of those days was of my dad and of Ferham Park where we used to play football, just pick-up teams with anything up to 20 a side sometimes. But, as anybody who ever played football as a kid will know, there is always a nutter in the park. This one decided to set up a football team and was going round taking subs. He tried to get me to join but I wouldn't because I knew he was a nutter. I was proved right the day his team was having a practice and I was behind the goal, kicking a ball about. It went on the pitch and I asked the goalie to kick it back. Next thing I knew, the nutter was shouting and swearing at me to get out of it. Then he picked up an iron bar, which he must have been using as part of the goal or a corner flag or something, and went to hit me with it.

I ran off, and I was quite quick in those days so there was no way he was going to catch me. I went home and told Dad, as it had frightened me a lot. Mum said, 'Roger – you get down there.' The park was only 600 yards from home so Dad, Mum and Colin rustled up a small posse to come back with me to the park. When we got there, Mum had a right go at the would-be football manager and he swore at her. Then Dad confronted the guy who, as park nutters tend to do, reckoned he was a bit of a karate expert but was doing all the bent-arm and straight-leg moves without getting anywhere near Dad. Unfortunately Dad was in his Seventies Rocker gear and he'd left in such a hurry that his leather platform boots were unfastened, too, which meant he was wobbling about all over the place and he too was having a lot of trouble getting near this would-be Bruce Lee. In the end, it was a bit like that scene in the Indiana Jones film when Indy waits for the Arab to do all his scimitar-waving moves before pulling a gun and shooting him. In this instance, Dad waited until the kung-fu moves stopped, then carefully stepped forward and decked him.

It's hard to imagine my dad as a Rocker now but when I was at school all the girls fancied him. He had long hair, a 'tache' (remind you of anyone?), and all the so-called trendy gear. He used to take me to some rock concerts, even down to London's Hammersmith Odeon. I liked the music and people used to reckon we looked more like brothers than father and son. Dad would sit there on his own while I'd be sitting a few rows back with my mates – all of us playing air guitar. We saw bands like UFO, Styx and Blue Oyster Cult, and I remember being really impressed with all the lasers and special lighting effects.

Although I liked the music I could never get up much enthusiasm for the motorbikes, but there was another spin-off of these outings that did appeal. It was then that I discovered that being tall didn't just help me in goal. When I was 15, I could pass for 18 so Dad used to take me down to his favourite Rocker clubs and bars. My eyes were out on stalks at the Rocker girls in their slit skirts but at first I was a bit confused why they could afford to buy drinks but not their own cigarettes – they all seemed to be sharing one fag. Still, my naivety didn't last long – about the waccy baccy or about girls in general and I didn't go short of girlfriends.

Sometimes there were even a few too many. One girl, Sally, was getting a bit too serious so, one day, when she came in the shop I hid upstairs and pretended to be out. But I was rumbled. Our living-room upstairs faced the road and as we were on a hill and the window was on the same level as the top deck of a bus, we used to look out of the window and see if any of our mates or any good-looking girls were on the buses that went by. Unfortunately, when Sally left she got straight on a bus and went on the top deck. And as it went by, she saw me hiding in the living-room. She got off at the next stop and came straight back – and did I have a lot of explaining to do.

The girls we abandoned Dad for on holiday at Skipsey were two sisters – Jeanette and Cheryl – who coincidentally also came from Rotherham and were the same ages as us. We had spotted them in another caravan and trained Dad's ex-army binoculars at them from our kitchen window. When we finally plucked up courage to ask them out, they said they had been watching us watching them with the bins.

Later, we went out with another couple of sisters – Teresa and Jackie. Teresa became my first real 'steady' when I was 15 and we went out for about three years. Later on, I met a few girls through Citizens Band radio. CB was a real craze at the start of the 1980s and I had a set at home – illegally, like most CB fans. My handle or call-sign was 'Green Giant'. CB girls would give you all the patter over the radio but then I found out why some of them were so good at it.

I arranged an eyeball (sadly, you never forget the jargon) but I had a car by then and I knew where this girl was supposed to be waiting. I drove up and saw she was a big – and I mean very big – girl so just kept on driving. But, although I had an eye for the girls and went to plenty of pubs and clubs, I wasn't a smoker or a drinker. I wanted to be a footballer – and I knew that drinking and professional sport don't go together. At least, that's what I thought then.

4

•••••

Choosing for a Bruising

When I first appeared on the scene as a schoolboy footballer with promise, clubs began sending people to knock on our door and try to sign me up on schoolboy forms. While it did not start quite as early as it does now – kids barely out of nappies are targets for clubs these days – and it was not as pressurised as it became in the 1980s and '90s, it was still a completely new and slightly unnerving experience for my parents. They had to deal with experienced managers like Bobby Saxton at Rotherham warning them that I would miss the boat if they did not let him sign me up. My parents may not have been football experts themselves but they had complete confidence in my ability. They did not have anyone to advise them and simply used common sense. If you are good enough, it is never going to be too late to sign up – that was Dad's view.

I was given a certain amount of advice by Bob Earnshaw at school – he had been a pro himself. But his advice was a touch biased because he wanted me to join his old club, Barnsley. You couldn't blame him – after all, he was scouting for them.

From my early days playing for Rotherham and Yorkshire schools, league club scouts would be at most matches but Dad would try to shield me from the pressure as much as possible. If he knew they were there to watch me, he would never tell me in case it made me nervous. When they started asking me to come in for trials, he would always come with me and the coaches would talk to him, not directly to me.

Between the ages of 14 and 16 I went for trials at lots of clubs. I had a good look at Rotherham, Chesterfield, Doncaster, Barnsley, Sheffield United and Wednesday, and Leeds. But I had made my mind up not to sign schoolboy forms for any of them. I wanted to try them all and choose the best one to join as an apprentice later on. I was fairly open-minded although, having always been a fan of Leeds, I did tend to put them at the top of my wish-list. They were still one of *the* teams of the time and it was my original dream to play for them, but I also had to consider how long it would take for me to be given a chance in their first team – and even how likely it was that I would ever get that chance. But when I trialled there, they had the most professional set-up of all the clubs. They had the best training facilities, the best changing-rooms and the best kits – and these things really impress you when you're a young player. They were also innovators – the first team to have number tags on their socks, and the first to go to the centre-circle and wave to the crowd before games. All the other clubs – including Sunday teams watched by two men and a dog – were quick to copy that one.

Because of my decision not to sign schoolboy forms, it meant the decision about my footballing future was in the balance for a couple of years before it all finally came to a head one evening when Dad fielded 20 calls from interested clubs in just a couple of hours. Barnsley were very keen for me to sign, and my favourite Leeds player, Allan Clarke, was their manager by then but Leeds were anxious for me to sign that evening because they wanted me to play a game for them straightaway. Other clubs were also sniffing around and I did think about going to a lower division club where I might get an earlier chance in the first team. But above all I wanted to go to the best club to get the best training. In the end, it was a straight choice between Barnsley and Leeds and after all the calls, Dad just asked me: which one? It was 50–50 but I didn't have to phone a friend to know my final answer: it had to be Leeds. They were the best I'd seen, I was a fan, and the club was only half an hour up the road. Looking back, I still think it was the right decision because at 15 going on 16 you are not going to break into the first team anywhere – especially as a goalkeeper when there is only one place up for grabs.

So the choice was made and, in case you're interested, no money changed hands. There were no bungs for me or my dad. I did not run into those until a lot later in my career, when a couple of transfer 'gifts' had disastrous consequences for one of my managers. But, although no money changed hands, there were a few perks going while Leeds were trying to sign me. My dad and his brother enjoyed hospitality at Elland Road which included directors' lounge and car park passes, and tickets for first-team games. As the two of them looked like refugees from the Bee Gees with their long hair, velvet jackets and jeans, this led to some interesting confrontations with the club commissionaires. Interestingly, the day I signed for Leeds, all that hospitality stopped. The courtship was over; now it was down to the serious business of treating football as a job of work, not a hobby.

But, at the time, my parents and I were just happy my future seemed to be settled. A successful career at the club I had supported all my life lay ahead of me – at least, that's what we all thought at the time.

Once I had signed with Leeds, I couldn't wait to get there. I left school as soon as I legally could – at Easter – without even staying to take the exams. In fact, I left Kimberworth on a Friday and was at Leeds on the Monday although there was still time in between for a local ice hockey team to contact me to see if I was interested in a pro career with them. I wonder how things would have turned out if I had changed my mind about Leeds and become an ice hockey goalminder instead. I doubt if I would have saved as many penalties, for a start.

But it was Leeds for me, even though it meant living away from home for the first time and switching from school to a fulltime job almost overnight – a hell of a change for a 15-year-old. But I was playing for my favourite club and earning the massive wage of £8 a week. Not much more than I got as a baker's boy, I know, but my digs were paid for and Leeds generously threw in a bus pass as well.

Despite having no footballing background, no contacts in the sport or any real idea of how to become a professional footballer, I had fulfilled my dream. Maybe I was a bit cocky but perhaps because I didn't have a background in the game, I just didn't realise how few of the kids who dream of being footballers actually make it. Either way, it had never really entered my head that I would not become a professional so, although I was well pleased to find myself at Leeds, I wasn't surprised. In fact, I thought: who needs exams, who needs another career to fall back on? It was onwards and upwards from now on. My future was secure – what could possibly go wrong?

I was about to find out.

5

· · · · · ·

Heroes and Villains

At first, everything went according to plan as I settled into my digs, which were in a vicarage in Morley just outside Leeds.

One of the other Leeds players living there was John Lukic, another goalkeeper whose career and mine would become interlinked right through to the present day. There were a couple of other apprentices staying there (Dwayne Percival and Simon Tait) and one of my clearest memories of the place is seeing the pad by the telephone covered in signatures. All of them were practising for the time when they were famous and fans would be asking for their autographs. I wasn't the only one to be super-confident about the future – and it wasn't long before my scrawl was on that same pad.

Apart from Lukic, the careers of the other apprentices I shared digs with never really took off. Dwayne, a right-winger, had a couple of first-team games but that was as far as any of them got and, as far as I know, they never had much chance to put their autograph-writing into practice. As I was to find out, being taken on as an apprentice is no guarantee of a successful career in football – it's the lowest rung of a very long ladder.

But, at the time, the biggest worry I had was trying to force down the goat's milk we were given by our landlady, Sue. She kept goats and never bought any other milk. The goat's milk tasted horrible – like watered-down skimmed milk – and I've never touched it since. Sue also took in a couple of police cadets, and I can remember being fascinated by their stories of the hunt for the Yorkshire Ripper which was going on at the time. For a young lad out on his own for the first time in his life, this adult world was an exciting place.

Also, although I had been confident about ending up with a big club, it was still a thrill to find myself out on the training pitch with all the star players around. I would look round and just think 'wow'.

Before joining Leeds full-time, I had spent a few days at its Elland Road ground in the school holidays so I certainly had no illusions about what apprentices spent most of their time doing. There was going to be hard graft and plenty of it – most of it nothing to do with training or playing games. I was made head apprentice, which meant that, not only did I have my own tasks to complete, I also had to check on all the other apprentices' jobs. Between us, we had to scrub and clean the Elland Road dressing-rooms, showers and toilets. This was a never-ending task as the dressing-rooms were used every day. Some clubs have separate training grounds away from the main ground but at Leeds they trained across from the car park at Elland Road.

A typical day for apprentices meant arriving early, before the senior pros turned up for morning training. We had to make sure all the kits were laid out and the boots cleaned. I had to clean boots for Kenny Burns and Neil Fern. They were both big, ugly centre-backs and, big as I was, too, I knew I didn't want to upset either of them if I could avoid it. When the senior players arrived, they would tell us which boots they wanted to wear – moulded or screw-in studs – and we would have to get them. Once we had sorted out their kit, we would get into ours and go out to train in our separate groups. But, at the end of the session, it was back to the grind. We would have to bring all the footballs in while the senior players showered; take their dirty kit to the laundry; lay out clean towels and bring their tea in for them.

Friday was the big one – the major clean-up before match day Saturdays. We had to scrub the floors with big, powerful machines. It was a blue lino surface right down from the dressing-room through the tunnel to the pitch and it was murder to try and keep the streaks off it. If you put too much washing powder into the machines, you had no chance. Our coach would tell me to come and see him when I was happy that all the work was finished properly. He would come out, check the top of the doors for dust and the floors for streaks. If it was streaky, he would go back into his room and get a tub of Flash which he would sprinkle all down the corridor, growling, 'Get that off.' And I knew it all had to be done again.

On Saturday mornings, we would play our youth team game but still have to be at Elland Road for the afternoon first-team or reserve game. We didn't have to put the kit out because there was a kitman for that on match days, but we would have to clean up afterwards. I don't suppose we enjoyed it much, but we all accepted it anyway. It was part of your career. It has changed now for young apprentices – at least at the big clubs – but it did make you appreciate your career more as you moved up the ladder.

There was loads of mickey-taking from the senior players but it was usually good-natured. We definitely knew our place on the totem pole, though. We had to knock before going in the first-team dressing-room. All the senior players expected us to show them respect but they also appreciated what we were doing because they'd had to do it themselves.

Away from Elland Road, I was happy enough in my digs but I still couldn't wait to get back to see my mates and girlfriends in Rotherham. Unfortunately, the only free time I had was after the games on a Saturday. I would get a lift from someone but I only had Sunday at home before having to get back for Monday morning.

I used to go out with the other apprentices in Leeds, but we were only 16 or 17 and still learning what the world was all about. We weren't really allowed in clubs but we did get out to a few. We kept our excursions pretty hush-hush, but it usually got back to the club – it was part of the landlady's job for the club to keep an eye on us for them.

In any case, as an apprentice, you had very little spare time what with all the skivvying on top of the training and playing. This punishing schedule, more than anything, kept us out of mischief. Which, of course, was the general idea.

I spent two years in the digs but I had a bit more freedom there when my parents gave me their car, a Vauxhall Viva. They had paid £300 for it and it was a bit past its sell-by date. But, foot down to the floor, it would do 70 – well, downhill anyway. When I could, I borrowed Mum's flashier but more reliable Escort Estate. I was driving that one day from Elland Road, heading for Rotherham with

Colin and another lad who we were going to drop off in Barnsley. As I turned out of the ground, White Van Man came right up behind me, inches from my rear bumper and hooting me. I put my foot down as we got on to a stretch of dual carriageaway but, as we approached a roundabout, the van came racing alongside me. As I turned to exchange a few friendly words and gestures with him, the Triumph Herald ahead of me stopped even though the roundabout was clear and I ploughed straight into the back of him.

Of course, there was a copper on the roundabout – isn't there always? It must have made his day. He came over, saw how young I was and said, 'Been driving long, then?'

'No, only passed my test couple of weeks ago,' I admitted.

'We can see that, can't we?' was his smug response.

I didn't dare point out that I had put in for driving lessons and my test at the same time only to get a test date straightaway. This meant I had only had time for a couple of lessons before taking the test – and passing first time. I don't think the guy I had hit would have been too impressed, either. He had only just picked his car up from the police pound after it had been recovered from car thieves. That wasn't the worst of it. Not only did I have to ring Mum and ask her to pick us up in the Viva, I also had to explain that her car was smashed up and in the garage and ... er ... 'Happy birthday, Mum.'

Colin was in the car because he'd been on two weeks' trial with Leeds. In fact, he'd had trials with all the local clubs just the same as I had. Much shorter than me, at 5ft 9in, he was a good midfield player and I thought he did himself justice in the trial games he played at Leeds, showing up well against the established players. But luck and good timing play a major part in sport, probably even more than in other careers. Although he was only coming along two years behind me, the state of the game had changed – and not for the better. Most clubs were struggling financially, tightening their belts, and they started to cut back the number of apprentices they took on.

Colin played for a year in the Junior Whites team under Leeds assistant manager Martin Wilkinson and alongside Scott Sellars. But, while Sellars was taken on at Leeds and has had a good career, the closest Colin came to a contract was at Huddersfield. He went several times for trials and at the end of one of them the coach in charge told Dad that, while in previous years he had been able to take on a dozen apprentices, this year the manager, Mick Buxton, was restricting him to two. He had chosen two other boys but promised that, if either of them did not take up the offer, Colin was next in line. Unfortunately for Colin, both agreed to go to Huddersfield.

This was in 1982. Four years later, the first YTS scheme was introduced which meant clubs could start taking on lots more apprentices. It was just too late for Colin, though. He was very upset although he admits that he probably wasn't as dedicated to making it as a professional as he might have been. But these days he still plays amateur football at a good standard having converted from midfield to right back. When football fell through for him, he immediately picked up an apprenticeship at an engineering firm. He is now working in insurance for the Co-op and is happily married with two children. I was a bit sorry when he left his previous job, which was dealing with surgical appliances. These included supplying hip replacements, which might have come in very useful for an ageing goalkeeper. Just ask Bob Wilson.

Colin has also kept up the cricket. When he was turning out for a local team, he played against Worsbrough Bridge in Barnsley and it doesn't get much more Yorkshire than that. The scorer had obviously been telling their players who Colin was, so, when he went to check his score, a group of scraggy-haired, snotty-nosed kids asked him, 'Are thee really David Seaman's brother?' When he admitted he was, they followed up with, 'Did thou used to wear his kecks when you were younger?' Obviously, where they lived it was first up, best dressed. Then they asked him, 'Does thee go and watch him – and does he pay thee in when thee go?' Only ten minutes up the motorway, and even Rotherham lads need an interpreter.

But, while Colin's football career never quite happened for him, mine was moving on up a lot faster and smoother than my Vauxhall Viva. At least, I thought it was. Less than six months after joining Leeds – actually on my 16th birthday in September 1979 – I was picked to play for Leeds reserves for the first time. But here my lack of experience at how things were done in the professional game embarrassed me big-time. The problem was that I had no real idea what I should wear to report for the game at Elland Road. I had put denim jeans on and cowboy boots and I was going to add my denim jacket to this tasteful ensemble but my dad said, 'No, take my blue velvet jacket.' I'm not sure which was worse but it was definitely a case of the colour-blind leading the fashion-blind. Not surprisingly, when I walked in looking like the all-time fashion victim, all the lads burst out laughing. In fact, it is a wonder I ever lived it down, but from then on it was regulation jacket, shirt and tie for me on match days.

Especially as that had not been my first sartorial stitch-up. I had no sooner joined Leeds than they told me I was going on a series of pre-season tours with the first team. The other goalkeepers ahead of me were all injured so I was the only cover for the first-team 'keeper. We had games in Spain, Canada, Germany, Switzerland and Ireland, which was an amazing prospect for a kid just turned 16 whose only experience of 'abroad' had been one school trip to Germany. It also put a lot of pressure on my wardrobe which at the time consisted of a few pairs of Levis, that denim jacket, Led Zeppelin T-shirts and some trainers. Dad thought he was doing me a favour lending me his only suit – a cream one left over from his hippy days. I wore it with a dark shirt and looked like John Travolta – quite cool really but you can imagine what the other, senior players had to say when I pitched up for the tour wearing that outfit.

Apart from the mickey-taking, my main memories from the tour were seeing Niagara Falls; disobeying the club ban on sunbathing by taking turns with John Lukic to lie on the floor in the room we shared to catch some rays through the huge window; and being amazed to see a top Yugoslavian international player turn up still drunk from the night before and then play for his German club against us. I didn't play in the games, but it was still a great experience and stood me in good stead when I did play that first reserve game.

Club managers and coaches don't have too much time to let apprentices know how they are progressing. At Leeds, the only way of knowing what they thought of you was their system of marking you out of ten for your performances in games. These marks were posted every Monday morning and it was nerve-wracking stuff looking at what you had been given every week.

For that reserve game against Preston, I was marked ten out of ten. It was one of those great days when everything – crosses, shots – just stuck. I don't remember being particularly nervous but, then, for me, nervousness comes and goes. Even now, I find I can turn out for England and feel confident and on top of everything and then, for a relatively minor league game, find myself feeling nervy when I get out there. Strangely, I was less nervous when I started out than when I progressed in the game. I think this was because, as I got older, I realised how important the team's results are to so many people and what kind of criticism could follow if I didn't play well.

But, when I started playing for Leeds reserves, even in front of some biggish crowds – nearly 10,000 once – I have to admit I wasn't as nervous as I was the first time I played for my dad's pub darts team. We had a board at home and I played a lot there and I had watched lots of games at the pub. The atmosphere was great, with the compere saying, 'Game on, gentlemen' and the lights going down. I thought I wouldn't mind some of that. But, when it came to it after Dad roped me in to play one week, I found myself more nervous than I had ever been in my life. My hand was shaking, along with the rest of me. I think I won the game but the whole thing was a bit of a blur. I just couldn't handle the pressure. Even World Cups are easier on the nerves.

Back at Leeds, although I played for the reserves from time to time especially in my second year as an apprentice, it was mostly the youth team for me. We were quite a good side but never won anything apart from one international tournament in Switzerland, an experience which made a big impression on me as it was my first piece of silverware as a professional footballer. I still have the photograph taken of us with the trophy but, looking at the team now, I realise that only one other lad made a name for himself in the game – Terry Connor, who was a good player and is now coaching. Although a couple of the others played the odd game for the first team, Terry and I were the only ones to make a real mark.

But that is the way it goes in football. Only a small percentage of apprentices even make it into the first team, let alone become top players. For that reason, the club makes sure you do have some educational qualification to fall back on if the football goes pear-shaped. All apprentices were sent on to college on day-release courses. I chose the only other subject, apart from sport and PE, that I had ever shown any ability at – Art. I took an O level in it and managed an A grade. For the exam, I had to do one pencil drawing, so I drew my right hand as a clenched fist; and one watercolour, which was of loads of flags that the teacher had put in the classroom. They both seemed to come out well.

I haven't done any drawing for ages even though my wife Debbie has bought me loads of materials to get me into it again. I did plan to do some while fishing but haven't had the inspiration yet. I do enjoy it, though, and I am sure I'll start drawing again one day. I have drawn people's faces from photographs and I drew one of the lads on the O level course with me, so I might try some portrait sketches. Villa goalkeeper David James does good caricatures of other foot-ballers and gets them to add their signature. That's when he's not at his playstation, of course.

But at Leeds, college was just a nuisance as far as I was concerned. I had no thoughts of any other career than football and was in a hurry to overcome the first hurdle for apprentices – being offered a full professional contract. When, on my 18th birthday in September 1981, this fell into my lap just like the apprenticeship, I thought, 'Nothing can stop me now.' This momentous moment in football received huge publicity – well, there was a write-up in Dad's works staff newsletter. Under the headline 'Soccer Dream Comes True', it starts: 'Most fathers dream of watching their sons run out on to the famous football pitches of Anfield, Old Trafford or Elland Road but one RJ employee doesn't have to dream. Only a few weeks ago, Roger Seaman's son David had his first game for the Leeds United first team.' It goes on to quote Dad: 'It's been like a fairytale for David. Ever since he could kick a ball, he's supported the Peacocks.'

That's a strange club nickname that seems to have disappeared now but it was not as bizarre as Dad's job title then. According to this article, he had been a horizontal borer there for 17 years. I've shared a dressing-room with a few vertical borers in my time. But the paper was right about my first-team appearance, as I had been picked for a couple of friendlies.

The first of these was a real eye-opener. We were playing Glentoran in Northern Ireland. The first shock was having armed guards on the coach. I'm only 18 and I'm thinking, 'What's going on here?' The streets seemed deserted and I started thinking about IRA snipers. There was more massive security when we went into our hotel and what really freaked me out was that there was a notice on the lift saying, 'Out of order due to bomb damage.'

And I was nervous enough already about making my first-team debut, more nervous than I had been before any game so far. It was my first taste of first-team football. Although I had trained with them for a couple of years, it still felt different to be playing in the same team as some of my heroes. I can remember seeing Frank Worthington, who was a legend by then, wearing all this flashy gold jewellery. He scored a great goal in the game. He could have sidefooted it in but, showman that he was, he flicked it up and volleyed it instead.

The regular first-teamers like Paul Hart, Trever Cherry, Frank Gray and John Lukic all did their best to help me before the match, but it was hard for me to focus on my own game, knowing that there were 14,000 fans out there – easily the biggest crowd I had ever played in front of. I also had my first experience of abuse from an away crowd as I clattered one of their players. With that notice on the lift still in my mind, I was glad to get off the pitch in one piece. But I can also remember feeling equally relieved at the final whistle just to have got that first game for the first team out of the way.

When I had joined Leeds in 1979, Jimmy Adamson was the manager (although it was one of his assistants, Maurice Lindley, who had actually signed me on) but he had been replaced in September 1980 by former Leeds star Allan Clarke, who had been the manager at Barnsley when they had tried to sign me as an apprentice.

At the end of the first year of my full professional contract, I went into the close season looking forward to establishing myself as the reserve team goalkeeper in the 1982–3 season. But, just before the new season began in July 1982, Clarke was replaced by Eddie Gray, one of the greatest players ever to wear the Leeds shirt and one of my boyhood heroes. In August, I was called in to see him and I was expecting to hear him tell me that my career path to the top was right on course. Which is why what he actually had to say came as such a shock. There was no preamble, Gray got straight to the point. 'I want a more experienced number two as cover for John Lukic,' he said. 'So we are going to have to let you go.'

I could hardly take it in. They were not renewing my contract. A month short of my 19th birthday, I was out in the cold. It looked like my dream was over. I went back home and cried my eyes out. What was I going to do now? Just about the only other career I was trained for was baker's delivery boy. Were all my eggs going to end up in one bread basket?

6

· · · · · ·

Scruff Turns Posh

I was not the only one who had been given a one-way ticket out of
Elland Road. Gray's arrival had also seen the club part company
with Martin Wilkinson, who had been Allan Clarke's assistant. He
had gone on to become manager of Peterborough United but he was
still in close touch with the comings and goings at Leeds and, when
he heard I was out too, he was straight in for me. He telephoned Dad
and said he wanted me to join him there and promised that I would
go straight in the first team, something that I had never achieved – at
least in the league – for Leeds.

But I was still shell-shocked by what had happened and, when I
was told about the offer, I have to admit I was not in the kind of
mood to show much interest. It was partly that I was so disappointed
by the end of my Leeds dream, the first real setback I'd had in my
sporting life, and partly that I genuinely didn't know anything about
Peterborough.

'Where is it, anyway?' I asked my dad. And when we found it on a
map and it seemed such a long way away, I was even less enthusiastic
about the whole idea. In addition, one of the few things I did know
about the club was that it languished in the old Fourth Division, just
about as low as you could get and still be in the league.

But Dad insisted I come down with him and have a look at the
club and meet up with Wilkinson again. He did not exactly have to
drag me kicking and screaming, but there was a distinct lack of
eagerness on my part. But I agreed to go and, using a bit of
psychology, Wilkinson, who still lived in our area, rang up to say he
was getting a new club car and would take us down in it.

It was a smart motor and my eyes started opening even wider as we were shown round the ground. Once a non-league club with a Cup giant-killing tradition, Peterborough had come into the league with a flourish befitting its 'Posh' nickname in the 1960s. It won promotion to the Third in its first season and, although it had never hit the heights after that, it was a decent, well-run club, especially by Division Four standards.

Then Wilkinson took us to lunch at a fancy French restaurant in a local hotel. The leather-clad menu was all in French and meant nothing to either of us so, after the waiter took Wilkinson's order, Dad caught my eye and said, 'We'll have what he's having.'

After that it was back to the club for the nitty gritty. As we sat in the manager's office, Wilkinson said he had a budget, a phrase I was later to become used to hearing from George Graham year after year when, along with the other players, I tried to squeeze some more money out of the Arsenal. Wilkinson offered me £130 a week plus £25 appearance money, £25 win bonus and a £1,500 signing-on fee. As I was on £100 a week at Leeds, the wage sounded good to me but it was the signing-on fee that really caught my attention. If Dad hadn't been there, I would probably have snatched his hand off. Instead, Dad told me to come outside to talk it over.

That was fine with Wilkinson because he had something important to do himself, i.e. explain what was happening to the goalkeeper whose place I was about to take – Eric Steele, who had been a good 'keeper for several clubs, including Posh. While he dealt with one of the trickiest parts of a manager's job, I walked around the pitch with Dad who told me that I should never, ever accept the first offer any more than I would if I was buying or selling a car. I argued with him for a while, telling him that this was good money I was being offered but he persuaded me to do it his way.

We went back in and said there must be a little bit more in the pot. Sure enough, Wilkinson upped his offer to £200 a week and a £2,000 signing-on fee (exactly half the transfer fee Leeds were getting for me). I think he also added a little on to the appearance and win bonuses, too.

But, to be honest, my first thought was what I could buy with £2,000. There was no competition – I was into cars and, at the time, the car to have was a Ford Capri, so that's what I got. It was yellow with trendy wide wheels although, even then, £2,000 only bought a second-hand one. It gave me as much pleasure, though, as some of the pricier and faster cars I have had since.

Everything happened so fast with the Peterborough deal that, in the end, I didn't have too long to dwell on being kicked out of Leeds but I will never forget that feeling of having no idea of what to do next with my life. I was still a bit apprehensive about living what seemed such a long way from home, though. Now, several club and house moves later, a 90-minute drive down the A1 to Peterborough does not seem such a long way, but I was still only a teenager and had only lived at home or in digs.

I had also only recently started to go out with a girl who was to become my first wife, Sandra. I had met her earlier that year in a nightclub in Rotherham but it turned out she lived near where I did. I had started spending most of my time round her place when I came back from Leeds at the weekend. In fact, like many mothers of teenagers, my mum had become really fed up with me treating home like a hotel. It was true that I was just dropping in and out with my washing before and after seeing Sandra. My parents had been used to me telling them what I had been up to at Leeds, but now they hardly saw me.

But, like all teenagers, I was oblivious to what they were feeling and more concerned about what was going to happen with Sandra when I moved to Peterborough. I was obviously not going to be able to get back as easily or as often from Peterborough so I had another big decision to make. It was helped by my new club's offer of a choice of three-bedroom houses to rent on a smart new estate in the town. The rent was only £25 a week so Sandra and I got engaged and moved down there together.

Mum and Dad were less than delighted by this development, not because they had anything against Sandra – they just thought I was settling down too soon. I was still only 18 (Sandra was 20) and, although they had married young and been happy together, my parents remembered their early financial struggles and just thought I should enjoy the freedom of being single for a while more. I still had some growing up to do, they thought.

Of course, it was exactly because I was 18 and still growing up that I didn't take my parents' advice and this caused a rift between us that lasted a fair few years. It was made worse when Sandra and I then got married in Peterborough. It seemed the natural thing to do at the time but my parents thought it was a mistake and did not come to the wedding. This obviously put something of a dampener on the day but it was one I remember well for another reason – it was Cup Final day, chosen because I had this strange premonition that Posh wouldn't be involved (it was actually Everton v Watford). Mystic Dave, that's me.

Parents always think they know best – and the irritating thing for their children is that they usually do because they have done it all before. In life, as in football, experience counts for an awful lot. After their non-appearance at the wedding, we didn't really speak at all for three years. Things then improved a little, but it was still a distant relationship for some years after that.

With experience, I came to regret what happened between us and was delighted that we became close again in time for them to enjoy the really big moments in my career at Arsenal, Euro 96 and the World Cup in France but, at the time, I was too wrapped up in my new home, new club and my first taste of league football.

The first big change I had to cope with was that I was now in at the deep end, swimming with the big boys. At Leeds I had played against boys in the youth team, and even reserve team football is mainly for younger players trying to break into the first team. Division Four was a complete contrast. Teams there were full of older, experienced pros. They were either on their way down, having played at a higher level, or players who had knocked around the lower leagues all their careers. Either way, they knew exactly what they were doing out there and how to put one over on younger players without their experience.

Players like Ray Hankin, who I'd seen playing for Leeds and Burnley. He loved to batter goalkeepers. Fortunately, he played for Posh but there were plenty like him in the teams we played against, all happy to smash goalies all over the place. I remember one hard player who could really put himself about. He played for Hartlepool but had also been in prison for killing someone in a road accident. After a couple of games, I realised that I would get a whack from him every time I went up for the ball. It was the same with Wayne Entwhistle, who was an experienced, well-travelled striker. In one of my first games for Posh, he was playing up front for the other side and went up for an early cross with me. Suddenly I felt a bang at the side of my head. He had elbowed me in the side of the temple. I was spark out but in those days there were no goalkeeper substitutes so I had to play on when I finally came round.

Another striker who took no prisoners and who I ran into for the first time when I was playing for Posh was Billy Whitehurst. He had a few clubs in his time and I ran into him again – literally – a few years later when I was playing for QPR. It was in the first few minutes and Billy was chasing a through ball. Although it was always a 60–40 ball in my favour, he kept going at full pace and went straight through me and nearly ripped my shorts off in the process. He tore them to shreds and there were stud marks all the way up my legs. 'Welcome to the game, Dave.'

The worst injury I saw during my time at Posh, though, was one I inflicted on another Posh player. I went out to take a cross but then landed on my own player. My knee went straight into his sternum and broke it. He was out cold, which was probably just as well, although the physio pulled his tongue clear to make sure his breathing was not restricted. He was carried off and you will not be surprised to hear that he didn't play for a while.

The physical side of the game at this level came as a shock, but I still enjoyed it because I did well from the start. I had made my mind up that I was going to be positive, particularly with crosses. I was taking them right at the edge of the box, despite being whacked from all sides and, in Division Four, that is exactly what your manager and team-mates want you to do.

I was only 19 in my first season with Posh and it was a great learning period for me. It still makes me laugh now when pundits say this or that goalkeeper is 'a good shot-stopper' because that *is* a goalie. If you can't stop shots, you shouldn't be out there in the first place but it is the other stuff that sorts out the good from the bad. It is calling, coming for crosses, dominating your area and sweeping up behind the defence that really counts.

The other big culture shock for me was getting used to playing in front of what seemed like very big crowds, week in, week out. I had played in front of the occasional big crowd at Leeds, for the reserves and in occasional first-team friendlies or tour matches, but this was different. For a start, these were league games and the result really mattered to the fans.

At Posh, there would be about 8,000 of them for home games and that was a lot in a smallish ground. They could make a great deal of noise but they were close enough to you – particularly when you played in goal – for individual shouts to be heard quite clearly. Especially the abusive ones.

Your first reaction to one of these is, 'Does he mean me?' and it is worse if it is your own fans slagging you off. They knew to wait for it to go quiet before giving it to you with both barrels – 'Seaman, you wanker.' The best response if someone keeps winding you up and shouting abuse is to turn round and say, 'What?' Then it's a competition to see how many times you can get them to repeat it before they get the message or feel like complete idiots.

But things went so well for me at Posh that I didn't get much stick, at least in home games. I started to get good reviews in the local and national paper reports, which was a big thrill as it was the first time I was written about as a pro footballer. Posh had a decent side at the time, too. In my two seasons, we finished high up the table but didn't quite make promotion. There were no promotion play-offs in those days.

The club was very professional about tactics and match preparation, too. But the major surprise for me was how big it was. Even though outsiders might have thought it a small club, it meant so much to the fans and everyone in the town. There are no other big clubs nearby, so there was good local support.

And playing in the league was so different to reserve team football where you just feel you are playing on trial all the time. Now results really mattered – and I loved the pressure.

I can remember playing Crystal Palace, who were then in the old First Divison, in the Milk Cup (now the Worthington Cup). We played at home and lost 3–1, but went to their place and won 3–0 to go through. That was a huge game for the club and the biggest I had played in so far. It was a great night. And it was everything I had hoped for from being a professional footballer. I was even able to turn all that signature practice in those Leeds digs to good use as people in Peterborough started asking for my autograph. I really did feel I had hit the big time.

That feeling increased when my first little bits of sponsorship started kicking in. Companies offered me free goalkeeping gloves but, although it seems daft now, the freebie that meant most to me then was the drink mixer all the players were given by one of the club's main sponsors, Sodastream. It seemed the height of sophistication at the time.

But the whole experience of being a pro was living up to all my dreams: going to away games on the coach, stopping for meals before and the chippie after the game – magic.

Posh had a tradition as a good family club and, unlike some places, the team wasn't cliquey. The rest of the players made me feel welcome, even though a lot of them were very experienced pros. It also helped that Neil Fern, whose boots I used to clean, had followed me down from Leeds. Trevor Quow was the up-and-coming star, and not just because of his trendy Afro hairstyle. He was a very good player as was Ivor Linton who had come from Aston Villa. I had replaced Steele in goal and, as I had been promised the number one slot when I signed, his number two, Keith Walsh, eventually moved on to Sheffield United. Although there was a good team spirit, we did not do a lot of socialising off the park. I was only 19 and it was my first time a long way from home so Sandra and I did go back to Rotherham a lot to see our friends.

But gradually we settled in Peterborough – we even bought three cats. Sandra, who had been an assistant PDSA vet, found a job as a lifeguard at the outdoor swimming pool. Her whole family were excellent swimmers. As that was a full-time job, I found myself at a loose end after our morning training sessions. I would be free by about 1 p.m. so I got into the habit of going to the nearby Thorpe Wood golf course and helping the assistant pro with all his re-grips and other repairs so he could finish early and play himself. In return, he would take me along. It started with just four or five holes, but it was every day and I was getting a lesson as well. I had played a little bit before but, as an apprentice, I hadn't had the time to make much progress.

My dad bought me my first set – or half-set – of clubs, but they were second-hand and after two or three hits they'd had it. With my new-found wealth, I bought my own new set in Peterborough. Eventually, I got my handicap down to eight and my best round was two under par, putting me well on the way to becoming a scratch player. It just goes to show how much free time I was getting then. Things have probably not changed too much for players in the lower leagues but, when you reach the Premiership, start playing in Europe and in internationals, and your club routinely reaches the later rounds of the cups, the games start coming thick and fast. Not that I am complaining, but the golf handicap is bound to suffer – although I had already changed hobbies midstream by the time I was playing for Arsenal and England. By then my other game was fishing.

But it was while I was still at Posh that I had my first taste of the England set-up. And it left the kind of bitter taste that made me doubt if I would ever play for my country.

I was called up for the England Under-21s and went for squad training to Macclesfield. At the time, Alan Hodgkinson, a former England goalkeeper of the 1960s, was in charge of England goalies and he trained us so hard I was thinking, 'If this is what it takes to be an England goalie, I have no chance.' It was so hard on me physically that I nearly passed out. After every exercise, I was falling over, totally knackered and thinking, 'I can't do any more.' But then I reasoned that the others (Gary Bailey and Alex Williams from the two Manchester clubs) couldn't be that much fitter than me and when I looked around I did see that they were in a pretty similar state.

It wasn't until later that I found out that this was just Hodgkinson's way of training – it wasn't the only way or even the best way to train a potential international goalkeeper. I know now that, if you are that tired, you can't produce real quality. You obviously need to be fit but that does not mean you have to be on your knees every training session. I talk to my trainer now, usually Bob 'Willow' Wilson, all the time about being fresh and making good saves and building up good habits. There is no point practising making mistakes. But, at the time, I was really disillusioned because I thought there was no way I was ever going to play for England or even the Under-21s if that was what it took to make it.

One aspect of playing at Posh that was no different from my Leeds experience was a complete lack of regular specialist goalkeeping coaching. That is a relatively recent invention as clubs have started to wake up to the real value of a goalkeeper to a team. In my early years, there were very few goalkeeping coaches around and most managers and coaches did not know much about the kind of training we needed.

When I was at Leeds, I did a lot of work with John Lukic, who was three years older than me, but it was mostly geared towards him as the senior keeper. There were a couple of other keepers at the club so sometimes all four of us would be given some coaching together in first-team training. Ironically, after getting rid of me to bring in someone more experienced to back up Lukic, Gray sold John to Arsenal and brought former Leeds favourite David Harvey back from playing in the USA. Hardly a long-term strategy, that.

At Posh, there was certainly no specialist training for us. The three goalies at the club would get together and decide what we needed and organise it ourselves without a coach. We would only be able to do that once a week, though, as the rest of the time we would always be needed for training with the other lads. As our squad was not very big, we would often be roped in to make up the numbers as outfield players. We could do extra training in the afternoons if we wanted to, but it was always down to us to organise it.

Martin Wilkinson was a friendly guy, but it was hard for the players to take him too seriously – especially for me, as he had been just a low-key assistant at Leeds. He wasn't even first-team coach there. If the manager has not made it as a pro player himself, it makes it harder for some players to accept him but it actually makes no real odds to me, because I know that hardly any managers have ever been goalies. Wilkinson was quiet and a bit too nice. He was also inexperienced as a manager but I thought he did OK.

He did have his occasional barnies with players, though. At half-time in a game at York, he had a real go at me. I had picked up a back pass (goalies were allowed to do that in the good old days) but then I tried to throw it over the head of the oncoming forward. I didn't throw it high enough and he headed it down and then put it through my legs.

Wilkinson really laid into me as soon as we went in at the break. What the hell did I think I was doing? Why didn't I throw the ball higher? I think he was testing me to see how I would respond, because it was the first real rollocking he had given me during a game. When we went out for the second half, he told me I had to prove to everybody that he was right to play me in the first team. It was embarrassing for me but in the second half I saved a penalty and we went on to win the match. I was even named as 'man of the match' and, to be fair, Wilkinson did praise me for playing much better in the second half.

Our results were OK under him but we didn't get promotion so, after a year, he was out and the former West Brom centre-back John Wile came in as manager. He immediately got more respect from the players because of what he had achieved in the game. He was a hard man but he treated me fine and, in any case, I wasn't there long. Like most new managers, Wile wanted to bring in a few new players and, as is usually the case in the lower leagues, he found he had to sell a few first to raise the money.

At the time I knew there was a lot of interest in me. The Under-21 call-ups had not done any harm to my reputation. I didn't have an agent because most players just didn't in those days but I knew Arsenal had come in for me. They wanted me, but the deal was dependent on John Lukic agreeing to move to Birmingham. Once again, our careers were interlinked. In the event, John went to St Andrews to talk but decided to turn their offer down and so Birmingham – then in the old Second Division – came in for me instead, offering £100,000.

John Wile told me of their interest and offered to come with me to negotiate my deal with them, which I thought was decent of him although I suppose he did have a vested interest in my signing. I did tell my dad what was happening but we weren't on close terms at the time, so now, apart from Wile, I was on my own.

The Birmingham manager was another well-known hard man, Ron Saunders, who had been a fearless centre-forward in his day.

But, remembering what had happened at Posh, I turned down his offer saying I wanted a bit more. Wile took me outside and said that, with Saunders, there was no messing about; if he offered you something that was all there was. I took his word for that and went back in and accepted the deal to become a Birmingham player in October 1984.

I'll never forget the day I signed. As soon as I had put pen to paper, Saunders said to me, 'Right, we'll have a training session.'

I said, 'What? I haven't even brought my boots.'

'Don't worry,' he said. 'We'll have all that for you.'

So we went on to the pitch and all the photographers and local TV film crews were there. I said, 'Now? In front of that lot?'

He just said 'yeah'. And you didn't argue with Ron.

So I had to do a full session. That was one occasion when I was really nervous because I was being shown off by my new manager. But, in fairness, after he put me through that ordeal he turned round and said to the camera, 'This lad'll play for England in three years.'

Considering I had played fewer than 100 league games, all of them in the Fourth Division, this was a brave prediction which put Saunders' own judgement in paying £100,000 for me right there on the line. But it was great for my confidence and my career. And, as it turned out, he wasn't far out in his prediction, although there were a few more twists and turns to my career before I became England's Number One for the first time.

7

······

Up and Down with Brum

It did not take me long to realise that my new boss was not just playing to the cameras when he predicted great things for his new goalkeeper. He had spent his playing career trying to put one over on goalies and, along the way, he had learned much about the art of goalkeeping. In fact, Ron Saunders knew more about goalkeeping than any manager I have played for before or since.

The move to Birmingham was a step up in every way – better club, better stadium, better facilities, bigger support, as well as that better-quality manager. Saunders was a character who had done it all in football. He was known for being hard and he was *very* hard. He was also fanatical about a player's weight, checking us all the time to make sure we had been looking after ourselves. If you were a couple of pounds over he would make you wear a bin liner under your shirt and then do extra running to sweat off the extra pounds. And the bin liner wasn't the worst of it. He would also make you wear a pair of what I can only describe as incontinence pants. Every Monday someone would be picked out. I can remember Ray Ransom, the former Manchester City full-back, coming in just a couple of pounds over and being made to wear this embarrassing get-up. I was always laughing at the latest victim and I think Saunders saw this and decided to cut me down to size – literally.

One weigh-day, I was just a couple of pounds over – and only then because I was still young and filling out as Ron and his staff well knew – but they had obviously decided it was my turn, come what may. This time, everyone else had a good laugh as I put on my plastic nappy with a bin liner inside it. I must have looked like an early model for the *Spitting Image* John Major puppet but I can't think of a better incentive for keeping your weight down.

And to be fair, if you did the right stuff for Ron on the field, he would look after you off it. He was good tactically as well as hard on us physically, but the best thing about him for me was his knowledge of goalkeeping. He'd never played in that position, but he just knew so much about what it took to be a good goalkeeper and what coaching and training was needed to improve our part of the game. He also clearly knew a good goalkeeper when he saw one. When he managed Aston Villa, he had Nigel Spink and Jimmy Rimmer and they were both top goalies. Before me at Birmingham he had Tony Coton, who was another good goalie.

Some people in football realise that goalies are important and some don't. It is as simple as that. But, for me, if you have a good team but just an average goalie, you are quickly found out. Yet transfer fees still suggest that we are not worth half of a good outfield player and that has to be wrong.

Ron Saunders passed his knowledge down through his staff. In a typical exercise, he or one of his coaches would volley the ball at me from close range. I was to catch it in front of my face without flinching or moving my head because Saunders understood one of the most important elements in good goalkeeping: keeping your head still as you make sure you watch the ball all the way. If someone throws you a tennis ball and you follow it right through its path with your eyes, you will catch it but, if you look away for a second, you will drop it. Good coaching is all geared to keeping your head still. In a game, you will often be playing from the floor – diving about, getting up quickly, all your body moving fast in a certain direction but, if your head is not fixed on the ball, you will not make the save. If your brain can recognise that the ball is coming towards you, your body will automatically move in the right direction. In other words, you must focus on the ball not the player striking it. The only time to watch him is if he is taking a penalty because then the ball is still. When the ball is moving, you need to watch that.

This is the reason goalkeepers have so many problems with free-kicks outside the box. There are so many bodies in front of you that your vision of the ball is blocked. You can't move until you see the ball and by then it may be too late. When you let one in, people criticise you because the free-kick was a long way out but it does not matter how far out it is if you only see the ball when it comes over or through the wall. Only then can you move but, by that time, it usually has too much pace on it for you to make the save.

Sometimes a defensive wall can push you out of position and strikers like to use that. When David Beckham is taking the free-kick, I just put two or three defenders in the wall so that I still have a good view. Beckham is definitely the best free-kick specialist in the country. Stuart Pearce was all power and plenty of it but Becks gets power, pace *and* swerve on it. He seems to strike a ball – especially a dead ball – in a totally different way to anyone else. In open play, he does not even need to beat anybody to fire in a dangerous cross. He just needs half a yard of space and then he whips it in. It is almost always a quality delivery and, because the strikers know that, they will always move in more positively because of it. They are also able to use the pace of his crosses to get better strikes on goal. For me, Becks should always be played wide because his kind of crosses are the hardest part of the game for goalkeepers to deal with effectively. They will produce more danger than anything else in the game.

Although there was no one about with Becks's crossing ability when I was at Birmingham, Saunders always made sure we had plenty of practice dealing with crosses. The coaching staff would make the youth team stay back with the goalkeepers for crossing sessions in the afternoons. I felt a bit sorry for them sometimes as they were young and still growing and all these big goalies would be crashing into them to catch or punch the crosses. I would see them limping off, counting their bruises, but it was all part of the learning process for them as it had been for me the first time I played in the league and had all those old pro centre-forwards crashing into me.

Two years at Posh had been a steep learning curve for me and the move to Birmingham proved that my career was going in the right direction, but it was not just moving up two divisions that made my start for the Midlands club a real challenge. That season (1984–5), Birmingham had moved straight to the top of Division Two but then they sold Coton to Watford. Saunders had bought a keeper from Sunderland to replace him but, for once, his judgement must have let him down because he immediately started looking for another goalie. Even though the club must have been unsettled with first John Lukic looking set to be their new goalie and then me coming along instead of him, their results had not been affected. In fact, my first game for them came on the end of a nine match-winning run. I went into the team for the tenth game, away at Brighton, and we promptly lost. Fortunately, I did save a penalty and make a few other good saves, so the blame for ending the run wasn't aimed in my direction by the team, management, or – most important of all – the fans.

We used to have big crowds at St Andrews and a good following away from home as well. I soon discovered that the most important part of supporting Birmingham was the massive rivalry with Aston Villa. It did not matter who we were playing, all the songs seemed to be based on our fans' hatred of the Villa.

At the time, Villa were in the First Division so there were no league derbies in my first season but we were drawn against them in one of the cups. We drew 0–0 at St Andrews but then went to Villa and won 3–0. Our fans were just ecstatic; it made their whole season. In fact, they would come up and say things like, 'That's a memory for life. Beating them like that at their place. I'll never forget it.'

We had a decent side, but probably with too many older players coming to the end of their careers, something which found us out when we reached the First Division. But there were some very good players including Des Bremner, Billy Wright and Gerry Daly. To look at him, you would never have picked out Daly as a footballer. He did not have any physique and you never saw him off the pitch without a fag in his mouth but in a match he showed great skill and always seemed to have so much time on the ball. Off the pitch, he was a great character, too – good fun to be around.

Other players there included Ken Armstrong, an experienced centre-half who had played for Southampton, strikers David Geddes and Wayne Clarke, wide players Robert Hopkin and Ian Benjamin (Benje had been with me at Posh) and full-backs Brian Borrows and Ray Ransom. In midfield, Martin Kuhl was a key figure. He was a decent player and scored a few important goals, too. But he was the kind of player you want in your own side and not to play against as he did like to leave his foot in when he tackled.

Although he was a hard man himself, Saunders liked us to play good football going forward. But he was always on at us not to take risks at the back. It was drummed into the back four that no one would score against us if the ball had been put into the stand or passed back to the goalie. (Those were the days . . .) It was a style of play that worked and we were promoted in my first season, going up behind Oxford who were champions that year.

I remember we celebrated with an open-top bus taking us through the city and thousands of fans turned out. They were very passionate fans – some of them too passionate. There was a nasty bunch called the Zulus who caused a fair bit of trouble in those days.

But, although I was obviously delighted with my first real success in the professional game, I was still only 21. I remember being pleased for the fans but I don't think that what we had achieved had really sunk in. There was so much going on in my life, what with moving to a new club in a higher division, buying a house and living in a big city, that it all seemed to pass me by.

It was the same the following season when we were relegated. It was the only time I have been in a relegated team – the only time I have ever been in a team that has been in a relegation battle, for that matter – but I don't remember too much about it. Apart from feeling sorry for the fans, I don't think my game was affected by it all and I have no real memories of that season. I suppose the bad memories do not stick as much as the good ones. Goalkeepers in relegated sides always have busy seasons and, looking at it selfishly, it can be good for your career as you have more chances to make saves.

Promotion and then that short spell in the top flight certainly did not do my international prospects any harm, either. In my two years with Birmingham, I was called up ten times for the Under-21s and I also played in a B international. And, as I mentioned, things were also happening for me off the pitch.

Professional footballers have to be prepared to up sticks and move house and family on a regular basis. It goes with the territory. So, although we had been happily settled in Peterborough, it was new club, new city, new house for us. Birmingham seemed such a massive place and, to be honest, I was a little scared of it. It was a big city, quite run-down at the time, and I had heard a lot of stories about what went on in the streets at night.

We decided to live outside the city and bought a house in South Yardley near Solihull. Detached with three bedrooms, it had a decent-sized garden with a duckpond and some incontinent geese. But there was a public footpath down the side of it, which I would not risk having now.

We would probably have been better off renting again but footballers always believe they are going to be at their new club for the rest of their careers. At least, that's what footballers used to think before a certain Mr Bosman came on the scene.

This house was the venue for my one and only attempt at plumbing. I decided I could plumb in the white goods myself, so I settled myself down with this kitchen sink unit and some flexible pipes and set to it. Five hours later, I was still at it. Every time I thought I had cracked it, I would turn the water on and there would be another leak. In the end, not knowing what to do next, I turned the water off and decided to sleep on it. All night I had nightmares about water all over the floor and furniture. Then in the morning, I had another two or three attempts before giving in and calling a plumber. It took him half an hour, tops. That was the last time I tried to do anything like that myself. I can do simple DIY but generally I prefer to call the experts in now.

And the nightmare turned out to be a premonition because, when we left Birmingham for London, we kept the house for a while. I was desperate to sell it, though, because we had bought another house and the two mortgages were draining my bank account. That first winter, one of the hot-water pipes froze and then burst. We came back to check on the place, opened the door and walked right in on it. From the attic down, all the windows were steamed up and the doors swollen, with all the paintwork scalded right off them. It was a right mess and I had to try and repair the damage, bodging it up so that it looked all right for potential buyers.

My two years in Birmingham are also memorable for two more major off-the-field events – the birth of my two sons Daniel (now 15) and Thomas (14). My roving football career means that they are that rare breed: Brummies with Yorkshire accents. Thomas is a keen footballer (and a goalie, as well) while Daniel is a very good golfer.

When I went to Birmingham, I started to play less golf and took up fishing instead. My brother-in-law (at the time) got me into it. He had just started fishing himself and, when he came down to stay for a weekend, he persuaded me to go with him to find some lakes. I started by catching small carp, but then I found my lines were being snapped by the bigger carp. So, as I wanted to catch them as well, I started looking into what equipment I needed – was it heavier lines or heavier rods? We went to a well-known carp place – Cuttle Mill, near Tamworth. It is actually opposite the famous Belfry golf course, so it was ideal. Sometimes I played golf at the Belfry, sometimes I went fishing, depending on how I felt.

But I still play golf now, often enough to have my clubs sponsored by Taylor-Made. I like playing the charity games, testimonials and pro-ams, especially when there is a good crowd there. I am competitive, after all.

But golf and fishing – especially carp fishing – are both very time-consuming so it is really a case of one or the other. Fishing is more solitary and more relaxing. I like the challenge of catching a fish but I don't feel frustrated if it gets away. You can go out on a sunny day for a round of golf on a beautiful course but still play crap which for me will ruin the whole day. Fishing is good for me as a player and as a person. I can be away from everything and my mind becomes absorbed. Nothing intrudes, not football, not the house. Whether you are having a good time or bad time in football does not seem to matter when you are sitting at the water's edge.

When Birmingham were relegated, I did worry that I might be treading water in my career so I was pleased when QPR, then in the old First Division, agreed to buy me for £225,000 just before the start of the 1986–7 season. I had played 84 games for Birmingham, 75 in the league, been in a promotion-winning side and in the process had more than doubled my transfer value to them. Saunders had left the club by then, to be replaced just before I left by John Bond, but he should have been proud that his judgement in goalkeepers had been justified yet again. And there was still a year to go for me to fulfil his prediction that I would be an England international within three years of signing for Birmingham.

At least I was moving in the right direction if I was going to prove him right – *up* to the First Division and *down* to London, the centre of sports media attention.

8

· · · · · ·

Bright Lights, Big City – Plastic Pitch?

I spent four seasons at QPR, which, as it turned out, was probably one too many. During my time there, the club had three managers which, as far as I was concerned, was also one too many.

Jim Smith was the manager who signed me and I liked him from the moment I met him in the then chairman (Jim Gregory)'s office. Jim Smith comes from Sheffield and is very friendly and down to earth. I enjoyed working with him because he was a good laugh and was always straightforward with players. You always knew where you were with him and what he wanted from you. He was also one of only two managers – Ron Saunders was the other – to show a real personal interest in the goalkeeping side of things. As a manager, he has become known for his ability as a motivator, but outsiders would probably be surprised at his tactical nous. Before all our games, he would go through the other team in great detail. Towards the end of his time at the club, he was also getting involved in the pyschological side of motivating players. He brought in a series of mental therapists who had different methods but were basically trying to put us into positive frames of mind, able to convince ourselves we would beat Liverpool 10–0.

We were one of the first clubs to go down this alternative road and, although it does not seem a very Jim Smith-like approach, he was definitely the driving force behind it. I have come to believe in the value of positive thought and visualising doing the right things on the pitch, but I find it easier to be self-motivating. Doing it as a group, I could not take it seriously. And I was not the only one.

A TV crew came down to film us in one of these sessions and when it was shown you could see half the lads killing themselves laughing.

They were trying to get us chanting, shouting, going into huddles, telling each other we were the best. But players are realists as well and we knew we were never going to be world-beaters and it was clear to us that, although Jim Smith was a good and ambitious manager, the club was not really going anywhere. Its ambition was simply to stay in the division, not to win it.

In fairness, QPR probably does not have a large enough base of supporters to match the big clubs although that was less of a problem then than it is now. But Wimbledon have proved you can go a long way without having many supporters behind you. During my four seasons there, we were never in any real danger of going down, but, equally, we never looked likely to win anything. The highest we managed was sixth in the league one year and we also reached the semi-final of the Littlewoods (League) Cup. And, although the club seemed happy enough to pay wages that were on a par with most of the other clubs, it was seen as a selling club. After I left, Paul Parker and Les Ferdinand were both sold off without big-name replacements coming in.

But, all that said, there were some good players there during my time and we were a decent footballing side as well. We had Alan McDonald, Warren Neill, Ian Dawes and Terry Fenwick in defence; Gary Waddock was a good competitor in midfield with Peter Reid and Ray Wilkins joining him later on; Wayne Fereday played out wide and Alan Brazil, Les Ferdinand and Gary Bannister were among the strikers we had.

Bannister signed for us from Coventry, where he had scored lots of goals. I remember him for two things: a bad car accident he had when driving back to the Midlands with his wife one time; and that he had one leg a good inch shorter than the other. For some reason, Gary did not have his boot built up to compensate, so he walked with a pronounced limp. But I don't think I have ever seen a ball hit harder than he could strike it with his shorter leg.

Then there was Mark Dennis, who played full-back at one stage. The Dennis Wise of his time, he was a good player and a great character. But, just like Wise, he was always being sent off and getting into scrapes on and off the field. I remember one game when he tried so hard to put a forward into touch that, when he flew across to tackle him, he missed him altogether and ended up clattering into the advertising boards himself. He knocked them for six and badly damaged his own knee in the process.

He could start a fight in an empty room but he was a funny guy. Once I saw him standing at the bar, having had a few. He started rocking backwards and, as he began to fall, put his hand up to the bar to stop himself falling. Instead, he managed to clear the bar of every drink there but, as he hit the ground, he bounced immediately back up, still holding his own pint. He had not spilt a drop. That's what I call a serious drinker.

Although there were not that many of them, the supporters were generally good to us, except for a section near the tunnel who really did like to moan. Apart from right at the end of my time there, I did not get much stick but some of the players were targeted for real abuse. And it did not stop after the game.

As QPR's Loftus Road ground in West London is small and in the middle of a built-up area, car parking was a real problem. There was no room in the club car park, so on match days we had to leave the cars on public roads and walk through an alleyway to the club. Fans found out what we were doing and the players they did not rate, like Colin Clarke, were coming back after games to find all kinds of rude messages written on their cars.

Despite his popularity with the players and most of the fans, Jim Smith was not to last out my time with the club. After I had been there two years or so, he was out and suddenly Trevor Francis was in as manager. As a player, he had been saddled with the tag of Britain's first £1million player; as a new manager, he was constantly reminded that Brian Clough had described him as being too nice to succeed. I don't know whether this made him determined to be extra-tough to prove Cloughie wrong but he was not the most popular manager I have ever played for.

I don't believe in getting too close to managers. However friendly they may be, the fact is they have to make decisions that affect your career and your whole life and that makes it hard to stay friends with them. But I don't go out of my way to be on bad terms with them, either. That said, I really did not get along too well with Francis. When he arrived, I had just over a year left on my four-year contract and was team captain, But when I refused to sign a new contract, he took away the captaincy. I thought that was petty as I had played well for the club and didn't feel that I was trying to hold them to ransom. The reason I wanted to leave was nothing to do with money. Like most players, I wanted to win things and I just could not see that happening at Rangers. It was a decent club, but a small one, and could not really compete at the highest level.

While I was there, the Thompson family (founders of Marley Tiles) took it over but, as far as I could see, never did anything for the club. They certainly did not put much money into it. It was almost like a plaything, an impression a meeting with Richard Thompson did nothing to dispel. Only 26, he had just been made chairman by his father when he sat in on some contract talks I had with Jim Smith. It had all been very friendly and, when everything had been sorted out, he suddenly said to Jim, 'Last game of the season, any chance of my getting on for ten minutes?'

Jim looked at me and we were waiting for him to laugh and say he was only kidding. But he didn't, and we realised he was deadly serious. There was an embarrassing pause while we tried to keep straight faces and then Jim managed to explain, tactfully, that something like that would not be possible. We tried to laugh it off afterwards but it is fair to say none of the players nor Jim could have much respect for Thompson after that.

When Francis became manager he made Peter Reid his player coach and I didn't get on much better with him. I can remember one time when we were both in the medical room, getting some treatment for injuries. Out of the blue, he just turned to me and said, 'Why don't you either sign your fucking contract or just fuck off?'

I said, 'I'd rather fuck off, all right, so just keep your nose out.'

And he was completely taken aback that I'd had the nerve to answer back.

But I was not having that from him. I was not talking about breaking my contract, just leaving when it ended. Yet, if the club wanted to sell me, they would – whether I was under contract or not. As it turned out, that is exactly what they tried to do the following year.

Francis also put his foot in it big-time when he tried to play hardball with one of the other players, Martin Allen. He had already upset us both when he put a block on a move to Tottenham. Spurs had made a bid for both of us and, although Francis initially let us know about it, he then avoided us for the next couple of weeks. We were left completely in the dark and, although we never found out what happened between the two clubs, the bid fizzled out. He obviously had not wanted us to go and made sure it did not happen.

This was a complete contrast to the way Jim Smith had handled a similar situation. He called me in one day and said, 'I've got some good news and some bad news for you. The good news is that Tottenham have come in for you; the bad news is that I don't have to sell you.'

I went away and thought about that and then came back and said, 'If you won't sell me, I'll have a raise instead.' Jim said there was no more cash but I could upgrade my car. I knew that Jim did not know much about cars so I said I would have a Ford Sierra Cosworth. Thinking one Sierra was much like another and not particularly expensive, Jim agreed straightaway but soon found out exactly how much the one I wanted cost. He came back a couple of days later and said, 'You did say a Cosworth?'

'Yes.'

'Mmm, thought so,' he grunted, and he gave me a very old-fashioned look. But he kept his word.

Francis's management style was quite different and it even became the subject for national debate during the saga of Martin Allen's baby.

We were due to play a game up at Newcastle at the time when Martin's wife was expecting her first baby. Martin wanted to stay behind but Francis insisted he travel with the team. Martin agreed but said that, if his wife went into labour, he was going back. Francis simply said he would see about that if and when it happened.

I was sharing a room at the hotel with Martin and I took the call from his wife at about two in the morning. She said that the baby was starting. I told Martin and he asked me what I thought. I told him he had to go back; it was their first baby and it was important he was with his wife. He went down to see the physio and told him he was going and caught the first flight home.

Francis was furious and I can remember him slagging off Martin in the team meeting, saying he had left us in the lurch and what sort of team-mate does that? I can remember thinking he had got it all wrong. And I was not the only one to think that.

It made all the newspapers (Martin made sure of that) and not just the back pages. When Francis fined Martin two weeks' wages, he found himself under attack from all sides. MPs stuck their oars in and it was even debated on TV. It was definitely a case of Francis trying to play the hard man and I am sure, with the experience he has had since, he would never handle that kind of situation in the same way again. Look at the stick Sir Alex was given when he fined Becks for missing training one day last season, supposedly because baby Brooklyn had a bit of a cold. What Francis did was like making someone play when one of their parents was seriously ill. Apart from anything else, if you do make the player turn out, what frame of mind would he be in anyway? He is hardly going to be focused on the game.

In the event, Francis suffered more than Martin, because he lost the respect of a lot of the players and the fans and it must have been a major factor in his sacking shortly afterwards.

The other aspect of playing at QPR that I was anxious to leave behind me was its infamous plastic pitch. I have a lot of time for Terry Venables – as a person and as a coach – but this was not one of his better ideas. Whatever its inventors said about how the plastic was a natural surface and better than playing on muddy, snowy or frosty surfaces, it was artificial. When it was dry, the ball bounced higher and higher and the bounce exaggerated the spin on the ball so you never knew where it was going to end up. When it was wet, it was like playing on a bar of soap. The quality of the games was definitely affected, but there was no doubt it gave us an advantage over the away side. We had learned how to play on it; most other teams hadn't and their players used to get some terrible injuries.

Teams would come and train for two or three days before the game but that was never enough to change their instincts and normal way of playing. On match days they would still be doing sliding tackles. We would see one of their players running full-pelt to the byline to get a cross in and be thinking, 'He's not going to be able to stop.' Sure enough, there would be an almighty crunch and he would be flat out over the hoardings.

Although people always used to say how bad it must be for goalies diving, it was far worse for outfield players. At least I could go out dressed for it with padded elbows and tracksuit bottoms. The rest of them could not wear padding because it would slow them down. But, ironically, the worst injury I saw while at QPR was nothing to do with the pitch and it happened to me, not an outfield player.

We were practising set-pieces, mainly defending corners, and the ball had gone dead when one of the lads hit a shot which I parried. The ball bounced down and I put my hand out to collect it. At the same moment, Les Ferdinand kicked the ball and his follow-through caught the end of my thumb. I immediately knew I had broken it and told the others. They did not believe me because I had not even taken the glove off to look. When I did, a piece of bone caught on the material and I shouted out in pain. The players looked and then immediately looked away. I looked, felt faint and had to sit down while they phoned for an ambulance. The ambulance men put a towel over it to stop me looking at it but, as I walked across, I felt faint again and they had to sit me down. It was a compound dislocation and the bone was out to one side so it was pretty bad. There again, my mum remembers me fainting over a simple injection at the hospital when I was a lad.

Fortunately, I do not think about the consequences when I am diving at strikers' feet. I would not be able to do the job if I did. Getting whacked is part of that job and I have had six or seven cracked ribs along the way, yet I never feel any fear when I am playing. I think you can spot the goalkeepers who do, and other teams will always play on it.

Apart from when I played on the plastic pitch, I have never worn any padding except shin pads. I did think about having a T-shirt padded to protect my ribs but decided against. Any padding would have to be very flexible and it probably still would not protect me from a big whack. I have tried different things, including the vests that racing jockeys use, but nothing has felt right. American footballers can wear padding because they are just whacking each other and running more or less straight up and down the pitch – they don't need to be as flexible as players in our kind of football.

It is elbowing that has caused most of my rib injuries. When goalies go up for the ball, we can't protect ourselves. Our arms are reaching up, leaving ribs exposed and vulnerable. This is why we need protection by the referee, not because we are wimps and just don't like being challenged, as some of the TV pundits would have it. Not that they were talking too much about me on the TV in my QPR days anyway – and that was a problem. Although I was playing in the capital and, because of it, becoming better known by the media and the football establishment than when I was at Birmingham, it was still fairly low-key stuff. QPR were just not featured on TV as often as the big clubs. In fact, the only times our games were shown were when we were playing one of the top sides. Any player will tell you that, if you want to get noticed, particularly by international managers, the more often you are on the box, the better. Forget Trevor Francis and the plastic pitch, the real reason I wanted a move was to win medals and a lot more caps.

I had enjoyed a taste of full international football while I was at QPR and I wanted more. I had received my first full England cap, two years into my QPR career, just a year later than Ron Saunders had predicted for me. Peter Shilton and Chris Woods were numbers one and two but neither was available for a friendly with Saudi Arabia in November 1988, so Bobby Robson turned to me.

It was a doubly memorable experience for me as the game was sponsored by British Airways and we flew out on Concorde. It was my first time flying supersonic and, on the return journey, the pilot re-routed us for a spectacular view of the Pyramids.

Unfortunately it was not a spectacular England performance. There were few chances for either side and then we went a goal down. It was a well-placed but not particularly fierce shot from Majed Abdullah. I scrambled across to it but it hit the underside of my left arm on its way into the net. I was very disappointed to let one in on my debut, but at least my future Arsenal team-mate Tony Adams helped me out by scoring an equaliser so the game ended 1–1. But, if the performances by the team and myself were less than memorable, there were good reasons for the game to stick in my mind forever and not just because it was my first full cap.

For a start, I had never played on a pitch like it. They had delayed the kick-off to the evening to avoid the heat, but this meant that the local wildlife was out and about. The pitch was covered in bugs, huge ones, and like nothing I had ever seen, even in the depths of that Rotherham canal. It was also my first time in the Middle East and I found it extraordinary the way everything in the streets and souks stopped at the call for prayer, which came many times a day. But perhaps my fondest memory of the game is that, as it was my England debut, it meant I qualified for a sponsored England team car. And that year it was an XR3. But sadly, a few of the lads wrecked theirs and this privilege was soon cancelled.

I won a couple more caps after that, but only when Shilts and Chris were out of the reckoning. In fact, the third cap only came along because Chris managed to cut his finger on a penknife while fiddling with the waistband of his tracksuit trousers. I knew that age and experience had something to do with my lack of opportunities, but I also knew that I would have a better chance of becoming England's Number One if I was playing for a bigger, more successful club.

It turned out to be easier said than done. Francis was still the manager when Arsenal first came in for me and I was put on and then taken off the transfer list without even being asked about it. The two clubs had already agreed my transfer before I was even involved. Arsenal wanted me before the transfer deadline kicked in towards the end of the 1989–90 season but part of the deal involved John Lukic – yes, him again – agreeing to go to QPR on loan. But John dug his heels in and refused to go. He was not at all happy about the way he was being treated by Arsenal manager George Graham.

This snag only happened at the last moment, on deadline day. I was actually at Highbury, with all the media waiting for the transfer to be announced, when Graham took me aside to explain that there had been a bit of a hiccup and it was all off. There is a photograph of me with a big long face, in front of the cameras, having expected to be telling the world I had joined Arsenal and instead having to go back to QPR.

It was something I never expected and, while Graham said he was disappointed, I was really gutted. What made it worse was that I had to go back to QPR on the Thursday to prepare for a home game two days later. Until then I'd had a good relationship with the fans but when I went out on the pitch for the next match, there was a very mixed reception for me. Half of the home fans cheered, the other half booed. It was not quite as bad as when Paul Ince was photographed in a Man Utd shirt before his move from West Ham went through and it was nothing like the reception Becks and Alan Shearer now receive around the country, but I was not used to being abused by my own fans. Some fans had turned against me because I had said I wanted to leave, but I was coming to the end of my contract and it was the right decision for my career. You only have one career so you have to be selfish in that way.

One compensation was that the clubs and I had a verbal agreement that the transfer would go through in the close season. The contract was signed the next day but not dated until the end of the season. There was another bonus, too. When I was on my way to Arsenal for the signing that never was, I had a call on my mobile from Clive Berlin, QPR's commercial director. He wanted to know when I would be returning the club car, which was a bit premature considering I had not even signed the Arsenal contract. Talk about giving you your hat and coat and showing you the door. I don't know whether he wanted the car for himself, but my first thought was 'bloody charming'. When the deal fell through, I took great pleasure in telling him that I would have to hang on to the Cosworth for a bit longer.

Other clubs were also sniffing around me at the time, although I never got to the bottom of the rumoured Celtic interest. An agent kept ringing me up saying Celtic wanted me but, like a lot of supposed approaches that agents say are on the way, nothing came of it.

I had parted company with a couple of agents myself because they wanted paying every week instead of just commission on deals and I felt I was not getting my money's worth. One of them also had a lot of players on his books and that does not help as it inevitably means there are fewer promotional deals and sponsorships to go round.

Even though I was an England international, I was doing very little outside promotion work, as anyone with anything to sell goes to the big clubs for the big-name players. I had a few glove deals but that was about it.

I finally signed with Jerome Anderson, who represented some of the Arsenal players. I thought it would be a good move to get in with him once all the rumours about Arsenal coming for me started. What happened in the end is that Francis was sacked and Don Howe became caretaker manager. He knew the Arsenal move was in the air and he just said that I should go there as quickly as possible and that it would be the best move I would ever make. He was brilliant, just wanting to make sure I did what was best for my career. He had already been responsible for me linking up with Bob Wilson, who is still my goalkeeping coach.

As usual, there was no specialist coach at QPR when I joined. One of the other goalies, Paul Barron, used to take some sessions and he was quite good, but then he left the club. I asked Don if I could have a specialist coach and through his contacts at his old club Arsenal, he arranged for Bob, who was coaching the Arsenal goalies, to come to Rangers once a week.

Players have a lot of time for Don Howe because they respect his knowledge and his enthusiasm for the game. After he had his heart bypass operation, he was only back at the club three or four days before he was running up and down, really out of breath and panting. We were all worried and told him to take it easy but he just kept running, gasping out, 'I'm all right . . . pant . . . pant . . . I'm all right.' Luckily, he has been all right ever since.

Manchester United also approached me once the Arsenal deal was out in the open and I even spoke to Alex Ferguson on that transfer deadline day, but he was talking about a future deal while the Arsenal offer was immediate.

I talked to Ray Wilkins, who was at QPR then, and he told me to choose Arsenal as I would win things straightaway with the team they had. As it turned out, he was right on the button. And that was what it was about – winning things, not money. They offered me more money to stay at QPR but Don knew I would go.

All players want to win medals. If we lose games, we are so upset we don't even want to go out and certainly don't want to read the papers. In fact I don't read the papers much at all now. It reached the stage where I was wondering what particular writers were going to say about my performances and I realised it was not helping. It was just their opinion, anyway. If it is praise, it does not matter; if it is flak, it is only going to upset me, so I only ever flip through game reports now.

It is a lot more important to have the fans on your side and that was my first problem at Arsenal. Although John Lukic had turned down QPR, Graham had made it clear that he wanted me in and John out so he finally agreed to a £1million move back to Leeds. Arsenal paid £1.3million, earning QPR more than £1million profit on me. At the time, it was the largest fee paid for a British goalkeeper and equalled the world record fee for a goalkeeper. Since I was only effectively costing Arsenal a net £300,000, it looked like good business to everyone except a hard core of Arsenal fans who thought there was no need for a new keeper at Arsenal because they already had a top-class one.

They had a point, because John had played a major part in the club winning the championship the season before but football is all about opinions and Graham thought I was a better goalkeeper. He was the manager, so that was it for John.

But it was down to me, not Graham, to win the fans over. It was the most pressure I have ever felt, at least as far as fans are concerned. At all my clubs, I have always tried to build a relationship with the fans, but every other time I'd joined a club, the fans were on my side to start with. Not this time.

9

· · · · · ·

One-Nil to the Arsenal

When Arsenal played the last game of the 1989–90 season away at Norwich, the fans knew that John Lukic was leaving and that I was joining to replace him. Most of them didn't like the idea – and that is putting it mildly.

The army of fans who follow their clubs away from home see themselves, reasonably enough, as the most loyal of the team's supporters and, if they believe one of their favourites is being badly treated, they let the management know all about it. The Norwich game had no other significance as Arsenal had long been out of the running for the championship, so the fans spent their time before, during and after the game chanting their support for John Lukic and, more worryingly for me, that they did not want David Seaman.

This was all widely reported, so I knew exactly what I was likely to be facing the first time I put on the Arsenal goalkeeper's jersey. I am a confident guy and I believed then, as now, in my own ability but I must admit I started to worry that I might have let myself in for a nightmare. And, although I was being paid more for the privilege of being booed than I had been at QPR, I also knew I would have been earning even more if I had decided to stay there.

My mood was not improved when I went to Arsenal to sign the contract. The cab-driver recognised me, guessed why I was going to Arsenal, and the first thing he came out with was, 'This lot, they're not the best payers, are they?' I had to keep reminding myself why I had made the decision. As a club, QPR was going nowhere. It *had* challenged for the Division One championship not that many years earlier but the reality – even before the Premiership came in – was that to make a realistic challenge was costing more money every year. Many millions were needed to bring in the top players.

QPR did not attract the crowds to generate that kind of money. Its Loftus Road ground would not have had the capacity to cope with them even if they had. Crucially, the club's owners were unable or unwilling to invest the necessary millions either. As a player, you can be playing brilliantly for a club like QPR but most people in the game will never see you. If you want an international career, you have to raise your profile. At that time, there were fewer games on TV so it was always just the top teams on show. Sky (now BSkyB) has made a big difference because of the huge number of games it shows, although it is still always going to be the big clubs which are featured most. Back then, if you played for a small club, you were virtually invisible. Managers, even international ones, are affected by the media. Press and TV coverage might not make them pick a player but it alerts them to his presence and there is a better chance that they will take a closer look at him. It is a build-up of factors. The press start writing about you and then people in the street start saying you should be playing for England, and that only happens because they have seen you on TV.

Ironically, given my reasons for joining Arsenal, my first move after signing for the Gunners was to fly to Italy to join the World Cup squad for which I had been selected while still a QPR player. I was going as number three goalkeeper, again behind Shilts and Chris Woods.

It was even more ironic when my former QPR team-mate, Paul Parker, broke my thumb with a shot in training at our camp in Cagliari. I did not see it coming and it caught me right on the end of the thumb just like Les Ferdinand's boot had done before. Paul definitely had it in for goalkeepers that tournament as it was his deflection of a free-kick that deceived Shilts for the Germans' opening goal in the semi-final.

I was long gone by then, though, replaced by Dave Beasant in the squad. The England team doctor, John Crane, was also the Arsenal doctor so, when we went to hospital and found out the thumb was broken, he said I would have to tell George Graham and Arsenal chairman David Dein straightaway. I asked him where we had to go

David Andrew Seaman, aged nine months. I was born in Rotherham on
19 September 1963, weighing in at a sturdy 9lb 2oz.

With my younger brother Colin, who had the talent but not the little bit of luck you also need to become a professional footballer.

My first encounter with a striker's elbow? If it was, it certainly didn't put me off wanting to be a goalie as soon as I was old enough to join the big lads' kickabout in the school playground.

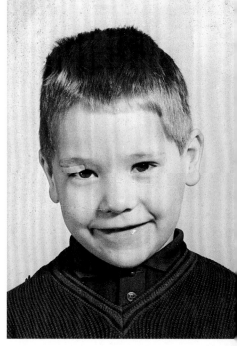

Mean, moody and moustachioed (well, almost) – the typical teenager look.

Cheers to Mum and Dad –
Pam and Roger – who did
so much to help me realise
my dream of becoming a
pro footballer.

There's no such thing as a quiet
night out at the movies once you
become a 'celebrity' but who's
complaining? Certainly not my
wife Debbie and I when we are
invited to star-studded premieres
like this one for *Judge Dredd*.

My winning the Elle style award in 1998
was one in the eye for those commentators (are you listening, Alan Green?) who
keep telling me my hair's too long.

Fishing is my escape from the pressures and tensions of bigtime football. I enjoy it even if I don't catch anything but when I reel in a big one – like this 32lb carp – it gives me the same buzz as saving a penalty.

I took up golf when I was playing for Peterborough and found I had a flair for it but it can be such a frustrating game that I now prefer fishing for relaxation.

Above With Debbie in the Wembley Players' Lounge during Euro 96, the tournament that changed my life. From then on, I found myself on the front as well as the back pages.

Right After Euro 96, TV companies started inviting me to appear on different shows such as ITV's *Wish You Were Here ...?* Debbie and I were sent to Florida to report on the holiday attractions of Captiva Island. A tough job but ...

It's a family affair. Debbie, my brother Colin and Mum and Dad join me in celebrating Arsenal's Double: winning the Premiership and the FA Cup in the 1997/8 season.

Debbie and her mum, Georgina, who was a lovely lady and so supportive to us both.

Calm as ever, Debbie's dad, Robbie, giving the traditional father-of-the-bride speech at our wedding.

If you invite your fellow England internationals Ian 'Wrighty' Wright, Paul 'Gazza' Gascoigne and Paul 'Incey' Ince to your wedding, your chances of a quiet reception are bound to be, well, snookered.

Just a perfect day – when Debbie and I married at Castle Ashby in Northamptonshire on 15 July 1998.

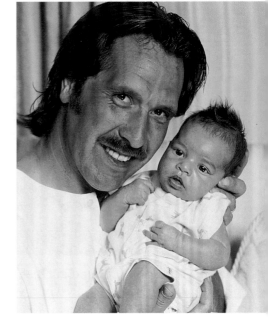

We decided not to find out which sex our baby was going to be beforehand so couldn't decide on a name, either. Having two sons already, I was especially delighted when Debbie had a little girl. Both Debbie and her dad, Robbie, were touched when I suggested we name her Georgina after Debbie's late mother.

to do that and I was surprised when he said the local port. When we arrived, there was a huge boat anchored in the harbour. It dominated the whole place and everyone was admiring it.

It turned out to be Dein's boat. He had travelled to Italy in it and now I was being taken on board to explain that, a few weeks after him sanctioning a £1.3million transfer fee, I was crocked. He and Graham took it well, though. After all, it was early in the close season and I would be fit for the new season. And, while I was disappointed to be leaving the World Cup squad early – we had only played two games – I knew that, as number three 'keeper, I was unlikely to have taken any active part in any of the games.

At least the injury gave me a chance to see for myself just how different Arsenal was from any of my other clubs. On board the boat, there were waitresses and uniformed crew all asking me and the other guests what we wanted. Nothing was too much trouble. It was exactly how you would imagine a millionaire's yacht to be and a completely different world to the one I had been used to.

I had played for some decent clubs but Arsenal was in a different league. I had thought that Leeds was a big club and, in its own way it was, but its on-field success only began in the 1960s and '70s. Arsenal, on the other hand, has always been a big club and anyone who joins it is immediately aware of its traditions and of its way of doing things. That way is to do everything in style, from the training through to the coaches the team travels in. Only the best will do for Arsenal.

I had been used to training in old T-shirts supplied by the clubs; when I arrived at Arsenal, we used to be given old first-team shirts and jerseys to wear for training. When I put one of these on, I always used to imagine what great games it had been worn in. It immediately made you feel good about yourself, as though the past glories rubbed off on you. But I still had to prove myself to the fans who would have preferred to see John Lukic wearing the current first-team jersey instead of me.

The club had a pre-season tour in Scandinavia and, my thumb having healed up well, I made my first Arsenal appearance against a small Swedish club none of us had ever heard of. Quite a few fans had followed us there but I just showed them what my goalkeeping was like and it seemed to win them over.

But before my first game in the UK, I was really nervous. It was against Wolves at Molineux in another pre-season friendly. There were a lot more Arsenal fans there but everything went well. I came out and caught all the crosses and made a few saves from local hero Steve Bull.

I took the same positive frame of mind into that first season. I reminded myself that I had been desperate to join Arsenal, so it was up to me to show the fans how good I was.

The first league game was against Wimbledon at its original Plough Lane ground. We won 3–0 and, although there were still some sceptics with reservations about my signing, most had disappeared by the end of the season. The clean sheet was the first of many and I only let in 18 goals all season.

The original back four was already in place: Lee Dixon, Steve Bould, Tony Adams and Nigel Winterburn, with David O'Leary and Colin Pates as cover. Martin Keown had been allowed to leave the club and would not return until 1992.

I was a little scared about how the players would take to me. Although none of them were the established internationals many were to become over the next few years, they had already won championship medals. I thought they would be looking me over to see if I was up to it, but there was none of that. In fact, they seemed to accept me straightaway.

Tony Adams has written since that I turned out to be a better goalie than he thought I was when I was playing for QPR. I thought I had always played well against Arsenal – both for Birmingham and QPR – but Tony had scored a couple of goals against me (from all of a yard out as I remember) so he was not quite so sure about me. But none of that doubt came through to me and I never felt as though I was on trial with the other, more established players.

A lot has been said and written about the 'great team spirit' at Arsenal in the 1980s and '90s. The reason it has developed is simply because the players would not allow any player to set himself up as better than anybody else. If a player starts trying it on, he is soon pegged back. Three or four of the other players will be at him all the time, cutting him down to size, and he soon realises that, 'Hang on, we're all in this together.' Or, if he doesn't, he's soon away – like a certain Nicolas Anelka.

When I joined, all I found was a strong team camaraderie into which I was immediately welcomed and, although he had helped create it, George Graham was never fully part of that. He deliberately kept himself aloof from the players. He was the boss and he made sure everybody knew it. He was not as personally interested in goalkeeping as Ron Saunders or even Jim Smith, but he did have a very clear idea of how he wanted his goalkeepers to play and this involved a lot of sweeping up behind the back four.

I had done some sweeping with QPR but it was much more part of the goalkeeping job at Arsenal. Graham believed in the back four holding the line well up the pitch and the footballing public were already used to Tony Adams's familiar arm-up stance appealing to the linesman for offside. It meant I had to position myself much further out from my goal than I had been used to at my previous clubs, ready to deal with any through balls that did beat the trap. I spent a lot of time sprinting out of the box to kick the ball into touch. My training changed to include a lot more practice at flykicking. I even learned to kick with my 'wrong' foot.

It was a different story when I was kicking out of my hands or taking goal-kicks. Graham always wanted me to kick these to a certain area of the pitch. I was mainly trying to hit our right-winger, and whoever was playing there knew he was going to get some heading practice during our games.

I practised kicking to that area a lot and Graham made sure that midfield and left-wingers pushed over into that corner of the pitch for the knock-downs. The downside of all that kicking is that I now have the scars of a double hernia operation to show for it.

We still revert to that style from time to time, but we tend to play more through the midfield now. When Graham was manager, we did kick it long and the team was given a lot of stick for it, although not by our fans while we were winning.

The early part of my first season at Arsenal passed me by to some extent because I was concentrating so much on my own personal performance. The previous season (1989–90) had been a disappointing one for the club especially as it followed the winning of the 1988–9 championship with Michael Thomas's dramatic winner at Liverpool in the last game of the season. After going out of both domestic cups in the early stages, a fourth place finish in the league might have been satisfactory for some clubs, but not for Arsenal – and definitely not for an ambitious manager like George Graham.

In the close season, Brian Marwood, Martin Hayes, Kevin Richardson and of course John Lukic had followed Niall Quinn out of the club while Graham brought in the Swedish winger Anders Limpar and centre-back Andy Linighan as well as me. Although my fee was large for a goalkeeper, these moves were a long way from the high-profile, high-priced and mainly overseas transfers in which clubs like Arsenal are now constantly involved. But, even at the time, Graham was criticised from all sides for breaking up the 1988–9 championship team without, people thought, bringing in adequate replacements. The team I joined was mainly British players with no real megastars but, as it turned out, Graham had the mix exactly right.

Andy Linighan was a good player, very steady and reliable and the fans took to him although his appearances were restricted by the form of Steve Bould and Tony Adams. Anders Limpar was another crowd-pleaser but in a completely different way. I always remember the tattoo on his shoulder of a mouse with its arms out saying, 'Nobody's Perfect.' That summed him up to a T. He could be brilliant or terrible, and what he was called by the rest of the team would change accordingly.

The rest of us usually had just the one nickname: Lee 'Dicko' Dixon, Tony 'Rodders' Adams (because he looks like Delboy's plonker brother, of course), Paul 'Merse' Merson, Alan 'Smudger' Smith, Steve 'Bouldie' Bould, Perry 'Grovesy' Groves and so on. There were not many dodgy nicknames – it is just my bad luck to have a dodgy name. As soon as I got there, the other lads were thinking of all the obvious ones about it but decided they couldn't really call me 'Spunky' when the younger fans are around. So they settled on 'H'. It's Cockney rhyming slang: Harry Monk – Spunk. So then all the kids were asking, 'Why H?' and I was having to say I couldn't tell them because it was an adult thing. It is better when they just call me 'Big Fella.'

Going to Arsenal had an immediate impact on all my life, not just the footballing part. I was receiving far more attention away from the ground than I had ever imagined happening. Before Arsenal, the fans were only a factor when I was playing or in and around the ground on other days of the week. Even though clubs like Birmingham have good local support and decent-sized crowds, the support is definitely limited to the local area. A club like Arsenal has fans all over London, all over the country, even all over the world. When you are an Arsenal player, fans keep coming up to you wherever you go – in shops, restaurants, the cinema. At first, this made me more nervous and certainly added pressure which I did not need with all the support still around for John Lukic. But, if I thought the attention was overwhelming at the start of that season, it was nothing to what is was like at the end of it.

Because I was so determined to impress the fans with my own form, it was not until after Christmas that I even realised we were in with a chance of winning the championship. And that was despite two major setbacks in that first half of the season.

First there was the infamous brawl of Old Trafford, which is always brought up by the tabloid press whenever Arsenal and Man Utd are playing each other. In fact, it was over-hyped then and now. We had made a good start to the season and were in second spot when we went up to Old Trafford in October. It was always going to be a hard, tense game between two top clubs going for the championship and it was hardly surprising that it all boiled over.

A couple of our players thought a couple of theirs were putting it about too much, and the niggling carried on until eventually it all blew up and then everyone seemed to want to be involved. Well, almost everyone. It was later reported to the FA that 21 out of the 22 players were in the 'brawl'. Guess who was the odd man out? Well, it was all happening a long way from where I was standing and I really couldn't be bothered to run all that way when I knew it would just be handbags at three paces.

Which is exactly how it turned out. Lots of pushing and shoving and mouthing off but nothing violent. But it looked bad with so many players involved and, because it was such a high-profile game between two big clubs, the FA thought it had to make an example of us. Both clubs were fined £50,000 and, although the players were not out of pocket at all, we suffered a worse punishment when the FA also deducted two points from our league total. Because Arsenal had a record with the FA, having been fined £20,000 for a similar incident with Norwich the previous season, this was a point more than was deducted from Man Utd.

But, if anything, this just made us even more determined to win the league. We had won the game with an Anders goal but the two points lost put us eight adrift of Liverpool. Our attitude was: stuff your two points, we'll win the league without them.

The second setback was a much bigger blow because it meant we lost our captain, Tony Adams, at a crucial stage of the season.

We all knew Tony had a court case pending for drink-driving after he had driven his car into someone's garden wall during the previous close season. It had caused a big stink in the papers because, as an England international and Arsenal captain, Tony was seen as a high-profile player who should be setting an example.

But the case had dragged on for months and, by the time he was due to appear in court, it was December and the last thing any of us expected was for him to go down. I know Tony never expected to go to jail. The timing of the court appearance was crucial. It coincided with the Government's annual pre-Christmas campaign against drink-driving and I am sure the jail sentence Tony received was imposed to give that a big boost.

I know drink-driving is a serious offence but we have all seen many cases when drink-drivers have been involved in accidents with people hurt or even dying and they have still walked away with just a fine and a driving ban. Granted it was more luck than judgement, but Tony had only hit a garden wall, hurting no one apart from himself.

Like everyone else, we heard about Tony's sentence – nine months plus a two-year ban and £500 fine – on the news and we simply couldn't believe it. There we were, halfway through the season and still unbeaten with an excellent chance of winning the league, and our captain had been banged up. Even when we heard that five months of the sentence had been suspended, so he was only serving four months and would probably be out in less, it was still hard to take in. Quite a few of the players wrote to him to try and cheer him up, but I am not a great one for letter-writing. If I have something to say, I prefer to talk to people face to face and, as his family were using his limited visitor allowance, I did not have the chance to speak to him until he came out.

Of all his stories of life inside – and the first thing he made clear was that there had been no funny business in the prison showers – the one that will always stick in my mind is of Tony being locked in his cell for 23 hours on Christmas Day.

And although I did not write, apparently I had still managed to cheer him up while he was inside. He listened to football on the radio and he told me that, when there was commentary from a game we played at Spurs, there was a great atmosphere in the nick. All the cons were shouting out for one side or the other because they knew he was in there listening. I had a blinder that day, making a lot of saves from Lineker, and Tony was shouting, 'Go on, goalie, show them' for the benefit of his fellow cons.

In the end, with time off for good behaviour, Tony served just two months. It still seemed a long time to us but it must have seemed much longer to Tony. But when he came out, he amazed us all because he was so fit. He had been given a job in the prison gym so had worked out all the time, doing endless press-ups and sit-ups. It was cheaper than joining a health club and, as he pointed out, what else was there for him to do?

We had managed to keep our good run going while Tony was out of action, losing just one game (our only defeat that season) at our jinx ground Stamford Bridge, where we never seemed able to win until the last couple of seasons. We were second in the table and his first league appearance on his return was a game at Liverpool, who were top, in March. We won with a Merse goal and from then on the championship was in our sights.

There are many important goals and saves which go towards winning a championship but a save I made against Sunderland stands out for me. It was right at the end of the season and we were playing on a freezing cold night at Roker Park. It was raining hard and blowing a gale from one end of the ground to the other. I remember

Jimmy Greaves telling me afterwards that the TV gantry he was commentating from was swaying alarmingly all over the place. And Greavesy is someone who knew all about swaying.

We were hanging on for a 0–0 draw when Sunderland midfield player Gary Owers struck one from distance, trying to curl it around me. He almost made it but I just got a hand to it at absolute full stretch. On the commentary, Greavesy said, 'How sickening is that? You get past the best defence in the world and then you come up against that goalie.' The point we won there and Liverpool's defeat at Chelsea the same day meant that our Anfield rivals needed to beat Nottingham Forest two days later on May Bank Holiday Monday or we would already be champions when we played our home game with Man Utd that evening.

Liverpool lost 1–0. When we came out of the tunnel one by one for our pre-match warm-up, the crowd gave us a fantastic reception. I can remember running out with clenched fists raised. It was a great feeling.

Almost immediately, ITV's Gary Newbon dragged me in for a live interview along with Anders, Nigel, David O'Leary and Mickey Thomas. Looking across at me, David said, 'I'm so pleased for this man here. It's his first season and he's done really well. This will be the first of many trophies for him.' I really appreciated him saying that and his words came back to me many times over the next decade.

I have since beaten my Arsenal record for goals conceded. In 1998–9, I only let in 17 goals compared with 18 in that first season, although I did play more games in that first season. But England goalkeeping coach Ray Clemence still holds the record, with just 16 conceded in one of his seasons with Liverpool. And, before he reminds me at our next England squad session, I know he had to play in more games then, too. Then again, the strikers were still wearing steel toecaps on their boots in those days.

But it was not all plain sailing for me. I saved my worst performance for one of the biggest games of the season – *the* biggest as far as the fans were concerned.

We had reached the semi-final of the FA Cup and were well on track to do the Double. We drew Spurs and, for the first time, the FA decided that Wembley should host a semi-final. I think that was the right decision. It meant more fans could see the game and gave the players an extra chance to play at Wembley. I don't think it devalues Cup Final day at all. Everyone knows it is a semi, not the final itself, so it is a different kind of atmosphere but it is still a great day out.

Except it wasn't for me that first time. It was a classic case of sod's law. I had been in top form all season but, when it came to an FA Cup semi-final against the club's biggest rivals and the first ever to be played at Wembley, I had a total nightmare.

We lost 3–1 and it was not a good team performance but it was my mistakes that stood out. Although Gazza's free-kick was a great strike I should never have been beaten from that range and then Lineker's shot went straight through my hands. His second, Spurs' third, was not down to me but it was still a scrappy goal. Nothing went right for me or the team on the day and I still think of the game as the semi-final I turned up for but never played in.

That game aside, I could not have asked for more from my first season with Arsenal. We won the championship and, through that, a place in the European Cup now that the ban on English clubs had just been lifted. My England career seemed to be taking off, too. Peter Shilton had retired from international football after the 1990 World Cup, and that, together with my form and higher profile with Arsenal, saw me picked for a friendly against Cameroon on a chilly night in February 1991.

It was one of the coldest nights I have ever experienced, so you can imagine how the Cameroon players must have felt. They all came out wearing gloves and did not look up for it at all. That did not help me keep warm as they gave me very little to do during the game. But I would take a clean sheet over a busy game, anytime. The temperature was −2 when we started and was dropping like a stone for the rest of the game. Wembley did not have undersoil heating, just a pitch cover. Once that was off, the pitch began freezing hard.

Looking back, I can't understand why I did not wear tracksuit bottoms unless it was some kind of superstition, not wanting to change what I normally wore for England. Or it might have been because goalies did still come in for some criticism for wearing bottoms then, just as foreign players do for wearing gloves now.

That kind of criticism had only begun to fade away when goalies like Dimitri Kharine, who wears them all the time, started playing over here. I have certainly worn them since for England because I have had to play on terrible pitches in some away internationals.

The one upside of having to wait, like most England goalies, so long to get in the side is that by the time it happens you have been an established member of the squad for several years. You have got to know the other players so you don't feel like the new boy when you finally start playing regularly. I had almost grown up with those players, and it was more a case of being desperate to play than being worried about how I would cope with it. In fact, I found the hardest part of being an international goalie was having to play behind a back four that changed from international to international. There are often long gaps between games and, by the time the next one comes along, players are injured or just not selected.

People think that England squads being together for a week before the game is enough to learn how each other plays. But we don't play games all that week, so it is difficult to build up the kind of defensive understanding you need to face international strikers. These days we have top overseas players in our league but even so there is a gulf between club and international football. When I first broke into the England side the step up was even greater. Not only were we playing against higher-quality players, we knew little or nothing about most of them.

I quickly realised that, while mistakes often go unpunished in club football, in an international almost all defensive mistakes lead to a goal. The fact that we now play against overseas internationals week in, week out in the Premiership and that we've also had to get used to different back fours in club football because of squad rotation has meant that the gap between club and international football has started to narrow, but it is still there.

At the end of the 1990–91 season, I played in a couple of Euro 92 qualifiers, against the Republic of Ireland and Turkey. We drew the first 1–1 and won the second 1–0 in Izmir where I made some good saves.

But it was the Ireland game that stands out now, not for what happened during the game but for what was said afterwards. I did not have a lot to do, just a couple of saves and a few difficult crosses, and there was nothing I could do about their goal, which Niall Quinn bent round me. Lee Dixon had won us a draw with a deflected shot and I walked off at the end, nursing a cut leg courtesy of Quinny but feeling reasonably satisfied with my own performance.

England manager Graham Taylor had a policy of not speaking to the press until the day after a game, so it was not until two days later that I saw the back-page headlines, including a real contender for *Private Eye*: 'Taylor: I blame Seaman'.

Like Victor Meldrew, I just couldn't believe it. Apparently, he had said that Shilts would not have let his defence back off the way he thought I had. But he was talking about David Seaman who, week in and week out, was orchestrating a back four famous everywhere for holding the line way upfield. He knew better, of course, and the press laid into me because of it. It was worse because the flak was so unexpected. You know when you have had a poor game and made mistakes but in this case, as far as I was concerned, I had played OK.

Apparently, Taylor phoned up to say it had not come out the way he said it. All the same, it was the beginning of a stormy relationship between me and the England manager. I did play in another friendly, against Argentina, a few weeks later but the following year my England career came close to ending before it had really begun.

Before that, I had urgent Arsenal business in England and Europe.

10

......

Now Follow That . . .

The season following a championship win is, in some ways, the greatest test of a team's credentials. If you can win the league again, it proves the first was no fluke and people are going to start calling you a great side, not just a very good one. Not many teams managed it when it was the First Division and only Man Utd have won two Premierships on the spin – three times. It certainly proved beyond us in 1991–2.

We were not helped by an injury to Steve Bould which kept him out of the side for most of the season, replaced by Colin Pates or David O'Leary. But we all found it hard to lift ourselves and never found the consistency that had won us the league the previous season. On the other hand, we had one newcomer who was to become one of the greatest players in the club's history: Ian Wright, who was bought from Crystal Palace by Graham for an Arsenal record fee of £2.5million a couple of months into the season.

Wrighty was super-lively from the beginning, although even he was a little bit in awe of some of the players when he arrived. But, as soon as he scored a few goals, he was off and running. Unfortunately, he was signed too late to be eligible for our European Cup games. Not that he missed too many as we were out of the competition almost before we had started to appreciate our first taste of playing in Europe.

When the team had won the championship a couple of seasons before I arrived, English sides were still banned from Europe so the rest of the team were no more experienced than I was. And it was the first time in Europe for George Graham as a manager.

He admits now that he learned a big lesson. In the first round we had few problems with Austria Vienna, winning 6–1 in the first leg to make the second leg a formality. But then we faced Benfica, who had been European Cup winners in their time. We did well to draw away from home and even scored an away goal, but at home they held us to 1–1 in normal time and then scored twice on the break in extra time as we lost our discipline pushing forward for the winner.

Graham said that it taught him that you can't play gung-ho football in Europe as the opposition is usually too strong. And he learned that preparation was all-important because we did not know most of the players and teams we were drawn to face. In the next chapter, I follow Graham's road to success in Europe.

Our Benfica experience was not, though, the last cup disappointment of the season. Arsenal have been on the wrong end of a few cup upsets over the years but not many more embarrassing than the one that saw us dumped out of the FA Cup in that season's third round. It was one of the games you dread when you play for a top club – away to a team in the bottom division. Our opponents, Wrexham, had even finished bottom of that division (the old Fourth) the previous season, so the press could fairly say it was a match between supposedly the best and the worst teams in the entire league.

At first, it all went according to form with Smudger scoring for us. It wasn't pretty, but we hung on to the lead until near the end but then Mickey Thomas (the ex-Man Utd player, not our Mickey T. who had just been transferred to Liverpool) scored from a free-kick. That changed the whole game and, with their tails right up, they threw everything at us and almost immediately scored another one. Even so, it looked as though we had equalised when Jimmy Carter put one in the net right at the death, but it was ruled out, wrongly we thought, for offside.

It was humiliating. A First Division or, now, Premiership team should be superior to a lower division club in every way – fitness, skill, organisation. In a top side, the players are at or very near their peak; in lower division sides, they will be a mixture of older players who have passed their peak (or have never been good enough to play at the top level) and younger players on their way up (many of whom will never make it to the top either).

But it is every big club's nightmare to be drawn away to a little club early in the FA Cup, because the game will be played in January or February when the pitches are not at their best. You try to play your own game and impose it on them, but it only needs some players not to perform to their best, a mistake that lets the little club get their noses in front and the crowd behind them and, before you know it, you're on the wrong end of a shock result. I never support the underdog in matches because I know what if feels like to be beaten by one.

What happened to us at Wrexham was, in some ways, worse than losing to Spurs in the semi-final the year before although I would not want to go through either experience again. The Spurs fans certainly reminded us of the Wrexham result whenever we played them over the next few years. Our own fans weren't very happy about it, especially those who had made the long journey to Wrexham to watch it.

But it was typical of a very disappointing season, especially as Wrighty had more than justified that record transfer fee by scoring 24 goals in his 30 games. Looking back, we certainly did not have the strongest of squads to cover players injured or suspended. It all added up to a season to forget and gave no hint of what was to follow in 1992–3. Another Arsenal double was on the way, but not the usual league and cup-winning combination.

In fact, there were no real signs that success on any scale was on the way. For a start, it was not as if Graham made any major moves in the transfer market. In the close season, he bought John Jensen from Brondby for just over £1million and during the season he bought Martin Keown back from Everton for £2million but, at the same time, David Rocastle was sold to Leeds – also for £2million.

Rocky and Mickey Thomas had been major parts of the championship-winning sides and the fans certainly did not think Jensen was much of a replacement, especially when it turned out that the winning long-range goal he had scored for Denmark in the 1992 European Championships was a complete one-off. John was a great character who liked his pie and a pint but I kept pulling his leg that he must be a different John Jensen to the one we had all seen on the TV because he did not even score goals like that in training.

But, if John looked as though he would never score again, Wrighty could not stop scoring. It did not seem to make any difference to him whether he was in the Second Division, the First Division or, now, the Premiership – he was, and is, a natural finisher.

Renaming the First Division the Premiership did not make any difference to the players but it made a huge change to the profile of the game. Sky began to cover many more games on TV in much more depth and detail. Andy Gray was a revelation as a commentator – so knowledgeable and with a real feeling for the game. The other main difference was the trophy. It was much larger and more impressive than the First Division trophy had been and I must admit that I started dreaming about holding it aloft.

However, that season we only managed tenth and it was to be quite a few years before I achieved my ambition but there were a couple of decent compensations in that first Premiership season.

The League Cup was called the Coca Cola at that time and it was treated more seriously by the top teams than the way some of them – including Arsenal – now approach the Worthington Cup. Lower division clubs have always taken it seriously as there is a Wembley final and a place in Europe at the end of it. Also, because even the early rounds were two-leg affairs, it meant the top teams always had to play away at some difficult places.

And they didn't come much more difficult than the old Den at Millwall, especially as we had only managed a 1-1 draw at Highbury. Things looked bad when Lee scored an own-goal, putting us on the back foot for most of the game with the crowd going berserk all around us. Millwall probably deserved to win it but Kevin Campbell equalised for us and it went to penalties. I saved three of them to put us through. The crowd were not too happy, to say the least, but I was. Most penalty saves are fairly straightforward blocks, but a couple of these were genuinely good ones.

After beating Derby in the next round, we had to go twice to Scarborough, which is one of the longer journeys for London clubs. The game was called off the first time, and even the second time it was a very foggy night and it was touch-and-go whether the game went on. We were all desperate for it to be played as we didn't want to have to make that long journey again and Graham and Tony made it clear to the referee that we wanted to play. We had our way but, to be honest, it should probably have been called off. When Nigel scored the only goal, I couldn't see it at all from my end. I was worried for the rest of the game that it might still be abandoned.

Goals from Wrighty put us through the quarter-final against Notts Forest, and then we easily beat Wrighty's old club Crystal Palace in the semi-final. Strikers can come into the Premiership and score a lot of goals early on while defenders are still trying to work them out and learn their tricks and turns. Often, though, they are found out in their second season. Defenders learn how to play against them and the goals dry up. That did not happen with Ian Wright, who proved he was no one-season wonder. His style is so out of the ordinary that, even at the end of his time with Arsenal, he could still surprise us with his cheeky finishes. In training, he was even more outlandish. He would try anything, shooting from miles out or chipping in from ridiculous positions. He put a few past me like that but, as I occasionally remind him, he has still never scored against me in a real game.

But he scored plenty in our FA Cup run that 1992–3 season. There was a hat-trick from him against those non-league giant-killers Yeovil in the third round and then a couple of goals against Leeds in a fourth-round replay at Elland Road. One of these was one of the best finishes I have ever seen when he chipped my old friend John Lukic. I had never seen Wrighty make that kind of finish even in training. He received the ball, went past a couple of players but was going across and away from the goal and there didn't seem to be any danger. But, suddenly, he just chipped the ball on the run and it was the surprise of it more than anything that beat John. He scored another cracker against Notts Forest in the next round when he smashed one from way out which dipped over Mark Crossley.

The quarter-final against Ipswich had Tony Adams in stitches – 29 of them. He played despite a wound he had picked up when falling down some steps outside a bar. He was still one of our scorers in a 4–2 win while I was pleased to save yet another penalty. This was getting to be a habit, one that was to lead me to more fame than I could have dreamed of then.

After Ipswich it was time for some revenge. We had to play Spurs again in another Wembley semi-final. It was not a great game but it was a great day for us. We played so well defensively that I did not have much to do apart from a couple of saves at Teddy Sheringham's feet. Tony scored the only goal late in the game, so we were through to our second major cup final in a season. There was more relief than elation in our dressing-room as it would have been terrible to have lost to Spurs in a semi-final for a second time. The fans would never have forgiven us.

Strangely we were now to play the same team in the final of both cup competitions: Sheffield Wednesday.

As the FA Cup Final was drawn we ended up playing each other three times. None of the games could be described as a classic, but we didn't care. We ended up with both trophies.

We won the Coca Cola 2–1 after being a goal down. Steve Morrow scored the winner but will probably remember the game for a completely different reason. At the end of the game, we were all celebrating and congratulating each other. Tony grabbed Steve, lifted him up and then lost his grip and dropped him over his back. Steve landed on his arm, breaking it and also dislocating his shoulder. Although the cameras caught it, most of us on the pitch missed it and only realised something was up when a crowd gathered around Tony and Steve. With a few of the other players, I went over to see what was going on. Steve had his arm hanging loose and his face rapidly going from pale to completely white. He seemed to be going into shock so we all took one look and quickly moved away. Footballers are a squeamish lot and we didn't want to see any more of that.

It was bad luck all round for Steve. Not only did he miss out on walking up the steps for his medal and the cup, he missed the FA Cup Final as well although he was allowed to pick up his league cup medal before the match. But worst of all for him is to be remembered more for the accident than his winning goal.

Mind you, I might also be remembered more for my medical condition at the time than for playing my part in our FA Cup Final win. I played both games carrying a double hernia or, as the *Mirror* so sensitively put it, 'No fuss, no truss.'

The run-up to the final was a fantastic time. It was just how you imagine it as a kid, from getting our new Cup Final suits to having the TV cameras on the coach on the drive to Wembley. But the tension does build up, especially in the last couple of days, and it is very draining. One of the reasons players tire and get cramp in many finals is that they are knackered before they start by the sheer nervous tension of it all. It's probably why the final is so rarely a classic.

There is also a big difference between playing at Wembley in an FA Cup Final and playing an England international. For a start, half the crowd hate your guts and want you to lose the game and they can make a hell of a lot of noise. If they have the seats by the tunnel, you know all about it when you walk out for the warm-up. I remember being given some terrible grief by the Wednesday fans who had the tunnel seats for both FA Cup Finals.

There were cameras in the tunnel itself so, when the two teams lined up before going out to play the games, I was careful not to be seen chatting to any of the Wednesday players. Fans always pick up on things like that and, if you lose the game, they will be quick to say that you weren't keen enough to beat them.

We drew the first game 1–1 and it was the same score in the replay until the last minute of extra time when Andy Linighan headed home from a corner. Chris Woods tried to palm it away but only succeeded in helping it into the net.

There had been a big crash on the M1 on the day of the replay and most of the Sheffield Wednesday fans were caught up in a huge traffic jam. Although the start was delayed, most of them still did not arrive until well into the game. It meant there was a strange atmosphere for the first part of the game as it was weird to see so many seats empty at an FA Cup Final.

The day was a good one for me. I made a good save from Chris Waddle and when I caught his eye and winked at him, the moment was captured by the TV cameras. The best moment, though, was that final whistle, when we knew we had won it. It was such a joyful, emotional time. Everybody went looking for their best mates in the team to hug, and then the goalscorers, the goalie, the coaches and finally the manager got the same treatment.

For a couple of minutes we were just thinking about ourselves but then we looked across at the losers and the contrast just couldn't have been greater. Some of them were crying including Chris

Waddle, who I knew well from England games. But there was nothing any of us could say to make them feel any better at that stage.

It was my first FA Cup win and I couldn't wait to walk up those steps and pick up my medal. It was a strange experience because the steps are right by the seats and a lot of the fans there were from Sheffield. I was half-expecting one of them to lean over and thump me. I wasn't the only one thinking that, either, as I saw some of my team-mates making sure they were climbing up as far across the steps and away from the fans as possible.

We went up in the order that we went on the pitch at the start of the game. I was right behind Tony when he lifted the cup and shouted out, 'You fucking beauty,' at the top of his voice. There are no TV mikes around but, of course, the cameras were right on him and viewers did not need to be experts in lip-reading to understand what he had said. I know he was really embarrassed about it later and I reminded him of it when we went up to collect the cup the next time we won it. But that's another story.

On the way back to our hotel after the game, we had to drive up the M1 for a few miles and all the Wednesday cars were passing us. They were giving us some real stick through their windows. One car stayed alongside us for ages so that they could all give us two fingers, so I just reached across the coach, picked up the FA Cup and held it up to them at the window with a big grin on my face. The car didn't stay there long after that.

But the grin didn't last too long, either. This double cup-winning season was over and I now had time to have that hernia operation I needed. I had played all season with a hernia on my right side. Then, because I was favouring that side, later in the season I developed one on the other side.

There was no doubt they were caused by all the kicking I was having to do as part of my sweeper's role, plus the deadball and drop-kicking to the right-winger. I took to wearing the long Vulcan shorts, which keep the affected area really warm. The pain of the hernia was not that bad and most of the time I was able to continue to train, play and take most of the kicks. But the pain from the operation – that was something else.

Tony and I were both booked in the same day for the same operation, although he only had a single hernia. We turned up at the hospital at six in the evening but, when we arrived, they said they did not need us there until much later, so we went out for a few drinks in Covent Garden instead. It was Dutch courage, and I would have had a few more if I had known how bad I was going to feel afterwards.

When I came round, I found that every time I moved I was tensing my stomach and it was agony. The pain came with a burning sensation and I soon learned that, if I felt a sneeze or a cough or a laugh coming on, I should do everything I could to stop it. I was still laid out when Tony came shuffling in. I was surprised to see him on his feet, although he admitted the pain was killing him. Foolishly I decided to see if I could get up, too.

I sat up, then stood up while the nurse was holding me from the front. I felt OK for a minute but then suddenly I felt sick and dizzy. I started to fall backwards and Tony just managed to push a chair under me otherwise I would have hit the deck. I don't even want to think what the pain would been like if I had.

I did not try that again for a while but, fortunately, we had the close season to recover. Hernias can easily recur but I've been lucky so far. Tony, though, had to have another operation in 1999 – and he was very welcome to it.

The important thing was that we were both fit for the start of 1993–4, the season when I was to enjoy what I still consider to be the biggest triumph in my club career.

II

······

Victory over Europe

Before the 1993–4 season started, we had a tour to a country which was new to all of us: South Africa.

We played three games, one against Man Utd and the other two against local club sides (including Kaiser Chiefs, I remember) and found the standard surprisingly high. Played in front of good crowds, all the games were tight, with us narrowly winning two and drawing the other.

As usual, we did not see as much of the country as I would have liked. Top footballers travel all over the world but see more of the inside of hotel rooms than they do of the usual tourist sights. We are there to play football, so training and then resting before the games is how we spend most of our time. In South Africa, there was the added problem of security. In some places, we were advised that it was not safe to go out by ourselves. But I do remember playing golf, slap-bang in the centre of Johannesburg, and being amazed to find this oasis of green in the middle of a big, built-up city.

My main memory, though, is of meeting Nelson Mandela. It was only a couple of years after his release from prison and we saw how popular he was when he came along to one of our games. He spoke to every player and was a very friendly and gentle man. I shook his hand and was surprised at how soft it was. It was an unusual start to an unusual season for Arsenal Football Club.

Once again, there had been little pre-season action in the transfer market with David O'Leary, now at the veteran stage, and Colin Pates leaving and Crystal Palace utility player Eddie McGoldrick joining for about £1million.

Our league form was nothing out of the ordinary, either. Although we eventually finished fourth, we were never challenging for the Premiership which Man Utd went on to win. We did not let in too many goals – just 28 – but only managed to score 53, with Wrighty grabbing nearly half of them. We also went out of both domestic cups early on, leaving us with just one trophy to play for – the European Cup-Winners Cup.

I can't speak for the other players but, when I came into the game, playing in Europe was not my major ambition. As well as wanting to play for England, I wanted my club to win the league and the FA Cup. Playing in Europe as a result would be just a bonus, not my main target. So, when we played in the European Cup after winning the league in my first season, I can't remember being particularly pumped up for it. Going out of the competition so early may have affected my memory of it but I was probably not as focused on winning a European trophy as George Graham.

Graham had won the European Fairs Cup (later to become the UEFA Cup) as an Arsenal player in 1970 and wanted to repeat that as a manager. I think he saw it as the ultimate test for a manager, winning against the top European sides and managers with their big reputations.

Now, having won a European trophy as a player, I have changed my mind and my priorities. Winning the European Cup-Winners Cup was the biggest achievement of my club career. I even put it above our two domestic 'Doubles' and the only way to beat it now would be to win the European Champions Cup. This is now the one every team wants to win because virtually all Europe's biggest clubs are guaranteed a place in its expanded league-style format, while the Cup-Winners Cup has now been merged into the UEFA Cup and is very much a secondary competition.

The Cup-Winners Cup had always been seen as second in importance to the European Cup because other European countries have never taken their cup competitions as seriously as we take the FA Cup. But it just so happened that in 1992 most of Europe's top sides won their national cup competitions, so it is fair to say that, for the two years we were in the competition, the European Cup-Winners Cup had an entry just as strong as – maybe even stronger than – the European Cup. When we reached the quarter-finals in

1993–4, other teams still left included Real Madrid, Ajax, Paris St Germain, Torino and Parma.

As I mentioned earlier, Graham had learned a lot from our quick European Cup exit a couple of seasons earlier. This time he was going to be prepared for anything and his tactics were going to be based on his belief that most of the other teams in the later stages would have more ability than us. As soon as we knew which team we were playing against in the next round, he would send an assessor from the club out to watch them play – once at home and twice away. We would be shown videos of them playing in their own league and also in Europe to see if and how they adapted to playing foreign opposition. Graham would talk us through these, pointing out their strengths and weaknesses as a team and then he would go through their side, player by player. As we had not played against most of them and only knew some of them through TV, the briefing would be very detailed. If they liked to run at defenders or lay the ball off early, were one-footed or two-footed – it was all covered.

And then Graham would make the youth team play against the first team in the style of our opponents. I thought this was very hard on them. They were nervous enough about playing against the first team without having to try and play like a top Continental team with world-class players. In fairness, Graham did not ask them to ape individual players but just to try and imitate their formation. I am not sure how much use it was but we did a lot of that kind of shadow-play.

There was little sign of the glory to come when we squeezed past Odense in the first round, drawing 1–1 at home having won the away leg 2–1, and we were apprehensive when we knew we had Standard Liege in the second round. They were a well-known European club and we thought we might have a tough time beating them but instead we turned on our best performance so far in Europe after winning 3–0 at home. Wrighty was rested for the second leg by Graham who wanted to prevent him picking up bookings which would see him suspended later in the competition. But, even without him, we turned them over 7–0. By the end, even their fans were cheering our goals. It was almost embarrassing as these were fellow pros getting slaughtered by their own fans as well as by us.

But this was a one-off. Our success in this competition was based on solid defence, with the back five (including me) coming into its own; hardworking midfielders including David Hillier, Paul Davis, John Jensen and Martin Keown, whom Graham had moved forward from the back four with some success; some magic from Merse and goals from Wrighty and Smudger.

In our nine games in Europe that season, we conceded only three goals but, apart from the Standard Liege tie, only scored more than one goal in one game (against Odense) ourselves.

No tie was tighter than the quarter-final against Torino who had a certain Benito Carbone in their side. David Hillier did a man-to-man on Beni and we won the tie the classic European way with a 0–0 draw away and a 1–0 win at home, the winning goal coming from a free-kick which Tony headed in.

Graham believed Paris St Germain, whom we had to play in the semi-final, were the best side in the competition. They had a couple of useful players of whom you may have heard – David Ginola and George Weah – but we just wore them down. We drew 1–1 away and won 1–0 at home with a goal from Kevin Campbell, who was one of the disappointingly few promising youngsters coming through the Arsenal ranks at that time. Wrighty scored our goal in France but he had picked up too many yellow cards and was suspended for the final against Parma in Copenhagen. That was not our only problem. Jensen, Hillier and Keown were also out injured or suspended. And I had my own problems – three of them, all cracked ribs.

In a league game against my old club, QPR, a couple of weeks before the final, I went up for a high ball in the area. QPR striker Bradley Allen, who is only a little skinny guy, went up with me and decided to get some leverage by elbowing me in the ribs.

With three cracked ribs, I was struggling to make the final. I have had cracked ribs three or four times in my career and I knew the only way I was going to play was to have pain-killing injections. Before the game I had four injections in the ribcage. These dulled the pain enough for me to be able to play and not show that I was in any difficulties. The club had left it up to me to decide whether to have the injections and play but there was no decision to make. A European final does not come along very often in most players' careers and, even if I had known I would be in another final the following season, I would still have played through the pain.

Nobody gave us a chance in the final. Parma were a class side with some great strikers who were all to play in our own Premiership later in their careers, although with varying amounts of success. These were Gianfranco Zola, Faustino Asprilla and a slimline Tomas Brolin.

Apart from our own fans who had travelled to Denmark, we had most of the locals on our side because of our own Dane, Jensen, even though he was out for the final. That gave us a lift, but what really fired us up was going to the stadium before the game and seeing Parma's name already on the podium board as the ultimate winners! The organisers were just testing the equipment and had to put up one name or the other and it may have been a 50–50 chance that they had chosen Parma, but we simply saw it as confirming that everyone thought we were going to lose. It made us all the more determined to prove everyone wrong.

Because of the players we had missing, we had to put out an inexperienced team, particularly in midfield where Steve Morrow and Ian Selley, who was only 19, came in for rare games. At the start, we were pushed back and they did hit the post once but we gradually got into the game and once Smudger had put us ahead, we had something to defend. Parma had plenty of possession after that but did not make too many clearcut chances although, from one, I made one of the best saves of my career. It may even have been *the* best – it was certainly one of the most important.

Zola has such quick feet he can hit the ball early and surprise goalies. This time he fired in a typically quick, fierce shot and I had to go full stretch to tip it over the bar. It was on my right side, too, where the ribs were cracked, so it proved the injections worked as well as keeping us in the lead and on our way to winning the cup.

Even with a full side out, we did not have a team of stars like half a dozen of the sides that were in the competition that season, so winning it was a brilliant achievement for us and for the gaffer. It should really have been the springboard for us to go and win more trophies in Europe and at home. But the club was still refusing to pay the increasingly high wages being commanded by top players.

In the close season, just three players came in: two reserve goalies, Lee Harper and Vince Bartram, and Swedish international midfielder Stefan Schwarz. Stefan was a decent player and a nice guy but he was not going to transform the side into world-beaters and, in the end, he did not settle in London, leaving after a year.

And there were problems ahead in the 1994–5 season which took all of us by surprise and meant that we lost Merse for part of the season and George Graham for ever. Both of these events, which caused major sensations in the football world far beyond just Arsenal, are covered in later chapters.

Our league form was disappointing with one of our lowest finishes for years at twelfth place. At one stage we were dangerously close to the relegation zone (four clubs were relegated that season) and we also went out of the two domestic cups early. But, despite all our troubles, we still managed to defend that Cup-Winners Cup all the way to another final.

We had a similar run to the previous year's, with an easy first-round win over Omonia Nicosia and then a stumble against Denmark's Brondby (Jensen's old club) when we only managed a 2–2 draw at home having won 2–1 away and were lucky not to concede a last-minute penalty which would have put them through instead of us. Except that I would have saved it, though, wouldn't I?

By the time we played Auxerre in the quarter-final, Graham had been dismissed and his number two, Stewart Houston, was in his place as caretaker manager. The match was another painful experience for me as I had to play with cracked ribs. Again.

I am not sure if goalies are better protected by referees than when I started, but I think more people are understanding more why we are protected at all. With all the games on TV and the extra camera angles, fans can see clearly what we have to put up with, especially those players who like to lead with their elbows.

Playing through the pain was worth it again for me, though, as we sneaked past Auxerre 2–1 on aggregate. We beat the odds again as Auxerre were a good side and we only drew 1–1 at home. But Wrighty scored the only goal of the away leg and we were through to a semi-final which was to make my name.

Our opponents, Serie A side Sampdoria, had plenty of star players and we did well to beat them 3–2 at home. Those two away goals would still make it difficult for us to go through and it looked odds-on we were out when they led 3–1 in the away leg. But Stefan got us out of jail with a long-range free-kick and, after extra time, it was penalties.

Although Houston, like Graham, believed in preparation there is not much a goalie can do to prepare for penalty shoot-outs. If your opponents have been awarded a penalty in one of the videos you have watched, then you take note of the taker and where he put it but you are only likely to see one penalty-taker at the most. In a shoot-out, you have to face at least five. In any case, a good penalty taker will change sides and styles from time to time. Alan Shearer is a great penalty taker and he does not always put them in the same place. Dwight Yorke even chipped one when he was at Villa. If the penalty taker has the bottle to do that, good luck to him. There isn't much a goalie can do about it except look pretty stupid when it goes in. But, then, Gary Lineker tried it when he had a chance to beat the record for England goals scored and he looked pretty stupid himself when the goalie read it and kicked the ball away to safety.

Against Sampdoria, I just watched the way they ran up to the spot. I focused on guessing the right way and not moving too early so that I make the taker's mind up for him. After that, it is just a case of trying to get something on the ball. A hand, foot, knee or elbow – it doesn't matter so long as it keeps the ball out of the net.

My theory worked in this game as I saved three penalties. The third, which won us the tie, was taken by Attilio Lombardo who made it a straightforward save as he placed it close to my hand. But the game was on TV back home and all the drama and those saves meant that I was suddenly a superstar.

If you don't believe me, ask my mum. *News at Ten* interviewed her after the game and she told them that, when I saved the last one, she felt like running out into the street and shouting, 'That was my son!' Dad was in the local pub when someone came in and shouted, 'Your Pam's on the TV – she's the "And finally" bit.' Yes, they dropped the Dead Donkey for David Seaman that night. I was soon being asked on national TV shows myself. It was the beginning of a build-up which ran right through Euro 96 and saw my career and profile move into a different league altogether

Before that, though, came our second Cup-Winners Cup Final, a game which gave me a profile I could have done without.

We played Spain's Real Zaragoza in France's Parc des Princes and were the underdogs again, especially when we went behind, but John Hartson, one of Graham's last buys for the club, equalised. I had a good game and made some important saves, including one I tipped on to the post and away. We had some good chances, too, but the score stayed 1–1 into extra time. But, after my Sampdoria experience, I was hardly going to be worried when it looked as though the game was going to end with another penalty shoot-out. As the last seconds ticked away, I could only see another chance for glory ahead of me.

Then Nayim did his party-piece.

In case there is anyone out there who has not seen it on TV, this one-time Spurs player picked up the ball near the halfway line, looked up and saw me where I should have been, well off my line to deal with any through balls that beat the back four. He then did what even the great Pele didn't quite manage in a World Cup game and chipped the goalkeeper.

As soon as he struck it, I knew I was in trouble. I backtracked as fast as I could and got a hand to it but it was the perfect lob, going in just under the cross-bar.

Debbie, her mum, my parents and my brother and his wife were all at the game. They were sitting near 20,000 Arsenal fans who had been singing and cheering us on all game and, when Nayim scored, it went from a huge noise to absolute silence in an instant.

They were all geared up to penalties and just could not believe the game was over and we had lost. Just imagine how we felt out on the pitch. It was not really my fault and none of the lads or management blamed me but I felt terrible and it took me a while to get over it.

The Spurs fans loved it, of course. They still remind me of it when we play them and the goal was the inspiration for their fanzine – *One Flew Over Seaman's Head*.

Still, no one said it was going to be easy being a goalie and it certainly wasn't if you played for George Graham.

12

......

Life with George

George Graham has to be the best club manager I've played for – just count the trophies he won while he was at Arsenal. I have been very impressed with Arsène Wenger and he could turn out to be even better but he has not been at the club long enough yet for me to rate him ahead of Graham. But, even if Arsène does eventually match or improve on Graham's record, they will always be totally different managers, with completely contrasting styles.

At first glance, Graham's achievements with Arsenal are already impressive, but a closer look at the club's playing staff during his time shows them to be even more remarkable. The facts speak for themselves: he won league and cup trophies in England and Europe with teams which had less all-round ability than Arsenal's main rivals.

Knowing this, he knew he had to make sure his teams were stronger than they looked on paper. To achieve that, it was important not only that all those individuals always functioned to the best of their ability but also that they always performed for the team and not for themselves. With his teams, if just one player did not produce the goods, the whole team would struggle. Graham made sure we all knew exactly what our team-mates were supposed to be doing so that, if anyone wasn't contributing 100 per cent, it would be obvious to all of us.

For example, he liked his wingers to track back and help the full-backs out. If the wingers or wide players did not do this, the team would run into problems and they would soon be on the receiving end of a load of stick from the other players, led by captain Tony Adams.

But there are times when handing out stick is counter-productive. Early on in my Arsenal career, I made a mistake which led to a goal in the first half of a match. Tony turned round and gave me a right rollocking but I just told him where to go and, at half-time, I made it clear to him that I was not going to stand for that from him or anyone. I told him never to rollock me out on the pitch and I would not have a go at him if he made a mistake. I made the point that it never looks good when team-mates are pitching into each other and one day I might just launch into him if he kept on doing it.

Ever since, the team policy has been not to have a go at each other after a goal has gone in against us. This is mainly because it is not the best time to do it. The idea is to bounce straight back, and you are not going to if you are wasting time having an inquest about the one you have just let in. Also, that kind of rollocking between players is noticed by the fans. They are already looking for someone to blame and, if they see the captain or some of the other players having a go at a particular player, they will reckon he is the one to blame and have a go at him, too.

I told Tony and the other defenders that, if a goal goes in, we should just return the ball to the centre-spot quickly and argue about it afterwards when we find out – usually from the match video – who or what was really to blame.

I see other teams where players are always going round blaming each other for goals, often when it was actually down to them. It used to be quite comical to watch Steve Bruce and Gary Pallister after Man Utd had let a goal in. They used to walk straight up the pitch without looking back because they knew that Peter Schmeichel was going to be pointing his finger and shouting at them. Usually the abuse from Schmeichel was worse on the rare occasions the goal was down to him. Man Utd were a good enough side to bounce back anyway but for most teams it is far better to leave the shouting matches until after the game.

Graham was not above launching into us at half-time, though. There were a lot of harsh words said if things were not going as planned. But I will say this for him – if you had a go back and he thought you had a fair point, he would accept it. He would listen and admit it if he had got it wrong.

We used to watch a lot of videos with Graham, especially after bad performances. It could be just like a schoolboys' outing – especially if one player was being singled out by the coaching staff. We would all have a laugh at him as well but it was not malicious because we all knew it could be our turn next. It was actually good for team spirit and also the players would learn how to avoid making the same mistakes again. As far as I am concerned, you never learn anything by having arguments in the middle of the game.

I was not as convinced of the value of the pre-match briefings Graham used to give. He would go through every player from the other side, detailing their strengths and weaknesses, whether they were right- or left-sided, their tricks, the way they like to play. I don't think I often learned anything from these briefings that I didn't already know but he will tell you that they were key to our winning games, particularly against European sides.

Superficially, Graham was friendly towards us but there was always that distance. He was the manager and we were there to do what he said and that was it.

He has been quoted as saying he would never have picked himself as a player. Although Graham the player was skilful and scored some memorable goals in his career, he did not earn the nickname 'Stroller' because of his high work-rate. Quite the reverse and, if there is one thing Graham the manager values from his players, it is work-rate and for that, they need to be fit.

No surprise, then, that pre-season training with Graham was a nightmare – it was just running, running and more running. We used to go to Trent Park near Cockfosters on the outskirts of London and our day would start with a 20-minute run. That was shattering, mainly because we all had to concentrate on keeping our footing as well as keeping up the pace. We were running from roads into woodland, so the surface was all over the place and we knew it would be easy to turn an ankle. Then we would stop and have a session of press-ups or sit-ups before doing a shorter, faster run.

This routine was repeated morning and afternoon and at the end of the day came 'the hill'. This we all dreaded as we had to sprint up and run down a steep hill at least four times. I would wake up next day sore and stiff, every muscle tender to the touch, knowing we were going to be doing it all over again.

This level of fitness training tailed off once the season was under way but there was never any let-up in coaching for the back four (or back five, when I couldn't get out of it). During the season, the training was not all that different from what I had seen at my previous clubs but the team-play practice was much more organised. Graham used to spend hours coaching the defenders in all aspects of defending, but particularly at set-pieces. The lads used to be pulling their hair out because the work was so repetitive and stop-start all the time.

The back four would be playing against six – two strikers and four midfielders – and still not let in any goals all session. In fact, the attackers would rarely even get a shot in. The defenders would work at holding the line – the offside ploy – and at covering if somebody was dragged out of position.

The lads did become very bored with it, doing the same routines season after season, but they knew it worked – the results and 'goals against' column proved that. And it was good for them as individuals as well as for the team as a whole. I am sure it is why the back four have gone on so long and not just at Arsenal. Bouldie is still playing well at Sunderland, while Andy Linighan has just played a full season for Crystal Palace and he has now turned 38.

With Graham, we always knew what we were going to be doing in training and it often lasted beyond 1 p.m. It was very demanding, physical work, too. Graham is intense because he knows what he wants and will have his players pay almost any price to deliver it for him. Sometimes he would have it fixed in his mind that a player was not doing something the way he wanted him to do it. With me, he would pick on something like I was starting too far back in my goal when I was sweeping behind the back four and he would go on and on about it, game after game. Even when I knew I was doing it right, he would still bring it up every game until I would finally have a go back at him. At that point, he would back down and let it drop.

This must have been a deliberate ploy because I saw him do it with other players. Nigel Martyn and Ian Walker have also both told me that he did exactly the same to them. It is hard to know just why he does this to players except that, as he obviously believes repetition in training eventually ensures players automatically do what he wants them to do in games, nagging on at them about some part of their game is probably just another way of getting the same response.

He was less dictatorial about how we lived away from the training ground. For a start, he was not a great believer in having the squad closeted in a hotel before games. I could not believe it when the lads told me that, when they had to beat Liverpool by two goals at Anfield to win the title, they had travelled up by coach on the day of the match.

We did travel up on Fridays for Saturday games outside London but there was no question of hotel stays before London games as happens now. For a home game, we would meet at the South Herts golf club at 10 a.m. For our pre-match meal, we could have anything we wanted: steak, fish and chips, scrambled eggs, beans on toast – there was loads of choice. Then we would have a team meeting before leaving about 12.45 p.m. But there was no coach to take us the 30-minute drive to the ground – we all went in our own cars. It was just like a Sunday football match convoy except that the wacky races we used to have on the way were in more powerful, top-of-the-range cars than the usual amateur team can muster.

Our diet would appal most club managers now but at the time we were not being put at any disadvantage because none of the other clubs were any different. These days, footballers have been educated about the foods they should be eating so that, even if Graham or some other manager is still operating the same easy-going policy on club meals, they'll be looking after themselves and asking for the food they now know is best for them before a game.

We are learning from the foreign players as they have been eating properly for years. When the French players came here, they could not believe the food we had in the week. Mind you, they think all English food is *merde*, anyway. They have never been able to understand the drinking culture there has been in British football, either. When I joined the club, there was a group of players – Bouldie, Merse, Tony, Grovesy, Lee and one or two others – who would go out once a week for a good drink-up. Tony called it the Tuesday Club. With all the midweek games we have now, especially if we are playing in Europe, there is no longer any time for a midweek night out but, even before the number of games increased and the Merse and Tony scandals broke, that drinking club had more or less broken up because it had started getting into the papers.

It was a time when the papers were nosing into players' private lives more and more. Everything you did was getting into print and the gaffer did not like it. It was not just the drinking that was a problem for Graham but the publicity that went with it. He went absolutely mad at Wrighty and Mickey Thomas because they had let a photo be taken at a club of them and the girl with whom David Mellor had (allegedly) performed in his Chelsea kit.

'You're Arsenal players and you're having your pictures taken with a **** like that – it's just not on,' he told them.

He was a bit of a puritan and did not like anything 'naughty' on the video when we were travelling by coach to away games. Anything violent or sexy was taken out of the machine straight away. He would not even allow my Roy 'Chubby' Brown tapes and they only have bad language in them. He used to tell us to cut it out if we were swearing loudly as well despite the fact that he swore a lot himself.

We did call him Gadaffi for a while, partly because they looked a bit similar but also because of the way he would act the dictator.

But, personally, I had no real fallings-out with him. There was one time when Tony, Merse and I had been away with England. We had won the game and had a few drinks, so when we arrived back we all agreed not to show up for Arsenal training that day. Nothing had been said to us about coming in so we thought, if none of us go, we would get away with it. Then Tony rings and tells me that Merse has gone in after all. Maybe because he had only been sub for the England game while both of us had started or maybe he just wanted to stitch us up for a joke. Either way, we were in trouble.

We went in but Graham said he had to fine us for being late. We were thinking a week's wages which, even at Arsenal, was a fair wedge, but then he said £100 each and I was tempted to say, 'Make it £200 and I'll have tomorrow off, too.'

The only real downside about his regime at Arsenal was the way he left, especially after the way he had treated us over our contracts.

Every time we went in to see him, he would say he could not give us what we were asking. The club had a strict limit on wages and he could not break it for us.

This was all through the time we were winning a lot of trophies for him and the club. He might say now that he gave us our chances, but you still have to take them and he was not going to give you a chance unless he thought you were good enough in the first place. It was also frustrating that we were being linked with so many top players but then never signing them because of the wage structure.

This wages cap meant that the team was not being strengthened to help us keep winning trophies, and also that we were not getting the money we should have been earning at the time. The club might say we were earning good money – and we were – but it was still a lot less than we would have been paid by other top clubs in our league as well as overseas.

Having said that, I was not seriously looking to move away although I did have a fancy to go and play somewhere abroad, preferably somewhere warm. No British goalie had ever played for an overseas club and the idea of being the first did appeal to me. There was some talk about various foreign clubs coming in for me but nothing concrete came of it.

For some reason, the stream of good players coming through from the youth sides had started to dry up as well so, although the first team was successful for most of Graham's time there, by the end of his era the cracks were beginning to show. Other teams were moving ahead of us because they could attract the big name players.

Everything came to a head in 1995. At the end of the previous year, the news broke that Graham was being investigated over payments made to him by the Norwegian agent Rune Hauge in connection with the transfers to Arsenal of Jensen and Pal Lydersen a couple of years earlier. Then, early in 1995, there was a flurry of buys: John Hartson for a couple of million from Luton, Chris Kiwomya for just over a million from Ipswich and then the Dutchman Glenn Helder for £2.3million, at the time the second highest transfer fee ever paid by Arsenal.

Glenn was a bit mouthy, so we soon found out what he was earning, which was a lot more than any of us. Arsenal had definitely broken the wage structure for him and what made it worse was that he was not much of a player. In his first game, he did this blinding trick down the line and the crowd thought, 'We've got something special here.' But it turned out he was a one-trick pony. After that start it was all downhill for him.

And it was downhill for Graham, too. A few weeks after signing Helder, he was sacked by the club even though, by then, he had paid the £425,000 given to him by Hauge into Arsenal's account.

When the first stories had come out about the money, we had not taken too much notice. As players, we never know anything about financial deals like that. We just read about them in the papers like everybody else. But, when Graham was sacked, we realised the stories must have been true and we were all shocked. There had been nothing in Graham's manner to suggest that he knew he was going to be sacked, but we knew something serious was happening when we were called into a meeting before training one morning.

Stewart Houston simply told us that Graham was leaving and that he was taking over as caretaker manager. The club had to tell us immediately they had sacked Graham because the press were on to the story and would have been asking us about it.

All sorts of thoughts then started going through your mind about the financial negotiations you had been through with Graham over the years. You couldn't help yourself thinking about what he had been doing with the club's money. He had been so mean with it as far as we had been concerned that it really did stick in the craw.

It was hard to believe that someone in his position, earning so much money anyway, would get involved in something like that. In every other way, we could not fault him as a manager but, for all that he had done with and for us, that ending is how most of us will remember him and that is a real shame. A lot of the players liked him but, like at any other club, it was the players who weren't being picked who were against him and were pleased that he was going.

I have no problems with him now and we say 'hello' when we meet but there will always be that distance between him and all the Arsenal players.

With Arsène Wenger, I believe he is genuinely sticking up for us now, trying to get us as much as possible. All the players believe that, and we never felt like that about Graham.

But I don't think his departure affected us on the pitch. There was a load of press coverage over it, but the more pressure we are put under at Arsenal, the better we play. When something like this happens, the players get together and agree to say 'no' to all interviews. That means there is nobody rocking the boat as we all just pull together and look to the future.

13

• • • • • •

Life after George

Although Stewart Houston took us to that second European final after Graham's mid-season departure, I don't think any of us thought he would make the jump from caretaker to permanent manager.

He had joined the Arsenal management team the same season that I had transferred from QPR, and he tried to become involved with the players by offering himself as a go-between if we had a problem to take to the manager. But Houston was very much Graham's man and we did not totally trust him to take our side. So, when he took over from Graham in February 1995, he did not have the same respect from the players.

At least he had the sense not to try and change the way we played, otherwise we might not have made that final. And he can hardly be blamed for our losing the cup to a goal like Nayim's, or even for our poor Premiership position – 12th – as we had been playing poorly in the league all season.

But it was well known that the board were looking for a new manager. They seemed to believe, as we did, that the job was just too big for Houston and it was no surprise that we started the next season (1995–6) with a new man in charge.

On our close-season tour to Hong Kong and China, there was an incident with a Hong Kong taxi-driver which saw Ray Parlour in the cells overnight and fined in court the following morning. Houston thought that this might have cost him the manager's job but I think the decision had already been taken. The incident was blown out of proportion, anyway. Ray likes to wind people up when he's had a good night and sometimes they just take it the wrong way.

I read all about it in the newspapers because, although I had been on the tour, I was back home by then. When I saw the pictures of the coppers taking Ray from jail to the court, I can remember thinking, 'Sooner him than me.' I could only imagine how bad the prison must have been because I had just experienced the state of the hospitals in that part of the world.

The trip had been organised by Sky through News International Asia. It had been a long season and I could have done without travelling all that way to play a couple of local sides but it was a fascinating experience, especially as the only part of Asia I had been to at that stage was Singapore, which does not prepare you at all for what you find in China.

In Beijing, we stayed in a huge five-star hotel but, within a very short distance of this luxury living, there was poverty like nothing I had seen before. There were also literally millions of cyclists but very few cars.

We were taken to Tiananmen Square, where we were told not to go around in big groups. Security was still tight after the violent putting-down of the 'Democracy' uprising. While we were in China, we were told by some of the people we met that a lot more had been killed that night in the Square than the official numbers released by the government.

We went into the Forbidden City, which was an amazing experience, especially as they had somehow wangled us permission to shoot a promotional video there for Nike and Sky. We were wearing our Nike trainers and Arsenal tracksuits and, when someone produced a ball, we took turns juggling it. I can't imagine many people will be able to tell their grandchildren they played keepy-uppy in the Forbidden City. It is one of my best travel memories.

One of my worst was of what happened when I was injured in the first game we played there. Halfway through the second half, I went right over on my ankle. It was a bad pitch and I put my foot on one side of a rut which gave way underneath me. Straightaway, I knew it was a bad one. I had dislocated the ankle and badly damaged the tendons and ligaments into the bargain. I was taken away in a Chinese ambulance – that is, a dirty old van without so much as a siren. The club doctor came with me but the physio had to stay in case there were any more injuries in the game. In any case, we had a travel medical insurance policy so I was covered for treatment there. But there's treatment ... and then there's treatment.

I was carried into the hospital on a stretcher and then switched to another one. When I looked back, I saw that the first one was covered in dried blood so I started looking around the whole place. I was horrified to see there was blood all over the walls and bits of broken glass on the floors. Fortunately, my wound was not an open one but it was swelling up fast. There were plenty of people around but none of them seemed to speak English until the specialist arrived. He had actually been watching the game at home and, when he saw me get my injury, he realised he would be the one called in to treat it so he came straight to the hospital.

He ordered some X-rays and said they showed I did not need an operation. Even if I had needed one, I was determined that I wasn't going to have it done there. I was left hanging around for what seemed like hours until I called the club doctor in. 'Doc, just get me out of here,' I begged him. I was in the Accident and Emergency ward and there were people around with all kinds of terrible open wounds and there was even more blood on the walls. I know the NHS has its faults but this was a real eye-opener. I told our doc that I just wanted the ankle strapped up and to be taken back to the hotel for our physios to check it over before taking the first flight back home to see a Harley Street specialist.

This is where Stephen Perry came into the picture as his company, London Export, had sponsored the game in which I had been injured. It had 50 years' experience of doing business in China and had been involved in the ground-breaking visit of West Bromwich Albion, the first England football team to visit the People's Republic back in 1976. Later it had also been involved in another China tour, this time by Graham Taylor's Watford. But Stephen and his company were Arsenal through and through, owning shares in the club and with an executive box at Highbury, as well.

He met me at the airport and immediately said, 'There is some good news and some bad news: the good news is that we have got you upgraded into first class; the bad news is that you are going to have to travel ten hours with three die-hard Gooners.'

They had arranged for me to go in the very front row of first class so that I could stretch my leg out and rest my foot on the front ledge. The cabin crew really looked after me, putting cushions under my leg and bringing me drinks, and I really didn't mind talking to Stephen and his colleagues about Arsenal; in fact we have become good friends since and I have been down to his son Jack's football club to present awards.

Before we landed at Heathrow, Stephen and the others drew lots for who was going to push my wheelchair and so be in all the news photographs. Stephen won, but the photos were cropped from the top so he ended up having just the second finger of his right hand immortalised in the *Daily Mail*. Mind you, he tells me he has been signing autographs on the strength of that ever since.

Back in England, I was on crutches for a couple of weeks and I still have problems with the ankle now because it was such a bad injury.

I was to see that pitch again when England had a similar tour before Euro 96. The surface hadn't improved. Although it looked good from the sidelines, there were ruts hidden in the green. We trained on it but I wouldn't go into the penalty area in case it happened again and did not play in the game. On this trip we also visited the Great Wall, which was an awesome sight, but nothing will match my memories – good and bad – of that first Chinese tour.

My 1995 injury meant that I missed out on England's summer Umbro tournament with Brazil, Sweden and Japan while, shortly after the rest of the team's return from China in June, Bruce Rioch was appointed Arsenal manager. His previous club Bolton had played well and beaten us in cup games in recent seasons and Rioch himself had been a top international player in his day.

He had the look and seemed to have the style of an old-style Arsenal manager. In other words, he dressed smartly and was strict with the players. Graham had the same look and style, of course, but then the Board must have recognised that he had been a successful manager despite the financial scandal that saw him on his way.

With Rioch, however, there were certain things I saw immediately which I just did not like. Although he had plenty of skill, he was known as a hard player who took no prisoners in midfield. Perhaps he thought it helped to live up to this reputation in training sessions but, whatever the reason, he definitely liked to leave his foot in when tackling.

Managers kicking their own players do not impress too many people, though. Once they cottoned on to him, the lads would deliberately take the mickey. There is a training routine where one player is put in the middle of a circle of players and he has to try to win it from the others who are passing it across the circle.

When it was the new gaffer's turn, they would try to nutmeg him, and every time it went through his legs, there would be a great shout of 'Ole!' They would keep this up until he cracked and took one of the players out with a wicked tackle.

Rioch also liked to give rollockings, especially to youth team players. He would lay into one of them for not bringing the water over quickly enough or something petty like that. He would do this in front of everybody, too, which made us all feel uncomfortable. This seemed all wrong to me. He was the Arsenal manager and should not need to behave like that.

He was also a shouter before, during and after games and I saw him throw a lot of bottles (plastic ones, fortunately) just to make his point.

Managing Arsenal is a massive job and, just as I had felt about Houston, I came to think that Rioch was not big enough for it either. Time proved me right.

Houston stayed on as his number two and, to start with, there was not too much difference in the way we were asked to play the game from the Graham days. Rioch did experiment with the formation, though, using three centre-backs and two wing-backs and Wrighty as a lone striker. He also encouraged us to pass the ball through midfield a little more. But, if he had stayed longer, I am sure he would gradually have changed the whole way we played – much as was to happen later with Arsène Wenger.

As it was, his first and only season saw us finish a respectable fifth in the Premiership and reach the Coca Cola Cup semi-final, which we lost to Aston Villa. That fifth position in the league also earned us a place in the UEFA Cup. All in all, it would have been a reasonable season for the majority of Premiership clubs but more is always expected at Arsenal. The fans were used to winning trophies in

Graham's time but, traditionally, the Board at Arsenal has been more patient than at some other clubs. Immediate results are not required and managers are usually given time to prove themselves.

After the Graham scandal, they were also looking to restore some stability at the club. But Rioch was sacked after just one season, making him the shortest-serving manager (apart from caretakers) in the club's history, and a lot of it must have been down to his feud with Ian Wright.

The Board had certainly backed Rioch from the start, by moving into the transfer market in a big way. After the Graham scandal, though, they kept a firm hand on all the transfer dealings themselves. Rioch's role was just to recommend the players he wanted.

Dennis Bergkamp, for a record £7.5million, and David Platt for £4.75million were both brought in for 1995–6. This was great for us, both because we saw world-class players being added to the squad and also because, as a result, we were now being offered the kind of wages that other top clubs had been paying for years.

The Board must have realised that they just had to break the wages barrier and go after the top players if we were to go any further as a team. The change of manager may also have helped, as it is easier to say 'yes' to a new one than to someone you have always said 'no' to in the past. But, then, maybe Graham did not try too hard to persuade the Board to buy big-name players. Perhaps he preferred to work with lesser players as they are easier to mould into a fixed way of playing. We will never know for sure. In any case, Rioch may have bought some big names but he still seemed to have trouble dealing with that type of player.

His troubles started when he called Wrighty 'a big-time Charlie' in front of all the first-team players in a pre-season friendly at St Albans. Wrighty went mad, effing and blinding, and it was not very nice for any of us to see one of our star players being slagged off for no good reason. That kind of pre-season friendly is just for players to get some match fitness. Scoring goals and winning are not important.

More rows with Wrighty and other players followed, often on match days at half-time or full-time when Rioch would go up to players and put his face right up close to theirs so that he would be literally spitting in their faces as he swore at them. It was just because they had made a mistake or not done something he'd asked them to do, but he turned it into a blazing confrontation.

He did it to John Hartson and Nigel Winterburn and also to Martin Keown, who has a real temper himself. I've seen Martin lose it a few times and knock a few doors off their hinges. But Rioch was just a very confrontational person and, as far as Arsenal were concerned, the wrong person at the wrong time.

Managers just can't treat players like that any more and not just because some players are bigger stars and higher earners than managers. It is wrong because we all have to get on together. It is a team game and it is hard to win games if there is no team spirit.

Although we had a reasonable season, there is no doubt that the bad atmosphere between Rioch and some of the players did affect the team. I am easygoing and I know it affected me. It did not make me play any worse – you don't go out to do that, whatever happens – but sometimes that little extra is missing which makes you and the team better than the rest.

Wrighty would score and run over and deliberately jump all over Rioch and we all knew he was taking the mickey. Eventually, he asked for a transfer because he said he couldn't play for Rioch any more.

The players were mainly on Ian's side but it was a strange time for us all. With a club like Arsenal, it is virtually unheard of for a player to go to the extremes that Wrighty did and I know he regrets some of it now. But, although Rioch had been a top player and was a very hard man with a regimented style, we all realised that he was out of his league as a manager. I don't think he got on too well with some of the directors, either.

Whatever the final reason, Rioch was out five days before the start of 1996–7 and, although Houston came in again as caretaker manager, he was off a month later to be manager of my old club, QPR. Bizarrely, Rioch later joined him there as his number two. It was an odd turnaround for the two of them but the QPR players told me that Rioch was soon acting like the manager and Houston like the number two. On match days, Rioch wore the suit and Houston the tracksuit. Nobody thought it could last – and it didn't, with Houston later being sacked.

Back at Arsenal, Pat Rice took over the hot seat. But he made it clear he was only keeping it warm for the next manager. A member of Arsenal's last Double-winning side, Pat was coaching the youth team when I first joined Arsenal, and all the players had a lot of time for him because he was so good, so enthusiastic with the younger players.

It was known almost immediately that Arsenal wanted Frenchman Arsène Wenger as manager and, when Pat came in, he made it very clear he was not going to play the big 'I am' just because he had the manager's title for a while. He had tried managing at Watford and had decided he preferred to work just as a coach.

Although he was a good coach in his own right, he made no changes to the system we were playing and made a point of involving players more in the tactical decisions and encouraging us to come up with ideas. We respected that.

Arsène was still out in Japan, where he was working out his contract with Grampus Eight but he must have been in touch with Pat. I imagine he had some input but, as he didn't know the players, I can't think he was suggesting too many changes.

We did not know very much about him, either, although we had heard players like Glenn Hoddle, Chris Waddle and Mark Hateley all saying fantastic things about their experience of playing for him at Monaco. We knew he had managed the French national side and that he had gone to Japan and done wonders there but the standard of the French and Japanese leagues were well below the standard of the Premiership, so there were a lot of question-marks against his name as far as we were concerned.

There was also the problem of the delay before his arrival, which seemed to be longer than the club had expected. When he finally arrived, in time for our game with Borussia Mönchengladbach in the UEFA Cup, he changed our defensive system at half-time when it was 1–1 and we promptly lost the game 3–2 and the tie 6–4.

He was also walking into a club with a striker still struggling to overcome drink, drug and gambling addictions and a captain who had just admitted to the world that he was an alcoholic.

14

· · · · · ·

True Confessions

If Tony Adams and Paul Merson could play like that as alcoholics, just how much better would they have been in their younger days if they had been sober and, in Merse's case, free of drug problems and the gambling bug? Once the dust had settled on their respective revelations, that thought occurred to me as it must have to Tony and Merse, too. After all, they had been top players for their clubs and full England internationals when things were at their lowest ebb for them off the field.

They say you can't fool all of the people all of the time but they had both managed to fool me. No one was more surprised by their confessions than the guy who had shared with them club and England dressing-rooms, a league title, an FA Cup, League Cup and European Cup-Winners Cup. And, let's be honest, I had shared a few drinking sessions with both of them, too.

When Merse admitted to his addictions at the end of 1994, I think all the players were shocked. We all knew that he liked a drink and could go haywire when he'd had a few, but we never realised it had reached those proportions. Some of the lads knew about his gambling but I don't think anyone knew about the drugs.

It was all news to me, but then they used to call me 'social' at one time because I often preferred to go fishing than be out drinking with the rest of the lads. When we did all go out together, we would have a good laugh and a drink but it was not serious drinking, or so we thought. I certainly had not noticed the effect of their drinking on their play and I don't remember ever seeing either of them come into training obviously drunk or seriously hungover.

The publicity after the first revelations was massive because it was not just the drinking with Merse, there was the gambling, the drugs and the problems with his wife, too. The press had a field day. But, as I remember it now, it seemed as though Merse went straight into the clinic and we did not see him again until he was out and clean. This meant the story died quite quickly – at least, until he tried to resume his footballing career.

There was massive hype about his first game back and it was a very emotional affair for all of us. The most noticeable change in him – and later with Tony – was that he looked so much fitter when he came out of rehab. They both lost a lot of weight and looked really toned up and super-fit. I have to admit it made me think, '*Is* booze that bad for you?' I had never noticed the extra weight on them before but, when I saw a photograph of Tony holding the two cups we won in the same season, his face tells the story: where it is all muscled-up now, he was Mr Chubby Chops back then.

Tony had been such a great player and captain that, when he made his confession, it was an even bigger shock than when Merse did it. Maybe it was also because, from what I had seen and known about him, it made me worry that, if he was an alcoholic, then so was I. I liked a drink and got drunk occasionally, which is what I thought he was doing. But then it came out that Tony had sometimes been binge-drinking every day.

I will never forget the day he told us: 13 September 1996. The season had just started, Rioch had already been sacked, caretaker manager Stewart Houston was leaving to manage QPR and Pat Rice was taking temporary charge. Tony asked for a team meeting and, once he had all the players lined up, he just said, 'My name's Tony – I'm an alcoholic.' There was a sort of stunned silence until he started to break down. There was a lump in my throat, too.

With both of them, once we were over the shock, the banter started again and it hasn't really stopped since. We tested the water to see how they would react to us taking the mickey. Merse was half and half about it – he took the mickey-taking OK but we could see that he still had serious problems. Tony was happier about it but still made it clear that, away from the club, it was not really something to joke about. But they were both very good about coming to the Christmas parties and other nights out that we had. They would come along and just drink coffee or soft drinks and none of us would ever pull their leg about that. In fact, we would tell them that we admired them for it – which we did.

The only time I saw either of them lose it with us was when, on separate occasions, champagne and beer were accidentally sprayed over them when we were celebrating winning important games. Tony went mad because he said the taste and the smell of it brought back such unhappy memories. He had such an extreme reaction to it that it really brought it home to us how serious his problem was.

Arsenal brought in Steve Jacobs as personal counsellor, first to Merse and then to Tony. Steve, who still travels to every game with Tony, was a member of Gamblers Anonymous himself originally but then became a counsellor to help others in a similar situation. In fact, it was weird at first because we would see Steve drinking when he travelled with us. But gambling had been his problem, not drinking.

Tony is very popular with all of us and it has been good to see him putting his life back together again. It is brilliant to see him in the mental shape he is in now. He can come out with the lads and it does not seem to bother him to see us having a drink but not to have one himself. In fact, he seems to take strength from it.

The only problem is that now he bores the pants off us with his philosophies, his piano lessons, the plays he has been to see, the books he has read. But, if it all gets too much for us, somebody will just say, 'Tony . . . phone call,' so we can make ourselves scarce.

His life has really turned around and it was great to see him awarded the MBE. We were even more jealous when we heard he had been out with Caprice.

I think it is fair to say that Tony has had a smoother ride to recovery than Merse, but that is because they are different types of people.

Once he had admitted his problem, Tony set about sorting his life out. He decided that a clean break with the past, starting with a divorce from Jane who had drug addiction problems of her own, was the right way ahead. He seemed to have worked out from the start how he was going to stay off the drink.

Merse is more of an addictive personality, which is why his difficulties did not stop with drink. After his rehab, he still had problems and my view is that he was giving too many interviews. These were not just quick quotes and soundbites, but major spreads in the papers. His wife was giving plenty of interviews, too, and there was just too much of his life being exposed in public. Everybody knew his business, every problem he had was out there for other people, other fans to pick over. It was probably because of the continuing pressure from the tabloids, which were running these and stories about his problems in recovery, that Merse left Arsenal shortly after Arsène Wenger arrived. I think he just needed a fresh start and a chance to put his life back in order.

It was not totally unexpected, either, as he had just had his testimonial and the club had a new manager with new ideas and new players he wanted to bring into the team. If there was a right time to leave it was then, although we were all a little surprised that he had agreed to drop down a division to join Middlesbrough. On the other hand, they were paying top wages, Bryan Robson was the manager and they had a good chance of promotion back to the Premiership.

But there have still been ups and downs for Merse ever since, with another move to Aston Villa and stories of him falling off the wagon. Again, a lot of these stories have come from Merse, himself, including another book that came out about his problems at the end of his time with Middlesbrough.

I just don't think it can be any help to have everyone you pass in the street knowing your private business. The temptations are hard enough to cope with for some players without them putting more pressure on themselves. And the wages are so high for top players at a very young age now. Players only need one good move early in their career and they are on huge money in their early twenties.

Glenn Helder was a classic case. He struck lucky when Graham signed him because, as we quickly found out, he was not much of a player. He was physically strong but he just could not deliver on the pitch. And, unlike some others who can't seem to perform on a Saturday, he did not even look good in training. After the stories about Graham came out, it looked a very dodgy signing indeed.

Glenn was a good lad but a flash dresser and a bit of a wide boy. He loved playing the drums and driving fast cars. He had a big 850

BMW, which is already pretty quick, but he was not happy with that and he had it souped up so it could run on aeroplane fuel.

We gave him plenty of stick, particularly for his clothes, but he took it well and seemed happy enough. But, after he left Arsenal, I was sorry to hear that he had he tried to kill himself over some gambling debts.

The one advantage young players have coming into the game now is that, at least at the top level, the drinking culture has started to disappear – although not completely as last season's La Manga incident with Stan Collymore and his new Leicester club showed.

But when I joined Leeds and then when I first travelled with England, I was amazed at how much drinking went on. I became used to seeing well-known England internationals very drunk when we were away for matches. Then there was the Tuesday Club at Arsenal. Now the influence of the foreign coaches, managers and players is changing everything.

Another factor is the way the higher wages have meant that players, once they have married and settled down, are often living in big houses well away from the city grounds so, after training, everyone tends to go their separate ways. And, as I've said, the number of midweek games we have to play now has also cut back on the socialising.

One side-effect of Tony's drinking problems was that I think, subconsciously, he felt guilty about what he was doing and so indebted to the club for continuing to employ him. This meant that, whatever money they offered him, he would just take it. As he was the club captain, this meant it cut the rug away from any of the other players who were thinking of asking for more. I am sure the club, and Graham in particular, realised this so made sure they went to Tony first every time.

Even after Graham left, this was still happening. I remember that I had to see David Dein for my contract negotiations the day after Tony had re-signed. I went to Dein's house with Steve Kuttner, my agent at the time, to see Dein and Arsenal managing director Ken Friar. I said I want this amount and they immediately said that Tony had already signed for this – a lower amount. I asked them if that was their limit, then. When they said it was, I told them that, in that case, I would not be signing.

We argued backwards and forwards and Steve and I went out four times to walk around Dein's garden while he and Friar discussed our demands. Every time we went back, they kept saying they could not do any more. We were at the brink of negotiations breaking down altogether when, eventually, they made a few phone calls and then said they could now pay what I was asking.

The next day, I bumped into Tony at the club and he said, 'Thanks, Dave.' I asked him what he meant and he told me that Dein had rung him and offered him a raise, just a day after he had signed his contract. He guessed it must have been because they had agreed to pay me more and knew they would have to raise his money to match it.

It was the complete reverse of what had been happening before and it spelt the end of their ploy of using Tony's willingness to accept anything that was offered him to keep all our wages down.

In some ways, we had all paid a price for Tony's addiction.

15

······

Three Lions on the Shirt

Well, Mum may have thought she was laying it on a bit thick with the local education authority to win me a place at a football-friendly school, when she told them that I was an international in the making, but she turned out to be spot-on.

To date, I have won nearly 60 caps, been to two World Cups and two European Championships and have played under several England managers. Looking back now, I could fool myself into thinking it was all just meant to be – but I don't. I know only too well that it has been a long, hard road. I have had to learn patience, and sometimes to bite my lip, or my international career would have been a lot shorter.

I have already described my first call-ups at Under-21 and full international levels and also the early end to my first World Cup in 1990 but even at that stage I was a long way off being England's Number One. And that had always been my ultimate aim.

I do not go along with John Barnes's view about nationalism that was widely reported from his autobiography. He apparently never really felt that it was that important playing internationals for England. But John still has lots of family in Jamaica and he has retained the accent, too, so maybe it was just England, not international, football that never quite connected with him. Maybe some of the lads who play for Ireland because they once bought a ticket for Riverdance (or whatever the national team qualification is now) find it the same.

But, for me and most English players, playing for England has always been the big one. When I was a lad, my target was to play professionally; then it was to play for a top side and win trophies and medals; and finally it was to play for my country.

I love playing for England. I think it shows, and I am not the only one. Most of the players who come into the England squad share the same passion.

Traditionally, England has always produced several top-class goalkeepers every generation, so being patient and waiting for your chance has always gone with the territory. Although I had become a full international two years earlier, I still went to World Cup 90 as number three to Shilts and Chris Woods, and I might not have made it at all if Gary Bailey had been fit.

But that first World Cup was still a memorable experience. Until you have gone to one as part of a national squad, you don't realise how big an event it is. I was only 26 and I was not too upset about only being third choice. I was just delighted and proud to be there with all the world's top footballing countries.

My first impression was of how tight the security was in Italy for the tournament. We would travel to games on the coach and there would be four or five motorbike outriders, two cars at the front and two at the back and a helicopter above you. I had never seen or been a part of anything like it. On the way back from one of the games, one of the coppers came off his bike. He went round a bend, hit some oil and lost it. Nobody seemed too surprised. After all, this was Italy – home of the boy racer.

Even going as third choice, it was a great experience to be at my first World Cup but, after breaking my thumb, it was to be a shortlived one. I would have my World Cup chance later but, for Bobby Robson, although he took us to the epic semi-final with Germany which we lost on penalties, that World Cup was the end of the England road, and he was replaced by Graham Taylor.

Peter Shilton also retired from international football in 1990. So I was then competing with Chris Woods for the number one spot. I thought I had a good case after that amazing first season with Arsenal when I only let in 18 goals and won a championship medal. I did play in friendlies against Cameroon and Argentina and those Euro 92 qualifiers against Ireland and Turkey but the comments

Taylor made to the press after the Ireland game made it clear that Chris was his number one.

Obviously I did not agree and I would love to have told him so quite forcefully but I bit my tongue instead and that was not the last time I had to do that with this England manager.

It seemed like you just had to move up stage by stage whatever your current form. Chris had been number two to Shilts so he automatically became number one while I moved up from three to number two with Tim Flowers now challenging me for that position.

At one stage, I didn't play in an international for 18 months, although I was usually in the squad. But the (almost) final straw was when Taylor decided to take Nigel Martyn to Euro 92 in Sweden as number two goalkeeper. I was in the original squad for Sweden but it had to be cut back to 22 players, and this meant three goalkeepers would be reduced to just two.

On the day the final squad was to be announced, we were all told to be in our rooms at the hotel and that each player who was being left out would be told in a telephone call to his room. The rest would meet up again in the main lounge to find out what was happening in Sweden.

Lee Dixon and I were waiting in the room we shared. We were both a little nervous, but that was because Lee was not certain of his place. Neither of us thought that mine was in doubt. All of a sudden the phone rings but it is just Merse winding us up. Nobody else phoned so we thought we were both going and were obviously delighted. We went downstairs to the lounge and everyone was congratulating each other when I noticed there were three goalies in the room. I thought, 'What's going on here?' A minute later, Lawrie McMenemy popped his head round the door and said to me, 'Come on, David, Graham wants a word with you upstairs.'

Taylor told me he wanted to take Nigel to give him some experience in case anything happened to me before the World Cup two years later. Was that all right with me? I was disgusted and said so. I told him it was a rubbish decision and I would have said more but he jumped in, telling me my England career was not over and not to say what I was thinking in case I regretted it later. So I bit on it again, just repeated that it was rubbish and stormed off.

I had played in qualifying games for this tournament so I could not see his logic at all and what really rubbed salt in the wound was not having received the promised phone call. Taylor never apologised for that and he will never know how close I came to telling him exactly what I thought of him even if it could have ended my England career – at least while he was manager.

When I went back to my room, England's goalkeeping coach Peter Bonetti was there. I had made it clear during training that I didn't agree with some of his coaching methods, and I was not sure if he had played any part in Taylor's decision to drop me. Whatever his role, he was there at the wrong time and I said, 'Pete, it's best if you leave now,' and I think he knew why.

Lawrie Mac came in and apologised for the mix-up and I was all right with him. In fact, the England business aside, I liked Graham Taylor as a person. After I received my MBE, he walked into a shop in Rickmansworth and, when he saw me, he got down on his knees and started bowing and scraping which was embarrassing but very funny.

In the event, Lee was injured and did not make Sweden either and we were probably the lucky ones. England lost every game and nobody in the team came out of it looking good, including Chris Woods. And it was from Sweden onwards that the press really began to get after Graham Taylor.

In fairness, he brought some of the pressure on himself as he did make some very strange tactical moves as England manager. For instance, he could be very negative. For one game, he told us he wanted one of the lads to kick it straight from the kick-off as far down the pitch as possible and directly into touch.

After this briefing, we were flabbergasted. This was the England team and the manager was telling us to kick it straight into touch?

We did this for a few games and then he changed tack for the vital World Cup 1994 qualifying match away against Norway. He told Gazza to dribble it straight from the kick-off all the way to their goal. He thought that, as we had been kicking for touch before, this would take them by surprise.

Although Taylor had deliberately chosen a secure airbase for our training camp, somehow the Norwegians found out our plans and they had four or five players waiting to ambush Gazza. It was embarrassing schoolboy stuff straight out of the Roy of the Rovers book of big match tactics. The rest of the tactics for the game were not much smarter and we were well-beaten 2–0. Nobody did themselves justice and Chris had a particularly poor game.

It came at the end of Arsenal's double cup-winning season when he had been a double loser playing for Sheffield Wednesday against us in both finals. He did not have the best of times and was blamed for palming in Andy Linighan's winning header in the FA Cup Final replay. After more poor performances from him on a summer tour to the USA that I missed, I was back in the team at the start of the 1993–4 season.

My first game for England in more than 18 months was a comfortable 3–0 win over Poland at Wembley in September but a month later it was a different story. We were away to Holland in Rotterdam and it was a game we really needed to win to qualify. What happened was immortalised in that notorious documentary on Taylor that effectively finished him as England manager.

Ronald Koeman should have conceded a penalty and been sent off for a foul on David Platt. He got away with it and then scored from a twice-taken free-kick.

The first time Koeman hammered the ball towards the side of the goal I was guarding and I had it well covered but the referee decided the England player who charged it down had moved too early. The second time, Koeman chipped it over the wall and into the opposite side of the goal to where I was standing. I was on the right side of the goal to defend the free-kick. If he had scored in my side of the goal, it would definitely have been down to me but as he chipped it up and over the wall to the other side, with no defenders on the line, there really wasn't much I could do about it. I might have been a couple of feet too far across to one side but even if I hadn't been, I don't think I would have saved it.

The reason I came in for so much criticism was Brian Moore's commentary on ITV. As Koeman readied himself to take the free-kick the second time, Brian guessed what he was going to do and kept repeating, 'He's going to flip it, he's going to flip it.' Which is exactly what he did.

I just wish Brian could have told me. But it looked bad, as though a commentator could see what was happening and not the England goalie. But he had a view from behind the player when I had the defensive wall in front of me.

Then my future team-mate Dennis Bergkamp slotted in a second and it was all over bar the embarrassment of the final match against San Marino. We needed to win this one by a cricket score to give us a mathematical chance of still qualifying. No one worried about San Marino scoring because they never scored against anyone.

Straight from the kick-off we passed the ball a couple of times in the midfield before Stuart Pearce decided to roll it back to me for an early touch. Unfortunately Pearcey scuffed the pass and San Marino's David Gualtieri nipped in to slip the ball past me.

It was just eight seconds into the game so it was the fastest goal England have ever conceded. We won 7–1 in the end with Wrighty among the goals but it did not help us qualify and, as far as the press and fans were concerned, letting San Marino score was the last straw.

Pearcey did apologise to me and the rest of the team later on but it was just one of those things. It was an unhappy day all round as it was also the first, and only, time I was aware of the National Front element making themselves heard amongst the England fans.

It was such a small crowd – just a couple of thousand – at the game, which was played in Bologna, that they obviously saw their chance to make a name for themselves. They spent the game having a right go at our black players. It was very unpleasant and I hope I never see that kind of demonstration at an England game again.

Our failure to qualify for the 1994 World Cup was a major disappointment for everyone involved and Taylor had to go. The one consolation, from my point of view, was that at least I was the man in possession of that England place.

Things can change rapidly, though, especially when a new manager arrives. Fortunately, they changed for the better when Terry Venables took over.

As a person, Terry is great fun and he creates a relaxed atmosphere around him. Players respect him because he is a footballer's manager, wanting to play the game properly. He would never ask players to kick the ball into touch from kick-offs. When a manager takes training, talks tactics and tells players what he wants, you can always tell whether or not he knows what he is doing. Terry clearly did and that won him immediate respect and that, in turn, bred confidence into the players. We were thinking, 'Yeah, that works,' when he introduced new tactics rather than, 'What's going on here?' which was often the case with Taylor.

He had told the papers before his first England get-together that it was between me, Nigel and Tim for the goalkeeping place but he quickly told me that I was his number one.

Starting with a friendly against Euro 92 winners Denmark in March 1994, I played 18 consecutive games for England under Terry Venables.

Terry's arrival and his decision to stand by me were to change my life forever.

16

· · · · · ·

Make that 34 Years of Hurt

No doubt about it: Euro 96 drew a definite line through my career. Before it, I was just an Arsenal footballer who had played a few times for England; afterwards, I was a national and international star, known far beyond just the footballing world.

And, to be honest, I had not played any better than I had before for my club and country, it was just that this time I had played on a far bigger stage. In fact, it turned out to be the biggest stage that any of the England squad had ever played on.

Because England was hosting Euro 96, it meant that we had the advantage of not having to qualify. That takes the pressure off the manager to some extent and also off the players although there is still the pressure of performing well enough to be picked for the squad to play in the tournament.

Terry was experimenting with formations and players during the run-up to the tournament. Sometimes we played with a back four, sometimes with a three plus two wing-backs and then there was his famous Christmas tree formation.

We had a long unbeaten run, winning most of the friendlies, so that, by the time Euro 96 arrived, we were ready and confident that we could win it. It was a happy bunch of players who set off on the pre-tournament tour to China and Hong Kong. For most of us it was the end of a long hard season so, after a week's training in the England camp, the tour itself was meant to be a welcome break with a few low-key games thrown in.

The evening after the game in Hong Kong, the management had arranged a trip to a bar they had been recommended as having a good party atmosphere. It was called the China Jump Club. At this stage, the players were being allowed a drink to wind down as this would release a lot of the stress that builds up before a major tournament. I was looking forward to going myself but, when I got back to the hotel after the game, I turned the TV on and of all things they were showing the 1993 FA Cup Final – Arsenal against Sheffield Wednesday. I thought I would just sit back on the bed for a few minutes and watch this and next thing I knew I was gone, fast asleep. Arsenal games have the same effect on other spectators, I've been told.

By the time I woke up, it was far too late to join them down at the club, which was a pity because I would have liked to be there. It sounded like a great night and there were some funny stories that did not make it into the papers. The trouble in Hong Kong is that everyone has a camera and a lot of photographs were taken of the lads in the club which did find their way into the papers, locally and back home. A lot of rubbish was written about the 'dentist's chair' drinking game but there's nothing wrong in players relaxing that far ahead of a tournament. Nights out like that are good for morale and team spirit, anyway. But the whole affair just underlined how little privacy is left for anyone in the public eye.

Even more rubbish was written about our flight home on Cathay Pacific. We were supposed to have wrecked the aircraft, but all that happened was that a card school was playing through most of the long flight. A seat tray was broken when one of the card-players sat on it and two of the small TV screens were cracked when one of the others knocked into them. There was a bit of a mess but no one from the airline said anything at the time, mainly because one of the Cathay Pacific staff was playing in the card game. That fact never came out when the airline suddenly started talking about thousands of pounds' worth of damage.

The press latched on to this, of course. They just love to build us up and then knock us down. But it all had the opposite effect. They wanted players to be singled out but we weren't going to play along. Instead, we drew closer together and, just as the Cabinet is supposed to do, we took collective responsibility. It was Terry's idea. He asked us if we all wanted to take responsibility or did they have to try and find out whodunnit? We could see that doing that would just play into the media's hands, so we all put our hands up.

It ruined the story for the papers and from then on we just thought, 'You're out to get us, so stuff you.' We limited our interviews with the press, either not doing them at all or keeping them very short, usually with one-word answers. England is just like any league club – there is always a player who is a press mole. Whether it is deliberate leaking or whether they tell their contacts in confidence and are stitched up, you never know, but this time no one gave anything away. It also helped that we felt the fans were really behind us and did not want to read the knocking stories.

The atmosphere in the country by the time the tournament started was fantastic. The 'Three Lions' song definitely played a major part in that. It hit the right note with everyone. The crowds really took to it and everyone seemed to be singing it. Before every game we would go out for our warm-up and near the end of it the song would always be played. The fans would start singing and I could feel the goosebumps coming up on my neck. It really fired all of us up for the games. The only time this didn't happen was before the Germany game when they didn't play it until we were back in the changing-room. Knowing what happened in that game, perhaps the Wembley DJ should take some of the blame. But I'm jumping the gun.

There was such a big build-up to Euro 96 that, while all those horses and dragons were charging around Wembley during the opening ceremony, I was just anxious to get started.

That first game against Switzerland was nerve-wracking because we were expected to win it comfortably. We had the perfect start with an Alan Shearer goal but then we fell away and hardly produced anything for the rest of the game. Pearcey gave a penalty away for the Swiss to equalise and the result was a total let-down for us. But, when the dust had settled, Terry just said, 'We have a point, we're unbeaten and we can go on from here.' He also pointed out that the hosts always play the first game in a tournament and, more often than not, it ends in a draw because there is so much pressure on the home side while the other side is always lifted by the occasion. The quality of the game is usually poor because there is so much at stake. For the same reason, as I've said, there are few great FA Cup

Finals. And the pressure was not going to be any less for our next game. Quite the reverse – we were to play Scotland.

Like many of the players, I had never played in a game between the two countries although I remembered watching one in Scotland for which I was third-choice 'keeper. I was up in the stands and not exactly among friends – I was sat next to Rod Stewart's dad. Or so he told me and, as he didn't offer to buy me a drink at half-time, I believed him.

For the Euro 96 game, the Scots travelled down in their thousands and were all over London like a rash. We knew we just had to beat them or we would never live it down. Also, Gazza was still playing for Glasgow Rangers then and he was going round telling us he would never be able to show his face back there for pre-season training if we lost. But, although there was pressure, we were having a laugh about it as well. We were still very confident about our chances of winning the whole tournament, not just the Scotland game. Whatever was to happen in the rest of the tournament, though, the Scotland game was a fantastic one to play in and it had the right result . . . if you were English. And for me personally it was a great game.

After a first half of few chances, we again went one-up through Alan's header from Gary Neville's cross and, although it was a fairly even game, they were still not making many chances. Then they broke through and Tony brought Gordon Durie down in the area for a clear penalty.

My first thought was that we had worked so hard to get a lead that, if we lost it so quickly, Scotland would have the edge. I knew their penalty taker was Gary McAllister and that he normally puts them away. He had not taken one against me (in fact, he has not taken another one against me since, either) but I had seen him take them against other 'keepers and he had put them both sides so there was no clue there.

But, like Baldrick, I had my cunning plan; to watch the run-up, not the ball, until the taker strikes it. It is the best way of judging where he is going to place the ball and it has worked pretty well for me.

McAllister put the ball down, started running up to it, and just as he struck it, the ball moved. Whether he had teed it up so much it shifted as his foot went towards it, I don't know, but he still managed a good strike on it. I guessed right and I remember thinking as I was diving to my right, 'I can't get my hands to this' – but by moving my elbow I got just enough on it to deflect the ball up and past the bar. It came off me at a strange angle, but probably the only one that would have seen it go to safety.

I will never forget the roar that followed with all the England fans up in the air and then Tony coming up to me and giving me the biggest kiss. Fortunately no tongues were involved, but it was nearly enough to put me off saving penalties. If I had known he was going to do that, I might have let it in. But, having given away the penalty, he was just so relieved.

It was a wonderful feeling then, and again when I saw the game later and all the photographs in the papers.

Penalties have generally been good for me. I have saved vital ones throughout my career, from Peterborough to Arsenal and England. Those I saved for Arsenal against Sampdoria in the Cup-Winners Cup had directly led to my first real taste of being a media star.

But I had no time to dwell on that after the McAllister save. Everybody was on a high but the ball had gone out for a corner, so I had to be ready to deal with that. When the ball came into the box, we were given a free-kick. I played it out quickly and Darren Anderton went down the line before putting the ball through to Gazza, and the rest is history.

It was just typical of Gazza to steal my thunder. I make a crucial penalty save but, within a couple of minutes, he has gone up the other end and scored one of the great international goals, turning one defender, chipping over another and volleying home.

It also overshadowed one of the best saves I have ever made. Although they were 2–0 down, the Scots were not about to throw in the towel – their fans would never have let them. John Collins put in a dangerous low cross which I knew I would not reach if I went for it. I just had to wait and hope I could make the next save. Durie reached it with a fierce diving header but I flew across to save it halfway up the post. I hit the post in the process but got a firm enough hand on the ball to flick it out. I had a massive bruise all down my arm but I didn't care. It probably did not look particularly spectacular but it was one of my best saves and certainly one of the most important because there was still enough time for the Scots to have come right back into it. The save was all about knowing the angles and quick reactions. I had to move across from one side of the goal to the other. The header was so near to the post that, not only did I have to stop it, I had to make sure I deflected it out of harm's way, otherwise there was every chance the Scots would have put the loose ball in the net. Knowing that the post was coming up quite sharpish also concentrated the mind.

After the Scotland game, the reaction from the fans was amazing. Listening to all the fans shouting my name – 'Sea-Man, Sea-Man' – was like a dream. Although we were then cut off from the crowds back at our hotel, we did see all the celebrations going on in London on the TV. There were some crazy scenes, with guys in the fountains at Trafalgar Square shouting at girls passing in cars to 'get them out for the lads' – at least one of them did, too.

Then, watching the game again on TV brought it home to us that we had four points and it was all down to the next game against Holland, exactly as Terry had always predicted. Even before the tournament groups were announced, he seemed to know that Holland would be the team we had to get a result against to go through to the final stages of the tournament. He had videos of their games and he had talked us through them time and again both before the tournament began and between the Swiss and Scottish games. All our training seemed to be geared to beating the Dutch.

We certainly owed them one. I wanted payback for the 2–0 defeat which put us out of the 1994 World Cup, when Koeman and Dennis scored and I did not have one of my best games. And Tony also wanted revenge for an earlier thrashing they had handed out when Marco Van Basten scored a hat-trick.

It was, we thought, our turn now. And this time the whole team had a 'cunning plan', devised by Terry. And it worked.

Most of it was to do with Teddy Sheringham playing in the hole behind Alan Shearer. They could not cope with him or Alan and the game went down as one of the best English team performances for years, probably since 1966.

We had an edge from the start because they needed to win to be

This is the day job. I'm quite happy if I don't see the ball all game but sometimes it can get a bit busy out there. I also like to keep a clean sheet but winning is more important. So this 5-1 defeat by Sheffield Wednesday, when I was playing for Birmingham back in 1986, was definitely not a good day at the office.

If you want to win trophies, it helps to play for a big club – and they don't come much bigger than Arsenal. But, when I joined the North London club in 1990, I didn't dream I would win the First Division championship in my very first season.

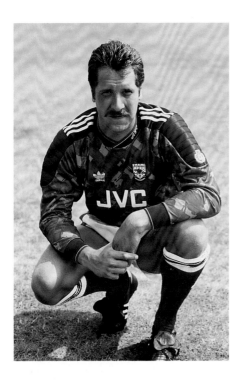

Feeling no pain. Despite having my thumb strapped up and three cracked ribs, I made one of my best saves (from a shot by Zola) to help Arsenal beat Parma 1-0 in Copenhagen to win the European Cupwinners' Cup in 1994.

It was a great night for the club and helping me celebrate after the game were Alan Miller and Arsenal goalkeeping legend Bob 'Willow' Wilson.

We reached the Cupwinners' Cup final again a year later thanks to this save from Sampdoria's Attilio Lombardo in the semi-final penalty shoot-out.

I didn't realise when I was celebrating it but that save would also put me in the media spotlight in a way that I had never experienced before.

I was in the spotlight again after letting in the last minute goal which lost us the final against Real Zaragoza. What made it worse was that it was a shot from the halfway line by Nayim who once played for Arsenal's North London rivals, Spurs. You can see how pleased all of us were about that.

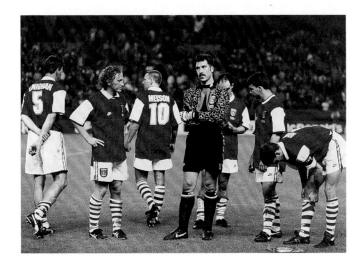

Winning the FA Cup is always worth shouting about, especially when you've had to play the final (against Sheffield Wednesday in 1993) with a double hernia. Just check out those Vulcan shorts.

"You f...ing beauty!" Our Captain, Tony Adams, opens his mouth and puts his foot right in it when he collects the FA Cup. His uncensored joy at winning is lip-read by millions when the TV cameras close in.

Willow and I – Arsenal winning trophies means a lot to both of us.

The 1993 FA Cup Final win was extra-special because it meant completing a rare double as we had already won the Coca Cola (League) Cup. We celebrated that one, too, but it was to be doubly tough on Sheffield Wednesday who were the losers both times.

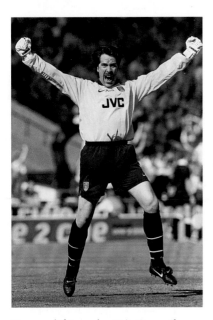

Forget lifting the FA Cup, the best moment in a final is hearing the final whistle when you're winning. We were 2-0 up against Newcastle when I heard it blow in 1998.

I didn't need any help smiling when we collected the Cup but Lee Dixon obviously wasn't taking any chances.

It doesn't matter how many times you win the FA Cup, it tastes just as sweet when you know you've done it again.

Especially when you have already won the Premiership – and for the first time, too. This was an even bigger thrill because it is so tough to win and it also means a place in Europe's Champions' League.

Going on to win the Cup meant we had won the League and Cup Double, finally matching the legendary 1970-1 Double-winning Arsenal team.

As my specialist coach at QPR and Arsenal, Willow has been a major influence on my career.

As you can see, we always take training seriously . . .

certain of going through while we only needed a draw but, although we expected a hard game, we went out confident we would win. In the crowd, I sensed a mixture of nervousness and expectation.

The first goal came from a great piece of skill from Incey, which fooled the defender into bringing him down for a penalty. Alan rarely misses from the spot and he didn't that day either.

From then on, people now remember it as plain sailing as we overwhelmed the Dutch 4–1 but, in fact, it could have all been different at 1–0 when Dennis beat the offside trap and was one-on-one with me. When I realised it was Dennis coming through, it made me even more determined than I usually am to wait until he committed himself to the shot before going down. If you go down too early against Dennis, he will almost certainly chip you. The only time a goalie should go down early is when he thinks the player is going to hit it early all along the ground. Schmeichel sometimes spread himself early but that was because he was so big and intimidating. It usually worked for him, particularly when he was at his peak with United. But trying to out-wait the striker is a real test of nerves especially when you know he is a brilliant finisher. Dennis had joined Arsenal by this stage and, if I had any doubts before about his ability, once I had trained with him I knew just how good he was. I told myself to out-wait him – make him make the decision – so I stood up and stood up until he finally put it down my left side. I read it and reached a good hand to it to put it out for a corner. It did not look as spectacular a save as the one from Durie in the Scotland game, but it was even better and just as important.

They did not score until we were 4–0 up. This one, from Patrick Kluivert, did go through my legs, which always looks bad but there was a silver lining (for fanatical England fans) to this setback as it was the goal that put Scotland out of the final stages. After that and the McAllister save, I dropped any plans for going to Scotland for my holidays in the near future. I seriously considered packing a crash helmet when we went up there with Arsenal for a pre-season tour but, even though I was given the bird from the Kop End during the warm-up for the game with Celtic, they actually clapped me when I went back to the tunnel. I think even the Scots appreciated the kind of tournament I'd had and that I had not just turned it on against their team.

After that Scotland game, we were all on a high and it was more a case of calming us down than hyping us up for the quarter-final against Spain. But it was easy for me to keep my mind off the games to come, as I was involved in another competition that was (almost) as important for me to win.

There was only one opponent but this one was as competitive as all the other teams in Euro 96 put together. Paul Ince does not like losing at anything. Neither do I, so our snooker challenge was played out as hard as any game in the Embassy world championships. The only difference was that we were playing for a tenner. We are both half-decent players and, because we stayed in the tournament so long, we had plenty of time to play frames. The final score was about 25–24. In Incey's favour.

My other way of winding down was, as usual, to go fishing, but this time I had company – Gazza (who is just as competitive about fishing as Incey is about his snooker) and Ian Walker. Terry was all in favour because he knew I was a sensible guy and wouldn't let Gazza get up to anything a couple of days before a big game. It would also be a way of stopping Gazza becoming too pumped up, which had affected his game in the past.

The press knew where we were going (a trout fishery near Maidenhead) but there was a kind of understanding that they would leave us alone.

It was Gazza's idea to take a boat out on to the lake and we were fishing quietly when, out of the corner of my eye, I saw this guy flyfishing on the bank. He had all the gear on and looked the part. Then I looked again and he had gone. The next second, this guy pops up behind a bush with a telephoto lens pointed straight at us.

I said to Gazza, 'There's a guy taking pictures of us,' and Gazza straightaway shouted, 'Oi! Pack it in.' Immediately the snapper gathered all his gear together and legged it.

He had obviously already taken his pictures, so Gazza started frantically rowing us in. While he was doing that, I called the owner of the fishery on my mobile and told him what had happened. He said he would lock the gates to the estate. Meanwhile we are rowing as fast as we can, hitting the riverbank with a thump. Gazza jumps out and chases after the snapper, who lobs his gear into his car and jumps in after it. He then puts the windows up and drives off. But when he reaches the gates, they are already shut. Gazza catches up with him and demands the film from his camera. The snapper says, 'No way,' but, as he opens his window to reply, Gazza leans in and swipes his mobile phone off the seat. 'I'll swop this for the film,' he tells him but the guy refuses again. Still hanging on to the phone, Gazza starts letting his tyres down.

At this stage, the snapper obviously panics and, revving up like a getaway driver, he guns it and drives straight through a five-bar gate, on to a road and across a junction without stopping. It was crazy, he could have killed himself or some other motorist just for the sake of a few snaps of the three of us in a fishing boat. Lucky as he was, he still smashed the gate and damaged his own car.

As he drove off, Gazza pressed 'send' on the mobile and, surprise, surprise, found himself straight through to the direct line of Piers Morgan, editor of *The Mirror*. 'If you print these pictures, I'm never speaking to your paper again,' Gazza threatened him.

But it made no difference. The next day, there we were on the front page under the heading: 'GAZZA'S ARMADA.' We had to admit it was a good headline, but Gazza still made sure the fishery owner had his gate paid for by *The Mirror*. Daft though the whole incident was it did show just how much Euro 96 had captured the media's attention.

The trouble was, after the Dutch game, the fans now expected us to sweep every other team aside and win Euro 96 at a canter. It was just a question of turning up and football would be 'coming home'. But there were some very good sides left and Spain, who we played next, were one of the best.

In the early minutes they played some very slick football and we all realised we were in for a very tough game. In fact, we were lucky when they had a good goal ruled offside. Another time, one of their players (Manjari) was put right through on his own but I had seen the trouble coming and, as he waited for the ball to arrive, I was 30 yards out of my goal and almost on him when he turned round with the ball. He must have been gobsmacked to be confronted by this vision in bright yellow. Although I was too late to get the ball, he panicked and hit the ball to my side. I got a foot to it and cleared it but I was very relieved. If he had chosen to go round me, I would have been in real trouble.

The game remained very tense as it went into extra time when the 'golden goal' rule would have applied. No goals came but, over the whole 120 minutes, we had just as many chances as Spain and a draw was a fair result at the end of it.

As usual, I was then looking forward to the penalties. I always enjoy them because a goalie has nothing to lose and it is the one time when the whole spotlight falls on the fella between the posts.

I don't expect the players having to take them felt quite as happy about it. Pearcey must have been particularly nervous after his miss in the 1990 World Cup semi-final. He strikes the ball well but his penalty against Spain was not the best shot he had ever taken. It went in, though, and that was all that mattered. He had shown tremendous character by taking it in the first place. Fans there and watching the TV at home could see what it meant to him. It was written across his face as he let out this fearsome yell. When he saw me coming to take my place between the posts, he clenched his fists again and screamed, 'Come on' at me.

One of their penalties hit the bar and went over and as we did not miss any of ours, we had the edge when a certain Señor Nadal stepped up to the spot. London's Capital Gold radio station sent me a tape of all of its Euro 96 commentaries after the tournament and just listening to it makes the hairs stand up on the back of my neck all over again. Its main commentator, Jonathan Pearce, is known for his over-the-top style, but he surpassed himself during this penalty shoot-out.

He led into that crucial penalty-kick with, 'Here's Nadal, the beast of Barcelona' and, when I saved it, he went into this tirade about stuffing the Spanish Armada, sticking it up their Julio Iglesias etc etc. It was like that Norwegian commentator going on about Maggie Thatcher's boys taking 'a hell of a beating' when they turned us over for the first time but I think JP got into a fair bit of trouble about what he said.

But, in fairness, Wembley and the whole country had gone mad at that moment. Ironically, the save was a fairly comfortable one to my left. I was not even at full stretch. And when I had made it I was still not absolutely sure we had won. Watching the video later, I could see myself hesitate for a moment but then spot all the other players coming towards me like that scene in *Zulu* when the warriors come over the hill towards Rorke's Drift. At that moment I knew it was all over – and it was, too.

Again the feeling in the England camp was brilliant. We only wished we could be out in the country, celebrating with the fans, instead of stuck in the hotel but we had another tough game ahead.

In fact, Germany did not play well against us in the semi-final but, being Germany, they still went away with the right result. We could not have made a better start, with another good headed goal from Alan in the opening minutes. We played well for a while but then gradually the Germans worked their way back into the game and scored a well-worked goal. Afterwards, until the end of normal time, we were well on top but just could not score. It was closer during extra time, as the golden goal rule is unnerving. Make a mistake and concede a goal and the match ends there and then, and it is all down to you. We are to used to playing that rule in training five-a-sides, but in the semi-final of a major tournament, it is a heartstopping situation. Or it would have been if the implications of it had sunk in at the time. But, because Euro 96 was the first time we had ever played proper games with the rule applying, I don't think any of us really appreciated what a knife-edge we were on.

They had a goal disallowed that was a marginal decision and it was only afterwards that I realised that the game would have ended there and then. I also had to tip one shot over the bar but we still had the better chances. Darren Anderton hit the post and then Gazza was just a stud's length away from toeing Darren's low cross over the line. Gazza said afterwards that he was expecting their 'keeper to get a touch to the cross so he hung back a fraction of a second waiting to readjust to reach the deflection. But the goalie didn't reach it, so neither did Gazza. If he had continued his run, he would have scored a truly golden goal to put us in the final. Forget the impact on the England team, who knows how that might have changed the way Gazza's career and life developed after Euro 96?

But he missed and once again it was penalties. I can remember walking towards the goal, passing Steve McManaman on the way and thinking to myself, 'Go on, save two and we'll get through' but I have to admit that I have never had so many good penalties put past me in a match situation.

I have never really been a great believer in teams practising penalties before games which could be decided by them. I have never thought that you can reproduce the pressure of a match on the training ground. But the Germans have such a great record with penalties, it is something we have to consider. It might be that they just have more experienced players taking them but perhaps they do practise them as well. It might be worth practising putting them in a particular spot as there is such a thing as an unsaveable penalty. That is one hit into the corner with so much power that no goalie's dive would reach it in time, even now that we are allowed to move before the kick. You could argue that we practise other techniques for games, why not penalties? Otherwise, if anything done outside a match situation is supposed to have no value, why practise at all?

As for saving them, whatever some pundits say, I don't believe 'keepers would save more by just standing still. This simply does not work because, as you are not moving, you cannot react quickly enough. Shilts tried standing his ground against Germany in the World Cup semi and he didn't save any or even get anywhere near them and those penalties were nowhere near as good as those that went past me at Euro 96. Of those, there was just one I managed to reach but I could not stop it going in. Like the others, it was just too near the post.

But we scored some good penalties and only went out when it came to sudden death. Everybody was sympathetic to Gareth Southgate when he missed but there was not really anything we could say that would make him feel any better about it. In fact, Tony Adams had the best idea. Once we got back to the changing-room, he put his arm around him, looked him in the eye and said, 'But Gareth, it was a shit penalty, wasn't it?' It really broke the ice and even Gareth laughed.

When we returned to the hotel after the match, there were about a thousand fans all cheering outside. It was a very emotional moment for all of us. Later, they broke through into the grounds. Security kept them out of the hotel but later, when we all returned from our rooms one by one to go for a meal in the restaurant, we had to walk through a glass-sided hall. As the fans saw us, they chanted our names one by one. God knows what they would have done if we had won.

I don't imagine I was the only one who could hardly bear to watch the final. But, with all the disappointment at the end, I came out of the tournament with many commentators rating me as one of the world's top goalkeepers and, for the first time, I had a profile outside the game, too. In many ways, Euro 96 did for me what the World Cup in Italy had done for Gazza. Maybe it was because I was so focused on the games but I don't think I realised quite the impact I had made during Euro 96. Until I paid a visit to Wimbledon for the tennis, that is.

Debbie was with me and Incey and his wife Claire. We had invitations to the Royal Box and we were just making our way there when the crowd suddenly all stood up and applauded. At first, we looked around to see who the standing ovation was for, then realised it was for us. It was a fantastic feeling. The players stopped and one of them, Pete Sampras, the defending champion, told me later that he could not understand what was happening until he looked up. He then recognised me because my picture had been in the papers all week. That moment even made the TV news that evening.

Debbie was probably less surprised than I was because, as Euro 96 had developed, she (and my parents) had found themselves under siege from the media. I was on the phone almost every half-hour to Debbie and she was filling me in on what was happening outside in the real world. Although we did watch some TV and had some idea of the hype, we did not realise just how big a story we were for the press and the public, because we were cut off from most of it.

Even for the games we were surrounded by security as we were driven directly from the hotel to Wembley, so Debbie had a better idea of the impact we were making than I did. So much so that I found I was having to calm *her* down before the games rather than the other way round. I could hear the excitement building in her voice as each one approached. She was also being asked to do interviews all the time. I remember one she did which had a photo of her wearing a pair of my gloves with a George Cross in the background with the *Sun* written across it.

I was signed up to do a column in the *Daily Mail* but it all had to be written over the phone because no reporters were allowed near us. At the end of the tournament, the *Mail* gave me a leatherbound copy of all my interviews and other stories from the games. When I look at it now, all the Euro 96 emotions come flooding back.

No doubt about it, that tournament marked a major change in my career and in my life.

17

• • • • • •

Arsène and the French Connection

If Euro 96 had been responsible for changing my life, the arrival of Arsène Wenger at Arsenal was to mark a major change in my lifestyle as a professional footballer. In fact, it was to change the lives of all the Arsenal players – and of the fans as well.

The club was in limbo at the start of the 1996–7 season as we all waited for our new manager to arrive. Pat Rice kept things ticking over, but he and we knew it was only temporary.

As if to make up for his delayed entry, when he finally did take over at the end of September 1996, Arsène made it clear that there would be total change straightaway. There was no messing about. He told us, 'This is how I run training and this is how I expect you to eat and look after yourselves.' He said we could not carry on eating what we had been used to stuffing down ourselves, as it was no good for us as professional athletes. And, in case we did not believe him, he brought in dieticians to re-educate us. It helped that they did not just tell us what to eat, but also why it was good for us. We also had doctors coming in with all sorts of vitamin tablets for us to take, and we found ourselves undergoing a series of medical tests which included having heart monitors attached to us while we were training.

It was fantastic to feel that the club was investing so much in our health and fitness, but I have to admit I was a bit iffy about it all at first. I had never needed to take tablets before; at least, I had never thought I needed to take them. But Arsène did not make taking the tablets compulsory so at first I opted out. Then I saw it was clearly doing the other players good and I joined in.

Our main concern at first was to know that all the tablets were legal and safe. We were assured that they were by the various doctors and dieticians and also by Arsène himself. Also it was – and still is – all carefully programmed. It is not a question of just taking the same tablets all year. At certain times of the season, this or that vitamin is required and it is doled out to us. There are also tablets to help us concentrate harder or for longer periods of time and sometimes we have vitamin injections straight into a vein.

We quickly realised that our new manager was an expert in his own right. He has made a study of the athlete's body and knows how it reacts to training, about the different chemicals it releases at different times, and how it is affected by tiredness. He also surrounds himself with a big back-up team so that every angle is covered.

The new regime had an almost immediate effect on the whole team. Our fitness and concentration levels were much improved. Other teams noticed that we were still flying after 80 minutes and, when Tony, Martin, Wrighty and I were on England duty, the other players started asking what we were taking. They copied what we were doing, carried on with it when they went back to their clubs, and most of them said they felt better for it. When this got back to Arsène, he made a point of warning us not to tell the other players exactly what we were doing and taking. At that stage, this was all new to the English league and he wanted to keep our edge for as long as possible.

He told us that the rest of the world had been using similar methods for years. The Brazilians had adopted these diets and pill regimes at least ten years earlier and even the Russians were up to speed with them. But it was all new to us – and this was as recently as 1996.

With more foreign coaches and managers coming in all the time, we did not have the edge for long. Chelsea and Liverpool were among the first clubs to catch on and then it really took off when Glenn Hoddle went from Chelsea to the England job.

Hoddle had seen the benefits when he played for Arsène at Monaco and wanted all the England players to change their diets and keep taking the tablets. Most of the players took it on board and even now Incey and Jamie Redknapp regularly ring up our physio to buy more tablets as most of them are French-made and not easily available in England. Of course, they could be Smarties for all we know – or worse. We have noticed that our French dietician keeps buying boats. Every few months, he comes in and says he has a new tablet for us and we all say, 'Yeah, yeah – you must want to buy a bigger boat.' Still, I suppose the time to worry is when one of us grows three breasts or starts glowing in the dark.

I am currently taking tablets every day, usually three in the morning and two at night. I don't take creatine powder, which is made up of pure food concentrates, but that is only because as a goalkeeper I don't need the amount of extra energy that outfield players use up. All the other lads were taking it, though, when the press started suggesting it might not be doing players any good. I don't know if any have stopped taking it but Arsène has always made it clear that any of us can say no to any or all of the tablets.

With diet, however, we did not have any option, even though the new rules involved a complete change of routine for us. On a Friday night before a match, we were used to having almost anything we liked – steak, fish and chips, whatever. Now we have steamed fish, boiled chicken or pasta. On a match day, it used to be something very light like scrambled eggs or beans on toast. Now we have a big meal, again usually pasta or something similar.

We were very reluctant to change at first. Arsène was telling us to eat all this food and we were thinking it would weigh us down and that we would never be able to run around and play properly afterwards. But we now know that pasta is the right kind of fuel – with a zero fat content it burns off straightaway – and that it is going to help our stamina. It is all geared to giving us more energy so our bodies will have more reserves to call on to help us keep going for the full 90 minutes – or these days, often 95 minutes.

The club likes us to have a varied diet during the week. Fast-food takeaways are not banned altogether but we are told just to have the occasional one at the most. Arsène would love to have us in a hotel the night before every game, home and away. This is because he knows that way the single lads will have a decent meal and the married lads will have a good night's sleep.

We have to stay in hotels the night before away games (for a couple of nights if it is a European game) and also before London derby games home as well as away for some reason. But we have told Arsène that, as the traffic in London is terrible on Friday nights, it would be stressful for us to have to travel in for hotel overnights before all our home games. We have got away with that one so far. When we do stay in hotels, at least we no longer have to share rooms. We started being given the option of single rooms four or five years ago. Before that, I usually shared with Lee Dixon. We get on well, but we are grown men and we have our own ways of preparing for games.

I am always up late on a Friday night watching the TV because, if I go to bed too early, I wake up early, which I hate. Lee was completely the opposite, and he was finding he was having to take sleeping tablets, otherwise he would be waking up in the middle of the night to see me still watching TV. Also, while I did not mind sharing that much when I was younger, now I have family and other private business that I need to talk about on the phone while I am away. I found I was having to leave the room to use my mobile, so I asked to have a single room and have had one ever since. Most of the other players have done the same, although there are a few who still prefer to share.

With so many midweek games, we do not have a lot of time to rest during the remainder of the week and so, when there is time in the hotel on Friday afternoons and evenings, it makes sense to take full advantage. You are not going to be able to do that if you are sharing with a snorer, for a start. There was a story about Neil Lennon being such a champion snorer that it was the other Leicester players who insisted on a single room for him.

England has gone the same way as the top clubs. The goalies always had to double up, but now we all have a single room when we prepare for internationals. Personally, staying in hotels – even five-star ones – drives me mad with boredom, and I think Arsène is too keen on us staying in them before games.

But, on the question of food and vitamin pills, I am convinced the new regime has worked wonders for us. I remember hearing Ron Atkinson holding forth at some function about how these new-fangled ideas about different foods and tablets were all a load of rubbish. A year later, we won the Double and Chris Evans rang me up to say he had Big Ron on his programme and would I like to ask him a question? I told him to ask him if he still thought this new way of looking after yourself was a load of rubbish. Unfortunately, the show's time ran out before he got to the question, but I know who is talking rubbish and it is not Arsène.

But, if a manager has not played the game at the highest level, it can be hard for some players to accept him or take seriously what he says. This was Martin Wilkinson's problem when he was manager at Peterborough during my time there, and it could have been difficult for Arsène, who only played as an amateur for Strasbourg. It never makes any real odds to me because I know that, even if a manager has played top-level football, it almost certainly will not have been in goal. Most managers know very little about goalkeeping so I tend not to take too much notice of them when they talk about that part of the game – whether they are ex-pros or not.

But outfield players notice that managers who have not been top players themselves seem to have different thoughts on some aspects of the game and also tend to take a more academic approach to things like diet and fitness. Now, whether top players-turned-managers don't feel the need to go through the kind of learning process that managers like Arsène have taken on or whether they simply don't believe in it, I couldn't say. It is possible that the likes of Arsène feel a little insecure about their lack of top-level experience and that is why they go all out for the academic approach. But I have seen both approaches work with the right managers and, although Arsène only had a modest playing career, the players at Arsenal have a lot of respect for him.

One possible weakness for managers like him, though, is a lack of appreciation of exactly what goes on between players during a high-pressure match. If you have never played a big game in front of a noisy crowd, you might find it hard to understand about retaliation. A player might be getting a dig every time he tackles one of the other team. This builds up until he gives him something back. The referee sees it and he ends up with a yellow or a red card. There were a couple of good examples last season. First when Nicky Butt was sent off for having a dig at Dennis Wise when Chelsea beat Man Utd at Stamford Bridge. If you watched the incident closely, you could see that Wise did not just grab at Butt, he said something to him as well, probably reminding him of another incident between the two of them in the tunnel after a game at Old Trafford a couple of seasons earlier. But, if the cameras were not there, no one would see that and a manager who has never played in a high-pressure game would find it hard to understand why his player had got himself sent off for retaliation.

It was the same when Patrick Vieira was sent off for us against West Ham last season. Although I don't condone what Patrick did – and I'll explain why later – Neil Ruddock definitely provoked him by deliberately walking straight into him after he had been given the red card. Again, a manager who had not played in such games might have thought that Ruddock's collision with Patrick was accidental.

When it comes to discipline on the pitch, though, Arsène's approach is similar to Graham's. Both tell players to tackle hard but fair and have also made a point of warning them that they do not want them clogging anyone. Maybe I have been lucky but I have never played under a manager who has told players to go out and 'do' somebody. I have no time for players who make tackles that can wreck players' careers. We all know what kind can do that: two-footed, full-weight tackles. There is no need for them in the game. I think players should be sent off for even attempting that kind of tackle. If they don't connect, it is usually only because the other player has jumped out of the way so they should be sent off for intent anyway.

Our new French manager had equally strong views on training. I have described the George Graham approach to pre-season, which was run, run and run some more, particularly in the first week. It was designed to work off any extra weight we had put on during the close season and lay the groundwork for the season right there and then.

As usual, Arsène's approach is a lot more scientific. It still involves plenty of running, but there are not many long runs or cross-countries; the emphasis is on timed running. There are different stages that you have to pass within certain times. He introduced plyometrics, which means running and then jumping, so we jog up to hurdles and then leap over them. The point is in the rhythm: bounce, bounce and then spring. This kind of training is deceptive. I finish one of his sessions not too badly out of breath and think it was not too hard. The next day, I am in absolute bits because it has impacted on every muscle. But it is effective training and we all believe we start seasons fitter than we have started them in the past.

Training during the season is also very different. For a start, there is much more emphasis now on resting. Arsène reckons you don't always need to keep training more and more; sometimes you should do less, to prevent boredom. He believes it is important to relax and so do I, which is one of the reasons I go fishing.

Arsène knows exactly what he wants when we do train, though. He is a tracksuit manager and he is out there with us every time. Everything is geared to his watch. He knows how long any training or tactical discipline should last and will stop it right on the button. Sometimes he drives us mad. We could be playing an eight-a-side game on a smaller pitch with a bigger goal. The score is 2–2 and it has been a really good, tight game but, when the time he has allowed for it is up, he will always step in and stop it. We all say, 'Let's go on until the next goal wins it,' but he never changes his mind. We have to stop and move on to the next exercise. There is no arguing with him.

With Graham, we always knew what we would be going to do in training; with Arsène, we come in every day and never know what he has planned. Some days, it will be just be stretching, massage and a spell in a jacuzzi. Graham used to spend hours on the back four, and who could argue that it did not pay off? But, by the end of his time at the club, the lads used to be pulling their hair out because it would be the same stop-start routines all the time.

But the biggest change of all was to our style of play. Graham's style had been effective and we had won trophies with it but all of us were a bit fed up with the 'boring, boring Arsenal' chants even if our fans now made sure they got their retaliation in first by singing 'One-nil to the Arsenal' when we scored what was usually going to be the only goal of the game.

But Arsène was determined to have us playing his way. Usually, that meant the ball being played out of defence and through the midfield. Outsiders might be surprised by this, but there was no resistance to his plans from the back four. I could see that Tony really enjoyed the idea. You could almost hear him saying, 'Play it out from the back? I'll have some of that.' He started going on massive charges forward and I would be shouting at him to get back. But he would be covered by one of the others, so I began to realise there was no need to be worried. It was a totally different pattern but it worked for us and much more quickly than I would ever have thought possible.

It was not so much that players were being told to do this and that but more that they were *not* being told *not* to do things. Everyone had more individual responsibility and, as they tried things and they came off, the players gained more and more confidence in the system and in themselves. To put it simply, they were now being told to express themselves; before it was a case of, 'You're a defender, just defend – all right?' We now had good players who did not want to play the ball long or have to fight for it in the air all the time. They wanted to play football on the ground, so they took to Arsène's new Arsenal style straightaway.

Another major change was our approach to games. Graham used to go through every player on the other side; Arsène hardly talks about the other team at all. Sometimes he will put on a video of our next opponents, but this is only to see their pattern of play and he does not even make it compulsory for us to watch. Occasionally, he might mention European teams we are due to play but only if they do something unusual in their team play. This is all part of building a belief in us that, if we play to our ability, we can beat anybody. I suspect that is exactly the approach Sir Alex Ferguson takes at Man Utd and it seems to have worked all right for them, doesn't it?

I have heard that Sir Alex does not throw as many tea-cups around at halftime. He has mellowed with age and success, they say, but I would not mind betting that, winning or losing, he still makes a lot more noise in the break than Arsène who has a real thing about noise at this point – he hates it. In fact, he does not allow anything to be said at half-time until just before we are going back out for the second half. When we come in, he checks for any injuries and then just sits quietly in the corner. We are expected to do the same. If anyone speaks up about something that has happened in the first half, he tells them to be quiet. This even applies to Pat Rice, who is usually dying to have a go about something. If Pat starts shouting, Arsène stops him dead and asks for calm. He will wait until 12 out of the 15 minutes have passed and only then will he say one or two things about the second half.

At full-time, he will say 'well done' if we have won or played well and nothing at all if we have had a bad game. He waits until the next training session to sort out any problems that we have had in the game. He rarely swears and, when he does, it always sounds odd with that French accent. He can look a bit dour but he is actually quite humorous in a dry sort of way and likes to crack a few jokes on the quiet. We have a few laughs at his expense, too and call him Clouseau because he is always knocking things over.

As part of his fitness regime, we find ourselves doing a lot of stretching exercises with him before and after games. We have to do these in a variety of hotels and you can bet that, if they have to partition off a ballroom for us, he will be the one to lean against the divider and knock it down. Or he will be bent over his shoelaces when the door opens on his head. He once went for a pudding at a hotel buffet and we all saw it fall off his plate as he was walking back to his table. As usual, his mind was on something else so he did not notice and just kept walking. When he sat down, he saw his plate was empty and looked completely bemused while one of the waitresses was out there cleaning it off the floor.

We don't call him Clouseau to his face, though. He prefers 'Boss' and we don't take any liberties, English not being his first language. When he arrived, his English was already quite good and it is even better now. He speaks so many different languages and I have seen him switch from French to English and then Spanish and German to put a point across to a group of players. He originally spoke to the French players in French because their English was not as good as his, but now he speaks only in English when we are all together. Sometimes he might go up to the French players if he thinks he needs to spell it out in French to make sure they understand, but the English players don't have any problem with that.

Pat Rice is a good balance for Arsène. He has had the English-style game bred into him, while Arsène has his Continental approach. They can both spot when a player is not happy with one approach or the other so they are a good blend. I think Pat's initial influence had a lot to do with Arsène keeping the back four together when he arrived. He must have come in thinking that they would be too old, or unable to adapt their game, but Pat will have told him different and after a while he could see that for himself. They were mainly responsible for the club managing to finish third in his first season, which meant we would be playing in the UEFA Cup during his second.

But Arsène was still determined to bring in a lot of new players and few of them were bigger names than most of Graham's buys. At least they weren't when he bought them. But, a Double-winning season and a World Cup later, Arsenal found it had a team full of international stars.

New Arsenal, New Double

If I had known back then how professional football was going to change in this country, I would have paid more attention to my French lessons at school. When I think about it, any attention at all would have been an improvement. I was not the only one at fault, though. If a certain Monsieur Anelka had worked a little harder at his English lessons 15 years later, that might have saved all of us a lot of grief. But I don't think I was being particularly short-sighted. I doubt if anybody back in the 1970s could have predicted that so many foreign players would suddenly come into the English league at the back end of the 1990s.

When I joined Arsenal at the start of that decade, the playing staff was 100 per cent British (and Irish). Graham bought a few Scandinavians but the club's wages policy meant that Arsenal was one of the slowest of the top English clubs to start looking to Europe for players. In 1995, Rioch bought Dennis Bergkamp for £7.5 millon but that looked to be a one-off deal for a world-class Dutch player until Arsène Wenger took over just after the start of the 1996–7 season. Then in 1997 Arsène paid £5 million for Marc Overmars, another Dutch international with a big reputation, but before that we were less than impressed by the arrival of a whole succession of European players, most of them French, who many of us had never heard of. It became a bit of a joke to us as every few weeks we would be saying, 'Here comes another well-known signing – Not.'

At that time, France had never won any major championships and nobody thought much of the general standard of their league. 'Small crowds, small teams' was what we thought, so we were not expecting too much from midfielders Patrick Vieira and Emmanuel Petit, defenders Remi Garde and Gilles Grimandi and striker Nicolas Anelka, even though most of them were French internationals. Arsène also bought an Austrian goalie, Alex Manninger, a Portuguese winger, Luis Boa Morte, and a Liberian striker, Christopher Wreh plus a couple of youngsters from German clubs. But, as far as we were concerned, that first wave of mainly French imports were all dodgy foreigners until they proved themselves in our league. Only one new English player came in, central defender Matthew Upson from Luton, but he was one for the future while Merse and, later, John Hartson were both sold.

You can't make all those changes, bring in players of so many different nationalities, without altering the atmosphere in a club, but I think the best move Arsène made was to keep the back five together. We were the backbone of the team, the core of Arsenal's legendary team spirit. But even so, at the start of one of the most successful seasons in the club's history (1997–8), none of us had very much idea of how we would perform as a team. Although we had finished third the season before, with all the comings and goings in the close season, we were all still getting used to new players as well as Arsène's way of doing things.

We had not won anything in his first season, yet it was a memorable season for one match that had an incident I have never seen before or since in a professional game.

We were playing Liverpool at home and needed to win to keep ourselves in with a chance of the Premiership. We lost the game 2–1 and, a couple of games later, we lost the Premiership to Man Utd, with Newcastle coming second. But the match was more significant for what happened when Robbie Fowler chased a long ball through our defence.

As he played it past me, I pulled out of the challenge. Robbie went down and referee Gerald Ashby blew for a penalty. I knew I hadn't touched him and I told the referee so but, amazingly, Robbie did too. He kept saying, 'He never touched me, he never touched me – it's not a penalty.' But Ashby said he had already made his decision, although I have seen refs reverse a decision after talking to the referee's assistant. But Ashby was so adamant I began to wonder if he had Liverpool down as an away banker on his Pools. In fairness, I have never played in a match where an opposing player has tried to persuade the referee not to give his side a penalty, and probably Ashby had not refereed one, either.

It was a strange thing for any striker to do but, then, Robbie and I were quite good friends through the England squad and he had been fishing with me and Gazza. Perhaps he thought he would get some stick from us if he conned a penalty. I would certainly have had a quiet word with him afterwards, if he had.

I saved his penalty but Jason McAteer put the rebound in. People said Robbie deliberately half-hit it; the record books will say that I saved a penalty and so I did.

The next season was both strange and memorable for other reasons. We were generally happy with the new manager's style and ideas on training and diets. With money obviously being made available for bringing players in, things looked good for the future. But that was where we were looking for our success – to the future. We were expecting something big to happen in a couple of seasons, but not right away. It looked as though we were right to think that, too, as the season began with a mixture of results, good and bad, in the league. We also went out of the UEFA Cup early to the Greek side, Salonika, losing 1–0 away and then only managing a 1–1 draw at home.

This 1–0 defeat had not been that bad a result, either, because the game was played in one of the most intimidating atmospheres I have ever experienced. Throughout the game, their fans kept up non-stop synchronised clapping which created a sort of Mexican wave effect but in noise rather than movement. It was very impressive to hear and see, but I could feel it affecting some of our younger, more inexperienced players. To only draw at home after that just confirmed what we had expected to happen that season. Lots of changes in players and team pattern usually make it difficult to achieve the consistency a team needs to win anything.

Despite those changes, we were still in touch with the leaders in this early part of the season and had some good results. It was not until we beat Man Utd 3–2 in November that I think we all realised that we could be in with a chance of winning something, after all. We just needed to find some consistency.

But we immediately lost three out of the next four games, including one at home to Blackburn and, as this meant we were falling well behind Man Utd at the top of the table, there were a few harsh words said by Arsène and the senior players in a special team meeting that he had called to sort things out. There were some obvious problems with the team. We were still swapping between playing a Graham-style back four and the three centre-backs with two wing-backs that Rioch had introduced. Tony was also struggling with an ankle injury and Wrighty with his form, even though, earlier in the season, he had broken Cliff Bastin's record (178) for most goals scored for Arsenal. But Arsenal fans are a demanding lot. They expect players to be doing the business all the time so, when Wrighty went a couple of months without scoring in the league, some of them were on his back.

It came to a head when they started shouting up at him when he came to the window of the dressing-room. He shouted a few things back and, as usual, it all went in the papers the following day. In January, he pulled a hamstring, and this was followed by a cartilage operation and then a groin injury which combined to keep him out for nearly three months.

Tony had better luck with his injury, which he took first to faith-healer Eileen Drewery and then to a specialist Arsène recommended in France. He returned fit at the end of January and, with Marc Overmars and Nicolas Anelka beginning to score some goals, results started to improve.

One of the main reasons was the partnership between Manu Petit and Patrick Vieira. When they arrived, they did not come with great reputations and, despite what people seem to believe, they had not played together before. Although they were both from France, they had played for different clubs there – Patrick for Cannes and Manu for Monaco. They also came to Arsenal at different times – Patrick in August 1996 and Manu a year later. Both took a while to settle down and find the pace of the game. It is so very fast in England compared with anywhere in Europe and particularly the French league. Manu was also having to adjust to playing in midfield instead of central defence, his original position.

In the clear-the-air team meeting held after the latest of our four defeats, against Blackburn, there were complaints that the back four was not getting enough protection, so Arsène asked Patrick and

Manu to do that job. Of the two, Manu sat back deeper, enabling Patrick to push forward more to make and score some important goals. Manu couldn't score to save his life to begin with but he finally broke his duck near the end of that first season and, since then, he too has scored a number of vital goals.

But as well as being good individual players, Manu and Patrick developed a partnership which began to be feared by the teams we played. It was not so much their skill as the power of their teamwork that was intimidating the opposition. I have talked to other English players who have played against them and they say it is unbelievable when they play together.

Their form was one of the reasons for our gradual improvement after Christmas. And it was not just our league form that picked up. We started making progress in both cups, only going out of the Coca Cola in the semi-final, losing 4–3 on aggregate to Chelsea after Patrick had been sent off in the second leg. We had also had the kind of luck in an early round of the FA Cup that makes you wonder whether your name is on the trophy. We beat Port Vale in a third-round replay but only after extra time and penalties. We could easily have lost either game in normal or extra time and, when Lee missed our first penalty in the shoot-out, it looked bad for us, but I saved Ian Bogie's penalty and Vale's Allen Tankard put his shot over the bar and we were through.

But it was in this game that Wrighty pulled his hamstring and the team's run of bad luck with injuries continued when, in the next game at Coventry, I broke a finger and was out for 13 games. I did it when I saved a shot from Darren Huckerby and, instead of palming the ball up, my fingers went into the ball and the knuckle was chipped diagonally across. The medical people warned me that, if I was not careful, the bone would come out and I would have to have an operation. Rest was the only alternative but it stayed swollen and painful for a long time.

But Alex Manninger, who was becoming a quality 'keeper, came in and did very well. He kept a clean sheet at Old Trafford when we beat Man Utd 1–0 and he even pinched my trick and saved a penalty (from Eyal Berkovic) in a shoot-out in an FA Cup quarter-final replay at West Ham. Although Remi Garde missed one for us, West

Ham's Samassi Abou hit a post with his kick so we went through. There was some paper talk about Alex keeping his place but Arsène had told me – and Alex as well – that, as soon as I was fit, I was in.

My first game back was home to Sheffield Wednesday, and we won it to extend our winning run. We had won the last two games and, including the Wednesday game, won the next eight. We had also been unbeaten in 10 games, so I helped extend that to 18. The run only came to an end when, with our minds already on the Cup Final, we lost the last two games of the season.

We had made it to Wembley having beaten First Division Wolves 1–0 in the semi-final with a goal made by man-of-the-match Patrick for Christopher Wreh. That was when we first started thinking about the Double. But we were mainly concerned that we did not do what Sheffield Wednesday had done in the season we won our two cups. They had made both finals, lost both and ended up with nothing. We were determined to win at least one trophy. Once we had done that, it would be time to worry about the Double.

And we wanted to win the Premiership most of all. Some of us were still around from the team who had won the league the last time and we knew what a fantastic feeling that had been. After being 13 points behind Man Utd nearly halfway through the season and still 11 points adrift at the beginning of March, that unbeaten run had chipped away at the lead until we overtook them in mid-April and still had games in hand.

It is always best if you can win it in front of your home crowd so to beat Everton 4–0 to win our first Premiership was brilliant for us and for the fans. Marc scored twice to make him our leading goalscorer for the season, with 12. Captain Tony even scored a goal with a superb volley – you couldn't have written a better script.

It relaxed us for the Cup Final in one way, because we knew we had one trophy in the bank, but we couldn't forget that it was a chance to equal the old Double-winning side. There was some definite rivalry there because we had all got a little tired of seeing Frank McLintock, Charlie George and the rest appearing on Sky to point out that they were the Arsenal team to have done the Double. This was our best chance yet of putting all that to bed for good.

There was the usual fun and games in the run-up. We were all fitted out for some snazzy black Hugo Boss suits. And a record was put out based on 'Hot Stuff' from *The Full Monty*. Fortunately, they did not rope us in to sing on it. Even better for *Top of the Pops* viewers, they did not ask us to get our kit off either. We did sing on our previous FA Cup record, 'Shouting for the Gunners', but the record company were smart and sent along a minibus which just happened to have a couple of crates of beer on board. That certainly helped loosen a few tonsils.

The final against Newcastle was like the semi-final, a bit of a stroll. Marc scored halfway through the first half and I had very little to do. My main memory is of Alan Shearer hitting the post when we were still only 1–0 up, but the video showed I had it covered if it had been going inside the post. Then Nicolas scored for us and it was all over. It was not a great final but the winners are never going to care about that. Going up the steps to fetch the trophy is one of the best feelings in football. I hate to think what it must feel like to be a loser in a Wembley final. Remembering Tony's foot-in-mouth performance the last time he had raised the trophy, I whispered to him not to say anything dodgy so he just lifted it up and screamed, 'Yeah!' The next thing I knew Lee was grabbing my neck and my head as if it was the trophy.

The fans might disagree, but I still did not rate winning the Double as highly as winning the Cup-Winners Cup. But it did mean another open-top bus tour to celebrate. These are fantastic to be part of as you see all the fans out on the streets and on the roofs, and all the faces at the windows. Finally we pitch up at Islington Town Hall where they put up scaffolding so we can go out and wave to everyone. I have been on three of these for Arsenal now and they are always a big thrill. One of my favourite photos is of Tony out on that ledge, holding up the two trophies with thousands of fans in the background.

But, after the Premiership and FA Cup Double, there was something even better for most of the team to look forward to: a World Cup.

Tony, Martin, Patrick, Manu, Dennis, Marc, Wrighty – we had just been through a long season together and come out of it with two trophies; now we were going to spend the summer trying to destroy each other's dreams of holding the greatest trophy of all.

19

· · · · · ·

Taking on the World

All the players were disappointed when Terry Venables lost the
England job. We had come so close to winning Euro 96 and Terry
had developed a pattern of play which we all believed could be
successful in the 1998 World Cup. But all the stories about his
financial affairs and the court cases led the FA to replace him with
Glenn Hoddle, who had achieved some early managerial success with
Swindon and then Chelsea.

Hoddle has a very different personality to Terry's and it was a big
change for us to handle. Both of them paid great attention to detail in
their preparation for games, but we felt Hoddle sometimes went a
little overboard with it, prying into everything we were doing off as
well as on the field. It is one thing trying to control players' eating
and drinking habits, but the Hoddle way seemed to go even further
into our private lives. He wanted to know what you were doing in
your own time. Then, if he was having a dig at you, he could suggest
you were not looking after yourself – going out too much perhaps.
Sometimes his attention to detail became a little over the top. He
even arranged for a bedding company to supply new mattresses for
all of us at the training camp hotel (Burnham Beeches) in England
and at our base in France.

His approach was stricter all round than Terry's. For example,
while we were out in Poland for a World Cup qualifier, we got bored
with staying in our rooms and watching the very iffy Polish TV and
we were downstairs playing cards and chatting at about 10 p.m. All
of a sudden, Hoddle's number two John Gorman came in and told us
it was time we were in bed. We were a bit taken aback as this was
Thursday evening, two days before the game.

Hoddle was not slow to give even established internationals real rollockings in training and, when we started the World Cup tournament, he made it clear that alcohol was banned unless he said otherwise. In contrast, Terry allowed us to have a drink after Euro 96 matches. It was certainly not allowed before a game but we would not have dreamed of doing that anyway. It just seems harder not to do something when you are actually banned from doing it.

But Venables and Hoddle just had different ways of handling players. When Terry was there, it was accepted that Gazza and I would go off fishing. We did get back late once and Terry told Gazza off because he thought it must have been his fault, not mine. But he basically saw it as a good way for both of us to relax before games and would let us go on Thursdays and Fridays before Saturday games. But Hoddle would not let us go fishing any later than a Wednesday before a game. He said it was too close to the game, yet the alternative for us was being stuck, bored out of our minds, in the hotel. The atmosphere in the England camp was just not as relaxed as it had been when Terry was there.

I admit that I felt a lot more at ease with Terry but I thought Hoddle was very sound when it came to the footballing side and he did well to see us through qualifying into the World Cup Finals, especially after we had lost at home to Italy. I was injured and did not play in that game. Ian Walker came in and was hammered by fans and the press for the goal Zola scored for Italy. This was very unfair because the shot took a deflection off Sol Campbell. I could understand the fans blaming him on the night because they would not have noticed the deflection but, once it was shown on the TV replays, all the criticism should have been taken back. No goalie has a chance when a shot hit that hard from close range takes a deflection, however small. You are already committed to going where the ball should be heading and, if it is diverted, it is almost always too late to change direction. Yet the press were still blaming him for his 'mistake' when we were preparing to play Italy over there.

Fortunately Ian is a level-headed guy so I don't think he would have let the criticism affect him. He was out of the Spurs side for a while under Christian Gross, with Espen Baardsen replacing him, but

I knew he would be back in when George Graham took over. If there is one thing Graham does not rate, it's a foreign goalie.

I was back for England in time for the game in Italy where we needed just a draw to qualify for the finals. It proved to be one of the greatest nights I have enjoyed as a footballer. We went into the game in a confident mood, but any professional footballer will tell you that the one sure thing in football is that there is no such thing as a sure thing. All you can do is hope that your own game is 'on blob' (on form), the whole team performs to their ability and that you get the breaks in the game.

We started well, got hold of the game and, most important, kept their crowd quiet. We really deserved to win it and would have done if Wrighty's shot had gone in instead of hitting the post near the end. But then, to prove just how easily a game can be won and lost, Italy went straight up the other end and nearly scored in the last minute.

But I can now reveal that the Vieri header which frightened a nation was never going in. When the cross came over, I moved back from the near post and, although he put a good header on it, as it flashed across me I just knew it was not going in. That's why I didn't even dive. Watching it again on the video, I can see that it was probably closer than I thought it was and, if it had been on target, I am not sure I could have got to it anyway but my initial reaction was that it was always going wide. It was just that the England fans in the stadium and the millions watching back home did not share my confidence at the time. But, after the euphoria of that night, it was down to the serious business of preparing for the finals. The players weren't happy with just qualifying, we wanted to go there and win the tournament. There are no medals for qualifiers.

Like all managers, Hoddle wanted to keep our preparations as private and secure as possible which is easier said than done as a man in a sausage suit demonstrated. We were at the FA's Bisham Abbey centre where we trained on two pitches separated from the changing-rooms by an entire golf course. A private security firm is supposed to ensure no fans or anybody unauthorised comes into the centre, let alone anywhere near where the players are training. Which is why we were all a little surprised to see this ten-foot-high sausage running all the way across the golf course to where we were having a practice match.

It was, of course, Giant Pepperoni Man with a photographer right behind him. The pictures inevitably made the papers and, although we had a good laugh at the time, it did show that our so-called security was pretty pathetic.

Something people forget is that it is not just from the outside world that players want to keep their secrets. We all play for different clubs and there are certain things you would rather not let other players find out in case they use it against you in club games. I know I don't want other players to know what I like and don't like about, say, the positioning of defensive walls. If I have a point to make, I always go through the coaches and make sure they don't tell the other players that a tactical idea has come from me. There is always that element of rivalry in an England squad. I have seen players from the same squad kicking bits out of each other in the next league game. Last season Jamie Redknapp and Paul Scholes had a big flare-up in a Liverpool–Man Utd game but then not everybody gets on with each other in the same club team, let alone at international level.

This rivalry is an aspect of coaching club players for internationals that fans would probably never appreciate, but a good international manager will always be aware of it. When players have had bust-ups in recent club games, he will take them aside when they arrive for England training and try to defuse the situation from the start. Apart from the club rivalry, there is also the fact that some players will be competing for the same position in the England side and that can make some of the challenges in training pretty interesting.

But, despite these rivalries, there was a good team spirit among the players in the run-up to the World Cup. We thought we had a manager who was tactically on the ball and enough good players to do well. But I don't think any of us really expected the bombshell dropped by Hoddle when he selected the final squad. Like Euro 92, I was to be closely involved, but this time I was not the unlucky player to miss out.

Hoddle had taken us to La Manga for a few days of light training and golf-playing, at the end of which he would announce the final squad of 22. This time, it was decided that he would speak to each player individually and we were all given appointments. I was pleased to be first off. I was not nervous as Hoddle had already told me that I was his Number One, and he just used our meeting to ask me to use my experience to help the younger players.

But I was equally confident of Gazza's selection, although there is always some uncertainty with Gazza. He is such a volatile character and he was certainly having some problems at the time, but he lives and breathes England and I expected Hoddle to pick him.

The story has already been told of how Gazza smashed up Glenn's room when he was told he was out of the squad, but I also heard that he actually tried to attack Hoddle himself. As soon as I heard what had happened, I shot up to his room as quickly as possible because I knew he would be distraught. But he was in an even worse state that I had imagined. I have never seen a man like it. He was so upset. It had come as so much of a shock to him, he could hardly talk. He was crying his eyes out and it was like watching a man totally destroyed. England was always his first love and he told me once that he only played club football so that he could play for England. For some players, the club comes first; never for Gazza. He was trying to make his own arrangements to get home and he couldn't even hold a conversation with the people on the other end of the phone.

A lot of rubbish was written at the time about Gazza's drinking being out of hand while we were at La Manga. He was certainly not in the best frame of mind but his stress was coming from home, not from a bottle. For a start, there was a lot of paper talk about his wife allegedly going out with someone else. When we had a night off, Gazza was in all the headlines for being drunk, but we all were. The finals were still some weeks off and the management had set up this bar just to help us to relax. No one was allowed in apart from players and staff and all the windows were blacked out. The whole point must have been for us to have a drink and a laugh and that is what happened but Gazza was the only one who was caned for it. This was the day before the naming of the squad, and people have said Hoddle made his decision because of that night, but I don't believe it. I am sure the decision was made well before.

There was some more nonsense spoken and written about what happened when we had a day on the golf course. Gazza was supposed to have been secretly drinking while we were playing, smuggling bottles of beer out in the club bags. This was rubbish because, for a start, beer was not banned on the golf course. The beer cart was coming round to all the players, courtesy of the management. If you don't want the players to have a beer, you don't send the cart round. Some players only had soft drinks, but it was our choice. I was playing in a four with Gazza, Ian Walker and Phil Neville and we certainly all had a beer; it was hot and thirsty work going round the course.

The press had been asked to stay away but there were cameras everywhere, most of them pointed at Gazza. But we all knew that, so we were hardly going to make idiots of ourselves by getting drunk. One piece of film that was used in the case against Gazza was of him falling about on one of the greens, doing his demented spider routine on his back. That was supposed to prove how drunk he was. In fact, he was just laughing his head off because he had put his ball on the green and then had to watch as first I chipped in with a wedge from 90 yards and then Ian Walker did exactly the same from 30 yards. The odds against that must have been astronomical and Gazza simply couldn't believe it. But his reaction just fuelled the witch-hunt against him.

I thought then and still believe that Gazza should have gone to France. I would not have hesitated to select him because he had a huge amount of skill and that ability to change a game with a pass. He also formed a great combination with Incey. Unlike the press, I have been on the same team when Gazza has turned it on. I have seen what Gazza can do and know what playing for England means to him. I still remember how delighted he was after the game against Poland which qualified us for the 1990 World Cup. It is hard for me to understand why he was dropped for France. He had always been the same, enjoying a laugh and a drink, but he had been a great player for England. I simply could not fathom out why he had been dropped and Hoddle certainly never explained his decision to us.

But, although we were surprised and most of us did not agree with the decision, it didn't have a negative effect on team morale. We were knocked back for the day, but only the day. It was a massive shock to everyone, but we were professional and we knew we had to roll our sleeves up and get on with it. As a squad, we felt we were close to doing something big in that World Cup and, if nothing else, what had happened proved we had a manager who was not afraid to make the big decisions. Even without Gazza, I still thought everything was in place for success. A lot of Hoddle's theories, tactics and training methods were similar to those of Arsène Wenger who had been Hoddle's mentor when they were both at Monaco. This Continental background gave us, I thought, a better chance to match the European and South American sides who had seemed to have the edge on England tactically in past World Cups.

And we made that all-important good start against Tunisia. I have played in a lot of big games – cup finals in England and Europe, championship deciders, a European Championship semi-final – but I have never felt so proud in all my life as when I walked down the tunnel to play for my country for the first time in a World Cup. It was such a brilliant feeling and I will never forget it. We were playing at Marseille's ground which has a long, deep tunnel to the pitch. We had to walk down a flight of stairs to it, and the officials stopped us at the foot of them and made us wait what seemed like hours before they let us out on to the pitch. That was the worst time because there were a lot of nerves about. We weren't talking to each other much as we were concentrating on what was to come, trying to focus on what we had to do. It was a good job Rob Jones wasn't still playing for England. He had the worst case of nervous cough I have ever heard. You could hear him coughing non-stop in the tunnel before internationals. Instead we had Incey, who always leaves his shirt off until he gets out of the tunnel, showing off his muscles – just knots in cotton, I always tell him.

It was baking hot as we emerged into the light. There were more England fans in the stadium, but the Tunisians were right by the tunnel so they were the first ones we heard and they were making a hell of a noise. I had goosebumps down both my arms and up my back and that was just walking out on to the pitch. When they played the national anthems, it was even more awesome and I really felt the responsibility, the expectation back in England. I was so emotional that I could hardly sing for the lump in my throat, but when the camera was on me I made sure I was miming loudly.

I was proud to be called up to the England Under-21 squad when still playing in the old Fourth Division (for Peterborough) but, after my first gut-wrenching training session, I thought I would never make it through to the senior side.

I was wrong. Despite competition from other goalies like Dave Beasant (he's the one on the left), I made my full England debut in a 1-1 draw away to Saudi Arabia (November 1988). Although it was not the best of games, it was a memorable trip for all of us.

Above A trip to Hong Kong and China with England before Euro 96 holds happier memories for me than my first visit behind the Bamboo Curtain.

Left During an Arsenal tour of China in 1995, I turned my foot over on a dodgy pitch, dislocated my ankle and damaged tendons and ligaments. I ended up in a Chinese hospital which frightened me so much I was out of there as fast as a person on crutches could move.

The atmosphere during Euro 96 was amazing and a lot of it was down to
THAT song sung by Frank Skinner and David Baddiel. The Wembley crowd
belting out 'Three Lions on the Shirt – Football's coming home' really lifted
us before every game.

We were 1-0 up against Scotland in our second game at Euro 96 when the Scots were awarded a penalty. I knew I had to save it as, if Scotland equalised, it would give them the edge and it could be them not us going through to the next stage of Euro 96 ... As Gary McAllister ran up, I guessed which way he was going to hit it but, as I dived, I realised I couldn't get my hands to the ball so moved my elbow up and deflected it up and over the bar. Wembley went mad.

I just knew it was a crucial turning point in the game.

So, it seems, did Tony. But what neither of us knew was that Gazza was about to steal my glory with a sensational goal just a couple of minutes later.

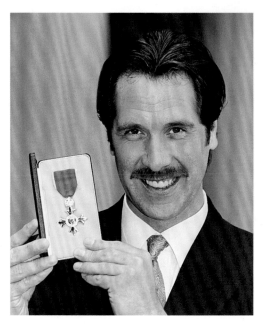

My MBE and my proudest moment. Receiving it (in 1997) from the Queen was also the most nervous I have ever felt. I warned Tony Adams about that when he was going up to receive his MBE. He didn't believe me – he does now.

World Cup 98 in France. Walking out onto the pitch for my first ever game in the World Cup Finals was another nerve-tingling moment. The atmosphere was amazing and I had goosebumps everywhere but, once the game began, I just focused on the game.

The result: England 2 Tunisia 0.

It has been a long road from playing by the murky canals and in the muddy parks of Rotherham to being England's Number One at Wembley and around the world. But I've enjoyed every minute of the journey.

But, although I was nervous then and during the warm-up because I was thinking about what I wanted to do and what I didn't want to do in the game, once we started it was just like any other match. It was what most professionals find: after that whistle blows, you just focus on the game. All the worries beforehand when the mind works overtime thinking 'What if I drop a clanger, mis-kick the ball to one of their players?' went out of the window once I started playing. Even though it was my first World Cup game, I felt fine from the start.

Before the game, we had watched loads of videos, so we knew what side they would play. Hoddle went through it player by player, but he was talking to us as a squad rather than as individual players and picking out our immediate opponents. He told us – and we believed – that, if we played our own game properly, we would have too much for them all over the pitch. They did have one early chance but they fluffed it, and that was it for them as Alan and Paul Scholes saw us home with something to spare.

The Romania game was disappointing because, having fought back to 1–1, we did not think we were in any trouble and a draw would have been a good result. But we were beaten in the last minute because Graeme Le Saux wasn't strong enough in the challenge. He was knocked and let it distract him, allowing Dan Petrescu in for a shot which went between my legs, the worst place for a goalkeeper as you really can't react fast enough to stop the ball going through. It always looks bad when it happens but you have to stand with legs apart to give you the purchase to dive either way. Stand with your legs together and you have no chance if the player places the ball to one side of you. If you adopt a stance to avoid a shot going through your legs, you are always going to be beaten by far more shots going either side of you than you are ever going to be by ones that nutmeg you. Sometimes, though, it will go against you and this time it lost us that game which put that much more pressure on the next one, against Colombia. That game now became the be-all and end-all of the tournament for us. The relaxed atmosphere in our squad started to be replaced by a much tenser feeling.

Until then, we had enjoyed staying in our compound with its underground car park converted into a games area with pinball machines, driving simulators, pool, slot machines. It was like a big amusement arcade just for us, as no one else was allowed in. We had some great races on the simulators. These were big cars you could sit in, with accelerator and brake pedals, and there were two side by side. Graeme Le Saux turned out to be the top boy racer.

We had also had some fun at the media's expense for a change, thanks to Alan Shearer and Gareth Southgate. They decided to see how many song titles they could work into their answers during the endless TV and radio interviews. Alan is a great Phil Collins fan so he was coming out with phrases like 'Against All Odds' and 'Another Day in Paradise'. He even got away with 'Something in the Air Tonight'. After the first couple of times, they let the rest of us in on what was happening so we used to watch the TV and cheer every time we spotted one.

Gary Newbon was the only reporter to realise what was happening but he didn't grass on the lads, just spent his whole time trying not to laugh on air when he heard one slipped in. My favourite was when Gareth was asked to comment on scurrilous press stories about the squad. He said they were just 'Careless Whispers'.

Sometimes it is better if we make our own entertainment. I can remember an unfortunate occasion when Graham Taylor brought a comedian into an England training camp. He is well-known now, so I'll spare his blushes and keep his name out of it but he was obviously very nervous of us. He started telling jokes during a dinner and they just weren't funny. It got even worse when Taylor's assistant Steve Harrison, a genuinely funny guy, started a bit of banter with him, and the comedian couldn't handle it. Suddenly he said he would have to nip out of the room for a minute. We thought this was part of the act, especially when we heard a loud thud outside. But when someone went to see what had happened, he found the comic out cold on the floor. The pressure had got to him and he had simply fainted clean away.

Nigel Kennedy did better when he came out to the World Cup in Italy but he did his show not just in front of players but their wives and girlfriends, too. That is a much easier audience than a bunch of lads on their own, so Nigel's concert went down well.

I have since taken Pearcey's place on the England team's

committee for the players, and the FA consulted us ahead of Euro 2000 on what kind of facilities and entertainment we would prefer. We were even given the option of having stars like Robbie Williams doing gigs for us.

But, back in France, things were getting serious. After the Romania game, there was less laughter about. We could be going home early and we knew it. The debate in the press about Michael Owen had also built up to a frenzy by then, with most of them having a go at Hoddle for not playing him from the start in games. The fact that Michael had scored the equaliser against Romania gave them more ammunition.

Unlike his Gazza decision, I thought Hoddle was right about this. Michael is very quick and a good finisher and looked good in training but I thought it was still a little bit too early for him to be starting and I think Hoddle handled his introduction to the team cleverly. Many pundits reckoned he ought to have started games to ensure we qualified but that would have meant leaving out Teddy Sheringham, who was much more experienced at this level. Everything that happened, I believe, showed that Hoddle was right to ease him into the team and not put too much pressure on him too early.

His first start was in our crucial game against Colombia when we turned in one of our best performances since Euro 96. We took control from the start and the result never looked in any doubt from the moment Darren Anderton put us in front. Becks, also starting a game for the first time in the tournament, scored a typical goal from a free-kick and it was game over. His mother was particularly pleased because the game was played on her birthday.

Winning the Colombia game settled us all down after the disappointment of losing to Romania. I don't think we were bothered that we now had to play Argentina rather than Croatia, who would have been our opponents if we had beaten Romania as well. Our view was that we would have to play and beat the so-called big teams at some stage if we wanted to win the World Cup and it might as well be now. There was also a feeling that there was still some unfinished business with the Argentinians over the 'Hand of God' goal.

The feeling in the squad was that we were good enough to beat them. We were quietly confident, but we did all feel tired by this stage, although probably more mentally than physically after the pressure of the Colombia game. That kind of game takes more out of you mentally than people realise. We were all taking extra vitamins to lift ourselves and make us a little bit more lively.

There were a few days before the Argentina game and the players' wives, who had flown out for the Colombia game, stayed a day and a night before flying home to leave us to prepare for the next big match. Some of the lads who had not played against Colombia had to train on the day they were there so they missed out on part of the family reunions. The wives, though, were flown back again for the Argentina game. We had to change our training location as we were playing Argentina in St Etienne, but our preparations remained the same as for the other games.

Unfortunately, it is hard to prepare for conceding a penalty and going a goal down in the opening minutes. I felt disappointed because I let myself get conned into giving it away. The ball was coming towards me followed closely by Diego Simeone and I came out to meet it. Maybe I should have stood up a little bit longer, but if I had he might have shot. But, once I had committed myself, Simeone knew exactly what he was doing. He tapped the ball to the side of me, ran into me and went over. No complaints – it was a penalty, but he definitely played for it.

And the penalty itself was also frustrating for me. I had watched him, and Hoddle and Alan agreed with me that he smashes the ball to the goalie's right every time. That is exactly what he did and I flew across to get a decent hand on it but there was so much power that I could only deflect it down to the ground and into the net. On another day, perhaps at Euro 96, I would have saved it. It was so close which made it even more annoying. Saving it would have been a big boost for us but, even so, we came back brilliantly.

Michael won us a penalty in much the same way as Simeone had done for Argentina, and Alan put it away. Then everyone remembers Michael's fantastic goal to put us ahead but, after that, Paul Scholes had an even better chance and put it just wide. If we had scored a third at that stage, that would have been game, set and match to us, even though we were still in the first half. But the chance was missed and, just before half-time, they hit us with a sucker punch from a free-kick just outside the penalty area.

It was a move we had never seen them work before – perhaps we should have hired Giant Pepperoni Man to infiltrate their training camp – and it caught us cold. Le Saux had been told to guard the left side of our wall but he had two players facing him there, one slightly further out and, as he tried to cover them both, he wasn't close enough to Zanetti who moved along the wall and then spun off the left edge and hit a great shot with his left foot.

It was a well-worked free-kick, but all teams are angry if they lose any goal from a set-piece and we were no exception. It meant we went in breathless at half-time. It was 2–2 and still another 45 minutes to go.

Glenn told us to stay tight in the second half and keep playing our own game because it was working. But, within five minutes of the restart, it was all turned on its head again because Becks was sent off. And, once again, it was a case of a player being conned into making a mistake. It was a bad tackle from behind by Simeone and, when he was on the floor, Simeone shoved Becks's head into the grass. The Argentinian has said since that he was deliberately trying to wind Becks up because of his reputation for having a short fuse which, if true, makes it even worse but it worked for the Argentinian. Becks did lose his head and flicked his foot up at him. Simeone would barely have felt it but he went down screaming and shouting. The sending-off was a harsh decision but Becks was stupid to react the way he did and put the referee on the spot like that.

It still makes me angry to see top-quality players like Simeone doing things like that. I was pleased to see that FIFA directive which now tells referees to book players waving imaginary cards to intimidate the officials into booking another player. Booking players for diving is a good move, too.

But none of that was going to help us out of the hole we were in then. Hoddle immediately sent instructions for us to go to 4–3 1–1 with our two strikers taking turns to drop back to help midfield.

From that point, I can't remember Argentina creating anything remotely like a scoring opportunity. I certainly did not have a real save to make for the rest of normal time or during extra time. We created a couple of half chances and then came one of the weirdest moments I have experienced in football. Sol Campbell went up for a corner and headed home superbly.

Half the team joined him celebrating on the sidelines. I jumped up and cheered myself but was still looking at what was happening. I'm thinking – hang on a minute, the Argentinians are playing the ball out, not just bringing it back to the halfway line. Suddenly, it was 'Shit – it's been disallowed, everyone get back.'

We only had half a team on the pitch but even then the Argentinians could not make anything of it and the move fizzled out.

At this point I know I am going to put myself at odds with every England fan by agreeing with the referee's decision to disallow the goal. Having watched the video, I'd say it was definitely a foul by Alan on the 'keeper. Alan has gone up for the ball and it's not his head but his arm that hits the goalkeeper and that has to be a foul. Still, as a member of the goalkeepers' union, I would say that, wouldn't I? Apart from that moment, very little went on in either penalty area and the game seemed to go on forever, with our lads getting more and more knackered.

At this stage it did not help that there seemed to be far more Argentinians off the pitch as well as on it. They seemed to have found more tickets and they were around more of the ground while the English were noisy but mostly confined to one section of the ground. I had spotted Debbie from the start because she had said she would be wearing a bright orange suit so I could pick her out and also let the other players know where their wives and girlfriends were sitting. In fact, the players' families found themselves surrounded by Argentinians as well. Debbie told me that their fans kept putting Argentine flags up across the rail in front of the seats where she was sitting with Claire Ince, Lorraine Merson and Lainya Shearer. She and the other wives kept undoing them and taking them down, putting up English flags instead. At first, the stewards tried to stop them when the Argentinian fans kicked up a fuss but they gave up in the end. At least that was one victory for the English that night.

Right behind me in both halves, it was all Argentinians and they were making a tremendous noise. They were also throwing stuff – plastic bottles and coins. This is a sad state of affairs but it goes on all the time, especially in Europe. Playing in Barcelona in the Champions League last season, they were spitting and throwing pieces of pie at me – and that was just during the warm-up. It happens in England, too, but it's not as bad as it used to be because police now have cameras to pick out the throwers so they can be turfed out.

As players, you have to rise above it. They are trying to distract you, so you have to try not to let them. It is not always easy, though. I was on the bench for England playing against Sweden, the game when Shilts was presented with a shirt for a record number of appearances. I came on as a sub but while I was warming up before the game this great big yellow dart about eight inches long landed right by my foot. It had a steel point on the end of it and, if it had hit me, would have done me serious damage. I've also had rocks, eggs and fireworks thrown at me. In Europe, fans seem to be allowed to bring huge red flares into the ground. One day, a player – probably a goalie – is going to be badly hurt.

It was the result of the Argentina match, though, that badly hurt all of us. I was half looking forward to the penalty shoot-out because it was another chance for me to be the glory man, and we started well with Alan hitting an unstoppable penalty. Then I saved the second Argentinian spot-kick. Although it was a decent save, I can't claim it was a great one but I thought it was going to be enough to win it for us. As I knew where Debbie was in the crowd, I remember looking straight at her, gesturing with my fists clenched and shouting, 'Yes!'

When I saw Incey stepping up to the spot, I was even more confident. It is important to score your own penalty immediately after your goalie has saved one and Paul was the ideal man to do it. He had plenty of experience and strikes the ball well. But he missed it.

Merse and Michael Owen then scored penalties for us, but there was nothing I could do about the next three Argentinian kicks so we were effectively into sudden death when it came to our fifth penalty. I did not know who was down to take this one for us but when I saw Batty stepping up, I just thought, 'No way.' I have never seen him take a penalty in my life and my instant reaction was that the odds were against him scoring. Sadly, I was right. He missed it and we were out.

I don't think tiredness was a factor in our penalty failure. Nobody worked harder in the game than Alan and Michael and they both scored. Once again, apart from Alan (our regular penalty taker), we had not had any specific penalty practice in training. The change of the rules about goalies moving did not help us either. Goalies have always moved before the kick was taken anyway but, although we are still only allowed to move from side to side and not off the line itself, most goalies now move forward as well and usually get away with it. Having said that, it is so frustrating when you see the goalie move out and then save it, which is what happened with Batty's penalty. It was bad enough that he missed, but the save was clearly illegal even under the new rules.

Afterwards, it was a very quiet dressing-room with a few tears around. We all felt we had come so close and that, if we had won the game, we would have had a great chance of winning the whole tournament. It was a desperate feeling for the players because we had played well in three out of the four games yet the statistics show that we went out in the second round. The bare facts are that we did not have a particularly good World Cup but, fortunately, that was not the way the English public saw it.

Their reaction was brilliant. When we came back on Concorde and saw all the people that were there to cheer us home, it really did lift us. The disappointing aspect was the treatment handed out to Becks, selected by the press as scapegoat for the latest England 'failure'. All the abuse was directed at him and we felt for him. After the game, he was in a room off the dressing-room with Incey. He came in to apologise to us but there was nothing much we could say to him. He is a quiet lad off the pitch anyway, which may have had something to do with Hoddle's reluctance to play him at the start of the tournament. He said Becks was not focused and seemed to be missing Victoria. He was given special dispensation to meet up with her but none of us had a problem with that. If it made him feel and play better, that was fine with us. We were playing golf when he went off to meet her, so it was not as if he was missing training.

We were more upset with what happened after the World Cup and the bombshell of Hoddle's book, marketed as his personal diary of the tournament.

I was not the only player who thought it was wrong for him to publish a book like that so soon after the event, especially as it was clear he had been working on it during the World Cup, using us as his material but without our knowledge. It was disappointing because it made you suspect that, if you had gone to him with a problem – something personal and not necessarily about football – the details would also have gone into the book. I also did not like the way it singled out players and picked on their bad points. These were players still in contention for England places and it did not help morale at all. It was something he did not need to do and left him open to the charge of doing anything for a little extra money. As with Graham Taylor, you just questioned his judgement in agreeing to do something which was obviously going to leave him open to so much criticism.

Some of the other criticism, though, was unfair, such as the flak over his association with Eileen Drewery. The truth is that Hoddle never put any pressure on players to go to see her, she was just there as a resource if we chose to use her. Despite all the negative reports in the press, quite a few of the players did go to her for treatment and the word was that she had helped them all. Then, after Glenn had left the England job, I saw a TV programme where players were swearing by her treatments. Some were players with injuries which they had been told would need surgery, yet she had seemed to be able to cure them.

At the time, I had a tendon injury in my shoulder that was simply not healing so I decided to give her a try. I went with a totally open mind, thinking that if she could do anything, it would be a bonus because I was getting quite desperate about the shoulder ever being right again.

She took me into this little room with a bed and chair. She sat me on the bed and started to stroke my hair, then the top of my head and then where the pain was in my shoulder. When she started doing it, I could feel pain from the injury yet she was hardly touching it, just smoothing it, lightly massaging it. What she was doing should not have hurt but it did. It had never been like that before and it felt like something was happening in the shoulder, a really strange feeling. Whether it was my mind or my body feeling that it was being healed or what, I don't know. But when I came out of there, I felt very tired and went straight back to the hotel and flaked out.

Before seeing her, I been suffering the same pain every time I did any goalkeeping. Although there was no sudden miracle cure, the shoulder did gradually improve from immediately after my visit. The injury is still there but it does not bother me anymore. Whether it is your mind or body playing tricks or maybe releasing certain chemicals because it is thinking it is healing itself, I don't know. All I can say is that it seemed to work for me.

I have not been back to her for anything else, but I would definitely go again if I felt I had an injury that she could help with. I know Arsène would be fine about it because he has allowed other Arsenal players to go to her. I was seriously thinking of going with my calf injury at the start of last season because it dragged on so long without getting better. I was initially out for eight weeks but eventually it did respond. I think it just needed rest as the calf is one of the worst muscles to damage because it has a poor blood supply and, unlike the thigh, there are no other muscles around it to take the strain.

Most players now have open minds about using faith healers like Eileen but it was not fair to accuse Hoddle of forcing her ideas on the players. On the other hand, the claims he made in his book and in the press were always going to be used against him once there was a move to shift him out of the England job. And he certainly could not have expected to have enjoyed the same trust from players after revealing so much personal information about them in his book. In fact, I am sure it was the book as well as the comments he was alleged to have made about the disabled that led to his sacking. Either way it meant another change at the top.

With Terry, we achieved something good at Euro 96 and the next thing you know, he's gone; then we have a half-decent World Cup, which could have been really successful with better luck, and we change managers again. No wonder we never seem to have any continuity in our national game. While I think all the players were sorry to see Terry go, there were obviously mixed feelings about

Hoddle's departure, but you always worry about who will come in and where you will stand with the new manager. And, when you consider how the last four managers had been treated by either the press or the FA or both, it was hardly surprising that there was not exactly a queue of high-profile managers lining up to apply for the vacancy.

In the end, there was a groundswell of support for Kevin Keegan but nothing is ever straightforward for England and initially he was supposed to be combining the England job with managing Fulham. Also, the contract was just for the four games we still had to play in our qualifying group for Euro 2000. It turned out that we would have to play six games to qualify but, even before that was known, it always seemed likely that Kevin would have to leave Fulham and take the England job full-time and long-term and that is exactly what happened.

While he was making that decision, I was back at Arsenal where we had two trophies to defend.

20

······

Now Follow That – Again

Patrick Vieira and Manu Petit will not forget 1998 in a hurry. First they won the Double for Arsenal and then just a few weeks later they were playing in a World Cup Final for France – and winning it. Manu even scored one of the goals which beat Brazil. They must have been on some high – and they did not have much time to come back down to earth and focus on the next season for Arsenal.

After we won the league championship in my first season with the club, it had been hard for us to lift ourselves to do it all over again the next season. This time, it was going to be even harder partly because we had two trophies to defend but mainly because, just like Patrick and Manu, the rest of the internationals in our squad were also recovering from the World Cup and, in our case, the disappointment of not winning it.

It was hardly surprising that we made a slowish start to the season. We were not being beaten much but we were drawing a lot of games – four out of the first five – and finding it difficult to score with just three goals in the five.

In the close season, Wrighty had left to join West Ham, David Platt had retired and the only major incoming transfer was defender Nelson Vivas, although Swedish international Fredrik Ljungberg, a wide midfield player, was signed a couple of months into the season. Freddie was to become an honorary English hero the following season for one special international goal, but Arsène had not bought him for his scoring power. Instead, he was looking to Nicolas Anelka to take over from Wrighty as our main striker.

As players, Wrighty and Nicolas were both lightning quick, but in personality they couldn't have been more different. Where Wrighty was the life and soul of the party, a bubbly character and a complete extrovert, Nicolas did not mix and hardly spoke to most of us. During the Double season, there had been press stories about rifts between the English and the foreign players in our squad. These were wildly exaggerated because there was only one problem and that was Nicolas.

He would be quoted in the French press, complaining that Marc and Dennis only passed to each other and never to him. This was rubbish, and Nicolas would deny that he had said it, blaming it on his brothers who acted as his managers. The lads took the mickey out of him when the stories came out. There was nothing malicious, but we were letting him know we knew about them and would take it seriously if he was really saying these things. It was fairly obvious that he was, as he was always complaining to our coaches that other players were not passing to him. He did it so often it was like a stuck record.

But his real trouble was that he kept himself aloof from everyone apart from the French players. All the foreign players Arsène has brought to Arsenal have made the effort to learn English and mix with the English players in the squad. All of them except Nicolas. The French players would say that was just the way he was, a shy person who lacked confidence in his English. But he wasn't shy with the French players. He was always talking to them. It did cause a divide in the squad.

His English was not too good but he could speak it. The trouble was he would not use it or try to improve it. And he had every chance as the club had language teachers to help the foreigners with their English. And as far as we were concerned, he had made the decision to come and play in England so it was down to him to learn the language and mix in with us. If one of us had gone to France or Italy, we would have been expected to learn the language. But, with Nicolas, it seemed as though he thought learning a language was too much like going back to school and he was not prepared to do that. Looking back, it was almost as if he knew he would not be staying long so why bother with English? Towards the end of the season, hardly any of the other players were going over to congratulate him when he scored. In fact, sometimes he looked even more miserable after he had scored than he did the rest of the time.

But compared with the scandals over George Graham's sacking, Tony and Merse's addiction confessions, and Wrighty's disciplinary problems, one sulky striker was not worth worrying about and once we had got the World Cup out of our systems, we went on to have a good domestic season.

We came close to retaining our trophies but ran into Man Utd both times – first in the FA Cup semi-final at Villa Park. This ended 0–0 and although it was still a very good game, the replay was a classic with Dennis missing a penalty in injury time which would have won it for us. But it is the constant TV replays of Ryan Giggs's extra-time winner that make me cringe.

All I can remember is seeing him with the ball and three or four of our defenders around him. I expected him to lay it off but he just kept on coming and it was a real shock when he beat the lot and was right in on goal. His finish was fantastic, smashing it straight above my head, but I did wonder afterwards if I should have stood up taller. He was so close, though, and the shot so fierce, that it would probably have gone in anyway. There was certainly no time to react and my only real chance of stopping it was if it just hit me.

At the end of the game, hundreds of United fans invaded the pitch. I was walking off, completely gutted, when I saw them coming and realised I had better get off fast. They started coming up and swearing at me. I was staring back at them as they did everything they could to provoke me into having a pop at one of them. Most of them gathered by the tunnel and one went up to Patrick, effing and blinding right in his face. Patrick thumped him out of his way and, when the fan complained to a policeman who had seen what happened, the copper told him he deserved what he'd got and to get lost. It was about the only thing that went our way that day and there was more disappointment to come – this time in the Premiership.

After our slow start, we had gone on a similar unbeaten run in the second half of the season to the one that had won us the Premiership the previous season. We beat Leeds in December 1998 and were unbeaten until we lost to Leeds in the second last game of the season in May 1999. That was 15 wins and four draws in 19 games, but it was not quite enough to stop United winning the Premiership for the fifth time in seven years.

We had our chances in that second Leeds game, too, but losing it gave the initiative to United. Even if we won our last game (at home to Villa), we needed United to drop points in their final game. And who were they playing? A team with our interests right at heart? Hardly. It was Spurs. There was some talk in the papers about Spurs doing us a favour but we couldn't see that at all, especially as George Graham was now their manager. There was nothing in the game for them and the idea of Spurs pulling out all the stops so that Graham could say, 'There you are, Arsenal – have the Premiership on us' – well, it was a complete non-starter in our minds.

Still, you always hope and we realised from our own crowd's noise that Spurs had gone into the lead. But, at that stage, we were not even winning our game and by the time we were, United were leading 2–1. Their game finished after ours, so we were back in the dressing-room watching the results on the TV before we knew for certain that they had won the game and the Premiership by a single point.

But at least it was a good season for me as I kept 19 clean sheets in 32 Premiership games and only let in 15 all season. Alex played six games and only let in a couple, too. Just 17 goals against in a season was another Arsenal record.

Whichever way you looked at it, the 'ageing' back five had done it again. Everyone expected Arsène to break it up after the Double but, although Nelson Vivas and Gilles Grimandi played the odd match, it was almost always a case of selecting the back four out of Lee, Nigel, Tony, Bouldie and Martin Keown while I remained number one ahead of Alex.

If we hadn't won anything in the end, at least we had played our part in making sure we had another chance in the Champions League. That season, we had gone out in the first group stage, losing away to Dynamo Kiev and then at home to Lens. We lost 3–1 to Kiev but we could have won it 8–3 but for their goalie having a great game. It was also the first time the club had decided to play home Champions League games at Wembley, and that may have had something to do with the Lens defeat. By the time we had to play

Panathanikos in Greece, we were already out and fielded virtually a reserve side. As the Greeks still had a chance of going through, I expected a real hammering but, in the biggest shock I have had in the Champions League, we beat them 3–1.

There were a couple of other shocks in Arsenal games that season. I was out injured for the notorious match at Sheffield Wednesday when referee Paul Alcock took a dive courtesy of Paolo Di Canio but I saw the funniest part on the TV. That was when Nigel was 'encouraging' Paolo to go off before jumping back like a scalded cat when the Italian suddenly turned on him. At the next England get-together, we were all talking about hard man Nigel acting like a big girl's blouse.

Even more bizarre was the FA Cup game against Sheffield United when Kanu scored the 'goal' that never was, after a United player had deliberately kicked the ball into touch because of an injury. Normal procedure on these occasions is for the ball to be returned at the throw-in to the side who kicked it out.

I had a clear view of what happened next and I couldn't believe my eyes. Although the papers picked on Kanu, I think it was more Marc's fault. He made the run to collect our throw-in, instead of allowing it to go back to them, and Kanu just reacted off his run and put away his pass. The worst thing was that I knew some of the United supporters who were behind my goal and I could hear them saying, 'Go on, Seaman, you're a gentleman, throw one in.' It did cross my mind to let them have a goal to compensate for the mistake, but I couldn't bring myself to do something like that. But I apologised to their players after the game and the first person I saw in the tunnel was David Dein. Straightaway I told him that the game had to be replayed. If we had let that result stand and then gone on to win the Cup, we would have been slaughtered – and rightly so. They decided to replay it and we all thought it was the right decision, even before we won it at the second time of asking.

At the start of last season (1999–2000), there were signs that Arsène had finally decided that new blood was needed. Bouldie saw the writing on the wall and left for Sunderland but the other lads have been written off before. As I point out whenever the press ask me about it, if they keep writing the oldies off every year, eventually they are bound to be right. But they are all strong characters and will not give up their places easily and they won't all disappear at the same time. Nigel, Lee and I are all about the same age but Tony and Martin are three or four years younger.

Of the original back four, Lee likes to take the mickey out of players. He enjoys the banter but otherwise keeps himself to himself away from the club. Nigel also likes to have a laugh but is much quieter in general. Tony is a strong personality and, as the captain, is a big talker on the training ground and in the dressing-room. Bouldie was the same kind of character but he began to see that, with Martin's development, he was going to be the odd one out unless Tony or Martin was injured. Nigel made the same decision joining West Ham at the end of 1999/2000.

It was difficult for Martin, having left the club and then come back later. He used to have a bee in his bonnet about Tony and thought that, because he was the captain, he always went straight back in the team even if Martin had done well in his place. Knowing this, all of us wound him up about it. It has always been easy to get a rise out of Martin because he is a bit like Dot Cotton in *EastEnders* – always moaning. He also gets bothered about the tiniest details with his boots and kit in his preparation for a game. Now, though, Martin has developed into a top player, an England regular, and he gives us back as good as he gets. He is even being used on a Puma advertising poster alongside Jaap Stam. If you put that on your front door, there would be no need for a guard dog or a burglar alarm.

Another problem for Martin when he came back to Arsenal was that he had been used to playing in a back five at Everton. Not used to holding the line, he was charging back here, there and everywhere. He would be chasing the centre-forward back in while Lee, Nigel and Tony would be stood there, arms up appealing for offside and then realising with horror that Martin wasn't with them. But he learned quickly and re-adjusted his game to our system.

It is much more of a problem for the foreign players who are now coming into the back four on a regular basis. Not only are they having to learn the system, they have to know and understand the shouts despite their limited knowledge of English. Last season, you could see the problems. We would be playing offside in a line and the three English lads would be well up and Gilles would be back in the six-yard box. Even after all these years, the defence takes a lot of organising and not just by me and Tony. Lee, Martin and Nigel also have to call the shots sometimes.

Although we would not want to go back to the Graham days of constant drilling of the back four in training, we seem to have gone too far in the opposite direction, especially as there are so many new players coming into our defence. We don't do any specialist training as a defence. Sometimes we might play four-against-four games, but that benefits the attackers far more than the defenders. Arsène's style is to put a lot more responsibility on individual players to make the systems work but it is hard to form a good defensive unit when it is made up of all different nationalities. In some games last season, we had a back four which included Argentinian Nelson Vivas, Ukrainian Oleg Luzhny, Frenchman Grimandi and Brazilian Silvinho. The shouting was a nightmare. Oleg is only just learning English. Shout at him and he just looks blankly at you – how is he going to know what you want him to do? And the only way Silvinho can call for the ball is by whistling.

We are not the only team with this problem. Look at Chelsea and Liverpool. Chelsea have already fielded a team with no British players in it at all and last season we played some games when there were just a couple of English players in our team. A lot has been written about squads and rotating players but, when we won the double with Wenger, the back five hardly changed at all. If you watch Man Utd's team selection, Sir Alex always picks his strongest team for the big games, especially away from home.

It will be interesting to see if the pendulum swings back in a few years and people start wanting to keep the same sides out there as much as possible again. But it is unlikely unless something is done about the number of games top players have to play – for their country as well as their club. Last season, we had Kanu missing for vital games because he was off to the African Nations Cup and there were other tournaments for South American, Australian and Asian players in the middle of our season.

Leeds are apparently reluctant to buy any South American players because of the fear of losing them for large chunks of the season and

I thought it was significant that George Graham went to Peter-borough in the 1999–2000 season to buy a couple of young British players for Spurs, Matthew Etherington and Simon Davies, at just £1.2 million. At that price, he can't lose and he knows the club won't find itself paying their wages so that they can spend weeks away playing for their country in mid-season regional tournaments.

But all of us have to get used to the fact that football at the top level has no borders anymore. Just look at the squad we had to pick from during 1999–2000. Having bought the Nigerian Kanu earlier in the year, Arsène used the close season to buy Oleg from Moscow Dynamo and a young German player, Stefan Malz, from Munich 1860. They joined the established French and Dutch players and the South Americans Silvinho and Vivas. Also on our books were Portuguese, Swedish, Austrian and Italian players. There were even a few Brits left. Then, early in the season, Arsène added another French World Cup winner, Thierry Henry, and the experienced Croatian striker Davor Suker.

I hope Nicolas did not spend his close season learning Italian, because the move he was angling for there did not come off and he ended up at Real Madrid. When we heard the £20 million-plus fee that was being offered, we thought 'bite their hands off' because, although he is a good player, he is nowhere near the finished article and the club had only paid £500,000 for him in the first place. He and his brothers obviously earned a lot of money from the move but, according to the reports from Spain, it does not seem to have made him any happier. His behaviour at Highbury was baffling because it is so important to get on as a team. Now there are all these stars coming in, it is vital that no one becomes so full of himself he thinks he is above the rest. I think it is fair to say that, at Arsenal, the English players are the ones who lead the banter and the mickey-taking that makes sure everybody keeps their feet on the ground. There is no one in the squad now who the rest of us think is a waste of space – which is how we felt about Nicolas in the end.

Dennis Bergkamp is a happy guy but quiet. He just wants to play his football and enjoy his family life. He didn't score goals straightaway for Arsenal and when that happens you do look for excuses. Maybe the two games a week we have to play here were hard for him at first but he is a quality player so it was only a matter of time before he proved it to us and the fans. He has a dry sense of humour and his English is good enough for him to take part in the banter when he wants to. I asked Dennis once about his fear of flying and he said he just gets ill even thinking about getting on a plane so I left it there. We all accept that he won't fly as we all knew about it when he arrived.

Off-field matters do affect players. For example, I don't want to be worrying about my family when I am playing so where they are sitting is important to me. Debbie follows the game now and understands enough about the rules to know what is going on. (Offside may be a bit of mystery to her but then so it is to some of the refs and their assistants, not to mention a few of the players.) But she doesn't go to away games because I can't control where she is going to sit. Once we played at Barnsley in the cup and I sent some tickets for my mum, dad, brother and uncle. Afterwards I found out they had been in the open end, getting rained on with the hardcore Arsenal fans. For England games, the tickets are for seats in with the fans, too, but at least they buy a whole block so all the wives are together.

This is probably less of a worry for Marc Overmars who is a great player but a bit of a loner. He wanders off on his own all the time. He also collects matchbox cars and other model cars that are big enough to sit in. That is one weird hobby and, before you even think it, yes it is definitely weirder than fishing.

Patrick and Manu are fairly easygoing, although Manu can be moody, especially when he picks up injuries. Patrick has settled down well, though, since he started going out with a steady girlfriend.

Outside the back five, the only English player in the running for a regular place is Ray Parlour. He is a very funny guy, full of practical jokes and he always has a good tip for you. His latest is, 'Never do your shoelaces up in a revolving door.'

Of the newest recruits, Kanu seems a friendly, easygoing type. His English was pretty poor when he arrived but he was obviously trying to pick it up quickly. Anyway, he knew enough to make his point when we went 2–0 down to Chelsea in one of his first games for us. Their fans were really giving it to us, singing, 'There's only one team in London.' But Kanu went up to Lee Dixon and said, 'Give me the ball and I will score,' and that is exactly what he did – three times.

Thierry Henry's English was better and he showed that he wanted to use it with us from the start.

Davor Suker (now with West Ham) is a great guy, very chatty and with good English. He has a great temperament as well. When we played over in Barcelona in the Champions League and he came on as substitute, the entire crowd whistled him non-stop until the end of the game because he used to play for Real Madrid. I have never heard a noise like it at a football match and it got even louder when he kicked one of their players and was booked for it. But it didn't bother him at all and he went on to set up Kanu for our equaliser.

But we still went out of the league in the qualifying stage for the second season running and this was a major disappointment, especially as we were unbeaten in what should have been the two toughest games: away at Fiorentina and Barcelona. We drew them both and should have won at Fiorentina, with Kanu missing a penalty for us.

It was our home form that let us down and again many of the fans blamed the club for switching the games to Wembley. The club's argument was a reasonable one as it gave more fans – over 70,000 compared with 38,000 – a chance to see the games live, although the extra revenue must have been another factor in the decision. But, although I love playing there because of its history and traditions, there is no doubt Wembley does give visiting teams a lift. At Highbury, the pitch is narrower and the crowd closer and more intimidating, so teams find it harder to play well.

Although it was losing to Fiorentina that finally put us out of the competition, the Barcelona game was the killer. We thought we had done the hard work over there and that we would show them what was what at Wembley. Unfortunately they showed us.

Attacking-wise they were very sharp, but they did look vulnerable at the back and we created far more chances. Apart from their four goals, they only had a couple of other chances. I did not have too much to do while their goalie was being worked all the time. The back four and I came in for a lot of criticism but their finishing was excellent, with most of the shots going right in the corner of the goal.

The Champions League is the toughest to play in because of the league format and the fact that they are the form teams you are playing. And, with all due respect to the UEFA Cup, it is the one everyone wants to win. But one European trophy is better than none, so when our exit from the Champions League meant a place in the third round of the UEFA Cup, we refocused on winning that.

We did not play that well at home to Nantes and we needed two late goals to give us the kind of lead we needed. We drew 3–3 in the away leg after being a goal down and then 3–1 up. Nantes were technically a decent side but Arsène predicted that they would not have the strength and the passion to beat us.

I had little to do in the home leg but when I went up for an easy ball I felt a twinge in my calf muscle and missed the away leg and several Premiership games. It was the same injury that had kept me out of the first nine Premiership games and four of the six Champions League games. It was that kind of season, stop-start, for all of us. With injuries, suspensions and the squad rotation, the team was changed every game. Lee and Nigel were saying that every time they began to feel they were getting into their stride, they found they were being left out. They felt like they couldn't get started and into a decent rhythm – and they are experienced players. It all meant that the team pattern never had a chance to develop, either. Martin was left out after we lost badly at Coventry because he lacked match fitness after an injury. He had a poor game and hardly won any headers but was dropping him the answer? How do you get match fit without games? Doing extra training does not help much with match fitness and there are not many reserve games at certain times of the season. And just when Matthew Upson, our promising young centre-back, had a chance of a run in the side in place of Martin, he damaged a cruciate ligament in a game at Leicester and was out for the rest of the season.

But we should have had a big enough squad to cope with injuries. I just think the whole team spent too much of the season on cruise control, winning here and there but rarely playing really well.

Ironically, the turning point in the Premiership for us should have been a game in which we did play well against all the odds. We were third behind Man Utd and Leeds and needed to win at Old Trafford in February as United also had games in hand, having been allowed to go to South America for the new World Club Championship. It was their first game back and, as they had been knocked out early, we knew they would be well-rested and without any major injury problems.

We, on the other hand, had a lot of players out. Marc, Dennis and Tony were injured, Davor was suspended and Kanu was away at the African Nations Cup. Everything seemed against us. Every time we picked up a paper, we saw pictures of the United players sunbathing in Brazil, as if they were getting ready for us.

We started well but the biggest nightmare was the pitch, the third one that season at Old Trafford. It was like a carpet that had not been glued down. If you pushed your foot into it too hard, it just came up in large pieces of turf.

Arsène had told us that we should take the game to them. His theory was that most teams go there to defend but virtually all of them still get beaten, so there was nothing for us to lose by being positive. His masterstroke was putting Freddie up front alongside Thierry. I had never seen him as anything other than a midfield or a wide player, and I thought Arsène might have brought in Graham Barratt, a youth player who has done very well as a striker in the reserves. But it was a massive game and it could have destroyed him. Freddie may have played up front for Sweden but not for us so it was a gamble but that is why Arsène is the manager. He put Freddie in there and he played very well.

Looking at the game, United did seem a little rusty while, for us, Patrick and Manu were tremendous in midfield, protecting the back four. Once Freddie had scored his goal, we had something to defend. It was a good finish, too, with Freddie putting the ball through Bosnich's legs. He claims he meant to do it – but strikers always say that.

Then Thierry went through one-on-one with Bosnich. If he had scored then, it would probably have killed the game. When Bosnich saved it, we knew they were going to come back into the game and have some chances.

I made a couple of decent saves near the end of the first half which made their second-half equaliser so frustrating. It was a great cross from way out on the left to beyond the far post. I had to go for it otherwise they would have had a free header but, under a challenge, I did not punch the ball as far as I wanted to. It went straight to Becks and he passed it straight to Teddy Sheringham and it was a simple tap in. I have to take some blame for the goal because I should have got more distance on the punch, but I was right to come for it.

Arsène didn't say anything to me after the game for one very good reason. He had told me when I came back from the calf injury that he wanted me to come for more crosses, take more risks in order to help the defence out more than he thought I had been doing. I thought, 'That's all very well but it will be me who carries the can if I come out and they score.' So I told him that, if he wanted me to do that, then at least he could tell the team that I wanted players on both posts for corners. Over the second part of the season, I came for a few more crosses than usual and I didn't miss too many. But the United goal was critical because it meant we had not closed the gap on them. In the dressing-room after the game, it was as though we had lost the match.

During the game it had been very noticeable that the home fans were really giving United players, Nicky Butt in particular, a lot of stick. It just shows how demanding fans are now. This was a team who were top of the league and champions of Europe but the fans were still not happy. A couple of weeks earlier when Leeds were leading the table, they went in at half-time a goal down against Aston Villa and they were booed off. The same thing happened to us when we were also top of the table one season. We were losing 1–0 to a bottom of the league team and were booed off. Even when we turned it on in the second half and scored five goals, they were chanting, 'We want six'. It brought it home to me just how fickle some fans can be. They pay their money and, as far as they are concerned, they are entitled to their views – however unfair they are sometimes.

Still, I couldn't blame those who followed us away from home last season for being unhappy with us. Our away form was dreadful and it was hard to know exactly why. We were going to places like Bradford, Coventry and Middlesbrough, where we knew we had to roll up our sleeves and battle it out for the first hour, and just rolling over for them. Some players were not doing their job away from home and this was clear because we were a totally different side at home. It had to be down to the players, not the manager. Our tactics home and away are much the same and, with the pace we have in the side, it should suit us more to play away because the teams have to come at us more. Yet it was much like Gordon Strachan's description of his side when asked if inconsistency was Coventry's problem. No, he said, because they were consistently good and then they were consistently bad. When we were beaten at Bradford, we couldn't believe it but I turned round to Lee and I said if we played like that we would lose at Watford, too.

We had always prided ourselves on being a difficult side to beat, and suddenly we weren't. A side that had only let in 17 Premiership goals the previous season was letting them in left, right and centre away from home.

The fact that the back five was not settled was probably a factor. Injuries to Tony, Martin and me kept us out of a lot of games while Nigel and Lee were being left out of some games, too. When a neck injury meant I could not come out for the second half of the game at Middlesbrough, it was the first time Arsenal had ever played a Premiership game without a single English player in the back five.

If it is the end of the road for the back four, at least Lee had a great night earlier in the season when Real Madrid came over to play in his testimonial. They brought a lot of big names but not Nicolas, who had a convenient injury. Perhaps he had heard that they weren't selling programmes but sticks and stones for the fans to aim at the striker who had deserted them. Tony, Martin and I could not play because there was an England international coming up, but Wrighty came back and stole the show as usual. Lee said afterwards that it had been 'an honour' for him 'to play in Ian Wright's testimonial'. But it was a great night for Lee with more than 22,000 turning out for him.

I am due a testimonial this season and, the way the game is going, it might be one of the last at Arsenal or any other top club. We earn a lot more now, so they are not as vital for our future financial security but it is also a fact that, after Bosman, it is hard to see too many players staying at a club for ten years in the future.

For the time being, I think the current Arsenal squad is the best we have ever had in my time at the club but whether it will produce the best team remains to be seen. The best I have played in was the one that won the Premiership: Lee, Nigel, and two out of Tony, Bouldie, and Martin at the back; Manu, Patrick, Ray and Marc across the midfield and Dennis and Wrighty or Nicolas up front. With the likes of Kanu, Freddie and Thierry, we should be even better but only time will tell. It is one thing to have the talent, another to have the mental strength to produce the all-important consistency throughout a season.

As last season drew to a close, our away results had left us struggling even to make sure of finishing in the top three to secure a place in this season's Champions League. We had been knocked out of both domestic cups and the UEFA Cup was my last chance of club glory. But I had my eyes on another trophy in the close season, this time for England not Arsenal.

21

• • • • • •

Rocky Road to Euro 2000

A change of manager in the middle of the qualifying games meant that England, like Arsenal, found consistency hard to come by in the 1999–2000 season. It nearly cost the nation the chance to compete in the Euro 2000 finals.

Not that there was a complete change of management and coaching staff when Hoddle left. As far as the senior England side was concerned, it was simply a case of Kevin Keegan, David Fazackerly and Arthur Cox coming in for Hoddle and John Gorman. And Ray Clemence, for one, stayed on as goalkeeping coach. But we immediately noticed the change in management style.

Kevin is very much a motivational manager and does not spend as much time as Terry and Hoddle did on tactics. It was difficult for him, coming in halfway through Euro 2000 qualifying, especially as we had already suffered a few disappointing results. The pressure was on him immediately and, although we had a good start with a Paul Scholes hat-trick winning us the home game against Poland, we were then only able to draw with Sweden (home), Bulgaria (away) and Poland (away) which meant we had to rely on Sweden doing us a favour just to qualify us for the play-offs. We needed them to beat Poland but, although they were at home, they had already won the group and had no other incentive to go all-out for a victory.

As luck would have it, we had a friendly to play the day after the Sweden–Poland game. It was the first international staged at Sunderland's Stadium of Light and we all gathered in the hotel lounge to watch the Sweden game on the TV. It was nerve-wracking stuff especially as we knew that, if Sweden did not do it for us, we would have to face an England crowd the next day having failed to qualify for Euro 2000. For a long time, it really did not look as though the Swedes were going to win. As we feared, some of them did not seem too bothered about the game and it was only my Arsenal team-mate Freddie Ljungberg who looked motivated. Perhaps it was the thought of facing Tony Adams, Martin Keown and 'H' if Sweden let England down that motivated him but, in fairness, his natural game is to get stuck in and work up and down the pitch.

We were all shouting at the TV screen, cheering Freddie and the other Swedes on, creating a really good atmosphere in the hotel. We just did not know how the game would go and it seemed an age before Freddie scored the only goal of the game in the second half. I did offer to buy Freddie a drink for that but he has not taken me up on it yet. It was a bit early for us to celebrate, anyway. The play-off draw could hardly have been tougher on us, setting us against a Scotland team still smarting from that Euro 96 defeat. It was not that Scotland were necessarily the best team in the play-offs but an England–Scotland game is like any other local derby – the form book goes out of the window. They are great games to play in but you go into them knowing that the winner will not automatically be the best team, just the one that plays best on the day.

On balance, we were pleased that the first game was away but we knew we had to get some kind of result – a draw or a win – at Hampden Park.

The pre-match hype was amazing. It seemed like everyone was talking about the games. Euro 96 and all the other key games between the two countries were raked over and a lot of tension built up. I was more apprehensive than usual because I had only just come back from my early-season calf injury.

Before the game, Kevin showed us a lot of videos on Scotland and particularly highlighted their set-pieces but no more than for any other teams we play. As everyone knows, Kevin's strength is as a motivator and this comes from having been there and done it all himself as a player.

We stayed in a hotel at Loch Lomond and the day before the game I decided to go trout fishing for a couple of hours. One of the security staff offered to take me to the same lake he had taken Gazza to when he was playing in Scotland. I went with Steve Guppy (you would have to be a fisherman with a name like that) and, when he heard about our plan, Kevin said he would come, too. He was delayed doing some interviews, though, so in the end we went without him. I did not really expect him to follow on but, sure enough, Kevin turned up. He even brought a couple of coats with him so Steve and I didn't catch cold. He was soon sitting on a bench by the lake, chatting to the local anglers about the fish they had caught and about the game ahead.

Before we left the lake, the owner invited us into his lodge. The entrance was very low and narrow but when we got inside it was like Dr Who's Tardis. He had everything in there: a TV, radio, even a cooker. We ended up having a cup of tea in this bizarre setting and Kevin has never forgotten it. I don't think he is really into fishing but he realised it was a good way for him to get away from all the hype.

There was no getting away from it on the day of the game. This was a huge match for both sides and the noise inside Hampden Park was deafening before the game. Alan had been quoted in the papers as saying that Scotland fans could whistle and shout all the way through our national anthem, it still would not put us off our game. This made a big headline and the Scots took him at his word. The band was right behind us but we could not even hear them. Kevin had told us he wanted us to sing it like the English rugby team do, to really belt it out. But we just couldn't hear the music and when we sang the last 'God Save Our Queen', we realised the band was carrying on at least a line behind, so we had to sing it again.

The Scottish crowd never really quietened down throughout the game but, although they were hugely outnumbered and confined to just one section of the ground, the English fans made a lot of noise, too.

It helped that we made a brilliant start, going two up in half an hour. After that, we were quite comfortable playing out the rest of the game but people tended to forget one turning point in the game. After we had scored, Scotland had a great chance to equalise when Kevin Gallagher was through on goal but I managed to save it with my shin and my knee. Almost immediately, we went up the other end and scored. Straight after that, they had another chance and Billy Dodds hit the crossbar but it was that first chance that could have changed the whole game. But at 2–0 in the second half, we had no problems holding out. I did not have a real save to make.

It was almost too easy for us, because this meant everyone expected us to win the second leg at Wembley quite comfortably. We knew that they only had to score the first goal and the whole complexion of the game would change. Scotland were a decent side and, because it was England, there was no chance of them giving up the game whatever the score.

Kevin told us to treat the second game as a one-off. We should imagine the match score was 0–0 and that it was important that we did not concede the first goal. We knew the tie was a long way from being over even if everyone else thought we were already through to Euro 2000.

There was not a huge amount between the teams. We had similar recent records and, if there was a quality difference, it was only among the strikers. Scotland have not had the choice of top-class strikers that England have enjoyed in recent times. But this was a match where technical ability was not going to be the only factor.

International football is totally different to league football anyway. The pressures are always much greater, and that applied even more to this game because of the rivalry between the countries and the prize that was at stake for the winners. I am very experienced at international level, but even I was feeling those extra pressures, and we had a lot of younger, less experienced players on the pitch.

Despite what the press wrote after the game, we played reasonably well in the first half and the game was fairly even with few chances at either end. But then, just before half-time, they scored the all-important goal with a fine Don Hutchison header from a good cross. This put all the pressure on us and it was always going to be difficult after that. Scotland had the better of the second half but still did not create many chances until near the end when they had one clear opportunity.

They took a corner and I can remember seeing a Scottish player flick it on and then having a clear sight of the ball as it went across me. Then I saw Christian Dailly power in for a header. Fortunately, it came straight at me. Instinctively, I threw my hands up, trying to make sure I blocked it and knocked it up in the air. I knew the most important thing was not to let the ball get past me by trying to be flash and catch it. Chris Woods had tried that with Linighan's last-minute header in the FA Cup Final replay and it went in off his hands. I managed to get strong hands on the ball and the rebound went to safety. It was Scotland's last real chance and we played out the game nervously but safely.

We knew it was not a great performance, but we had still done the business and we were through to the Euro 2000 finals. The Scots have made a lot out of having beaten us at Wembley but it was a two-leg tie and the only score than mattered was the aggregate one. Imagine what the press would have done to us if England had tried to boast about winning one game 1–0 if we had lost the other 2–0. And from my point of view, the games had been good. I made vital saves in both of them and had not had much chance with the only goal I let in.

Before the games, there was a lot of paper talk about who would be playing in goal. A lot of pundits suggested or recommended that Nigel Martyn would be brought in. The papers definitely tried to get me out, just as they have tried with Alan and he is England captain with a superb scoring record for clubs and country. Nigel had played well for Leeds in the first half of the season and I had missed a lot of games with my calf injury. But people in the professional game know that for big games you always pick your most experienced players. Kevin told me on the day of the game that there had never been any decision to make, that I was always going to be playing. But he did not tell me until then. Before the selection, I had not been totally sure that I would play.

Even after we qualified, some pundits started saying that Euro 2000 should be a test period for England, a time for bringing in new players with the 2002 World Cup in mind. That is just crazy. Euro 2000 is a major tournament in its own right and it was certainly hard enough for us just to get to the finals. England's recent record in qualifying for major finals is not so good that we could afford to sacrifice an opportunity to do well in one tournament in the hope of doing better in the next one. We might not even qualify for the next World Cup and, if we did bring in younger, inexperienced players and ended up playing badly in Euro 2000, we would be slaughtered in the press. The fact is, England are not allowed to have test periods. The fans and the press expect us to do well in every competition.

And managers can be affected by the press. I have seen players picked for the England squad on the back of a campaign in the papers. While not quite the same thing, the inclusion of Coventry's Steve Froggatt in the squad for the Scotland game seemed to be based only on the fact that he is a left-footed player, which all the papers were saying the England team lacked. He was not even a regular in the Coventry first team and the club's own fans seemed as surprised as he probably was at the call-up.

I try to avoid reading articles about me in the press. I have the *Sun* and *Mirror* at home, and if I see an article about me, I won't read it. I know whether I am playing well or not – I don't need a journalist or an ex-player to tell me. And I will also know why. Last season was one of my worst for games missed through injuries. Halfway through it, I had only played 11 Arsenal games. Goalkeepers are no different to outfield players. We need to be playing matches to keep our sharpness. However much you train, you can never recreate the pace of a real game. Even the pace of the ball is a lot different, because players never go full out in training.

When I came back after my first calf injury, I started being given a lot of stick for not being at my sharpest, and I was being blamed for goals which were not down to me. One journalist asked me if I thought I had made any mistakes. I said, 'No' and they then ran an article with that quote set against a list of about eight mistakes I had made which had led to goals. But none of them were from that season; they were ancient examples, such as the Nayim and Koeman goals.

I did have a run last season when a succession of sloppy-looking goals went in. They were mostly deflections, which never look good but were not actually my fault. These runs happen, but the beauty of being experienced is that you know it will change. When we beat Leeds, who were then top of the league, I made a crucial save but very little was written about it because even the TV did not show how good a save it was, low down to my left. But I knew I had made it and I took a lot of confidence from it.

Perhaps it is a problem that I am not a spectacular 'keeper. I always do just what is necessary. You don't see me flying about, palming shots over the bar instead of catching them simply because it looks better. Some goalies get away with being flash but the way I see it, goalkeeping is all about judgement – knowing where your goal is and making the right decision.

Kevin had given me no guarantees that I would be the Number One for Euro 2000, but I believed my place should be safe. I played well in the Scotland games and I would have to have a really bad run, throwing in goals for Arsenal, for my place to be in any doubt. Even then, there is an argument that only a player's form for England should count. There was a time when Shilts was not playing well for his club but playing well for England and the England manager at the time said that his England form was all that mattered.

The team's form took an upturn when we drew 0–0 with Argentina in a friendly early in the New Year. Kevin changed our shape to a three in the middle at the back with two wing-backs and we looked a solid outfit. I had a few saves to make, but we made more chances and we came off feeling we had played well against a very good side. There would be just three more friendlies (Brazil, the Ukraine and Malta) before Euro 2000.

Looking ahead to that tournament, we saw that the group we had been put in was a tough one, but the reality was that all of them were going to be tough ones. The good thing was that there was no one country in the whole tournament that overshadowed everyone else. Even World Cup winners France had struggled to qualify. None of the teams in our group – and that included Germany – had been in the best of form so we believed we had every chance of doing well.

22

· · · · · ·

Goalkeeping in Safe Hands
with Willow

Goalkeeping can be a lonely business. With one or two exceptions like my manager at Birmingham, Ron Saunders, the only people at a football club who understand goalkeeping are other goalies, and not all of them make good coaches. As a young goalie I was almost completely self-taught because there was simply nobody around to teach me about goalkeeping. I was in my early twenties before I started receiving any regular specialist coaching and even then that was only because, for some reason, former centre-forward Saunders took a special interest in goalkeeping.

At QPR, the specialist coaching took a back seat again until my last year there when, at my request and on Don Howe's recommendation, Bob 'Willow' Wilson was employed one day a week to coach me and the other QPR goalies. His main coaching role, though, was at Arsenal and one of the reasons I was so pleased to move to Highbury was that I knew I would be able to work with Willow all week. Although I knew he was a great goalie for Arsenal in his time, it was – as I keep reminding him – before *my* time so I don't remember ever seeing him play. But, of course, I knew him from his TV presenting work. My first impression of him was that he was exactly as he came over on TV – friendly, lively and with a similar laid-back personality to mine.

He told me later that coaches and other people in the game were putting it around then that I was too laid-back and even too lazy in training to realise my full potential. But he knew they had just been taken in by my easygoing manner which tends to mask my competitiveness. I want to win at everything I do, whether it is football, golf, snooker or whatever.

At the time the fashion was for rapid-fire training for goalies and I have never been a fan of this because it is not realistic. Only very rarely do goalies have to make a second or third save in quick succession, so I think it is a waste of time to spend too long training for it. Fortunately Willow was right with me on that one and, at that stage in my career, I was delighted not only to have my own coach but one of his stature.

I felt the benefit straightaway, because the way he coaches goalies is designed to build confidence as well as fitness. When you finish one of his sessions, you come off feeling tired but also happier about your game. The first thing I noticed when I started working with him was that, although he has his own routines, he is always willing to listen to what you have to say and, if you want to work on something specific, he will incorporate that into the session. If I think the routine he has set up is not a realistic match situation, I will tell him and he will always take it on board.

I like coaches who will adapt, because all goalies are different. For a start, his style was completely different to mine. From what I have been told and occasionally seen on old videos (he just made it into Talkies, I think), he was always up on his toes and liked to dive head-first at people's feet. He is always showing me the scars on his head, but I just say more fool him for doing it. He was also a big talker on the pitch, the Peter Schmeichel of his day.

He knows I am a different kind of goalie so he never advises me what I should or should not be doing in a game. He sees his job as helping me improve my technique. We do a lot of work on shot-stopping, training to keep my eyes on the ball, not the player. Mostly this starts with me on the ground having to get up to save, down and then up to make another save. Although, for the reasons above, we don't overdo this it is important to do some reflex work and there is another side-effect.

When I was coming back from injury last season, I had to spend a lot of time in the gym doing tough fitness routines. The coaches reckoned at the end of it that I had never been fitter but, when I started to do the specialist goalie training again, I found it was knackering me. It is very hard work and it uses different muscles to those the gym exercises work on.

In the old days, managers liked to see their goalies training in all weathers and in all conditions although diving around on rock-hard pitches is an easy way to pick up injuries. When Willow was the subject of *This is Your Life*, they showed a film of him supposedly training when he was Arsenal goalie. He was throwing himself about in pools of the sloppiest mud on a bog of a training pitch. There is no point at all in that as the conditions are not realistic. You would never play on a pitch in that state, so why train on one?

Although his wife Megs was the one most involved with setting him up, I was also in on his 'Life'. I had to distract him as Michael Aspel mingled in with the other players as they ran round the pitch towards where we were training. I kept shouting things to him so that Michael could get right up behind him with the Big Red Book. It was a great way to set him up because we had always had a running joke where, every time a helicopter flew over the training ground, he would wind me up by telling me that it was Michael coming down with the Red Book for me.

He was amazed when he realised he was the 'victim' and it could not have happened to a nicer guy even if he is the oldest Best Man alive (but that's another story). We have mutual respect and he tells any journalist who asks that he is my biggest fan and that he now rates me alongside such greats as Jennings, Banks and Shilts. When George Graham was looking for reassurance that he was making the right decision in bidding for me, Willow told him that I was certain to become England's Number One. In fact, Willow was almost more upset than I was when Graham Taylor left me out of the Euro 92 squad. With no disrespect to Chris Woods, Willow believed that I should have been England's Number One several years earlier than it actually happened. When Taylor left me out, he even went to the trouble of setting up a goal near where he lived, so we could have coaching sessions while the tournament was on, just in case I was called up after all.

Willow said that I reminded him of Jennings because of my calmness, belief in my own ability, presence on the pitch and the way I seemed to fill the goal. He also liked what he saw as my ability to make game-turning saves as well as the bread-and-butter ones. At the same time, he admired the way I played the percentages even if it meant that goalies like Schmeichel would gamble more and sometimes bring off the more spectacular saves. Willow admired the Man Utd goalie but always reckoned I would let in fewer goals over a season.

As it happens, in almost all my seasons with Arsenal, I have been either first or second in the Divison One / Premiership table of goalies letting in the fewest goals. That is because my first rule is to keep the ball out of the net. That seems obvious but what it means is: catch the ball if you can but always remember it is more important to keep it out than to make a flashy save.

Willow believes I can play at top club level until I am 40 and I know he has been advising Arsenal not to be too hasty in pushing Alex through to replace me. And he can fairly claim to have the club's interests as much as mine at heart when he says that. Although he coached at QPR and also had spells at other clubs including Southampton and even (whisper it quietly at Highbury) at Spurs, Willow is Arsenal through and through. So much so that Chris Waddle gave him an earful after one of our cup finals with Chris's Sheffield Wednesday team.

Working for ITV, Willow was sitting behind one of the goals and when we won I went straight over to him and he celebrated with me. Not unreasonably, Chris took a dim view, pointing out he should stay neutral if he was going to comment on the game for TV. But once a committed goalie, always a committed goalie.

It was before that FA Cup replay that I discovered just how much he thought of me and the club. Pulling my kit out of the bag in the changing-room, I found an envelope with his writing on it. Inside was a pair of thin, faded green gloves. Willow had written: 'If I could play brilliantly in these in 1971, think what you can do tonight with your gloves – play well.' I knew he only had a couple of pairs of gloves left as mementoes of his playing days at Arsenal and to give me one pair and send a message like that was a great gesture. It gave me a real lift before such an important game.

Before another big game, I found a note which simply read: 'Swift, Banks, Trautmann, Yashin, Jennings, Seaman – you've earned your place amongst the greatest-ever – keep proving it' while, before the Euro 96 semi-final, Willow smuggled a copy of Gordon Banks's autobiography into my kit with a note pointing out that Banks had been the only England goalie – so far – to have won anything. Well, Willow is a Scot after all. And for the World Cup in France, he hid a photo of himself holding the World Cup trophy, with another note: 'You've done everything and much more than I've ever done. Now I want you to repeat the last photo on view but for real.'

But the gesture that meant most to me was when, for the Cup Final against Newcastle that won us the Double, he tucked in a photo of his daughter Anna standing between goalposts when she was just three. With it, he had written a note: 'Do it for Debbie, do it for your family, do it for yourself – and please try and do it for this beautiful girl. This is Anna at Highbury in 1971, the Double Year. Good luck, play well, keep 'em out – Bob (the Double keeper).'

Anna was seriously ill with cancer at the time of that Cup Final and tragically died last year, aged just 31. She was a lovely person with a great sense of humour and Debbie and I got on very well with her and her husband, Mitchell, who gave her the same nickname as her dad. That lives on now in a charity – the Willow Foundation – which Megs and Bob launched after Anna's death. Anna was a great Arsenal fan and loved her days out at Highbury so the charity is designed to fund special days out for other seriously ill people aged 16 to 40. It is a typically generous move by a couple who have been great friends to Debbie and me over the years.

Life has changed a fair bit for goalies and professional footballers in general since Willow was playing, though. To give you some idea of what it is like for those of us still playing in the 21st century, here was a typical week out of my life during last season:

We played Everton at home on a Saturday, and normally Sunday would have been a day off for everyone except the subs and squad members who didn't actually play in the game. But, as we had a game against Barcelona on the Tuesday the rest of us had to come in as well, although only for some stretching, a bath and a massage. This was all designed to get the lactic acid out of our muscles.

We all had to be in at the normal time on Monday morning. Along with the other five goalies and Willow, I arrived as usual an hour before the rest of the players at about 9.45. It is our chance to do our specialist training before the rest turn up and we are roped into theirs. It is much harder if we have do our training after doing theirs.

We start with a warm-up, just keeping the ball with one-touch passing between all of us. Then we put some difficult passes in to make it harder to control the ball. This gives the exercise an edge and is very useful for me as, with Martin Keown in your team, you know you are going to be on the receiving end of a few dodgy pass-backs. Martin can't just roll it back to me nicely, he has to chip it up so I have some work to do to clear it. If I complain, he says, 'You're good enough to deal with it, aren't you?' I say, 'Yes – but it would be a lot easier if I didn't have to.'

After the warm-up, we will go into basic handling. We stand in a circle, kicking it at each other and it develops into a competition. We can kick it as hard as we want and the other goalies have to catch it without letting it hit the ground. But, like in baseball, if you kick it too far wide to left or right, you are out of the game. It is a good exercise because the power of the shooting makes it realistic and also helps improve our own kicking. We repeat this exercise four times.

Willow used to join in, but hasn't since he had his artificial hips fitted. Before that, he would still be making diving saves even though it would take him ages to get up again. He is moving a lot better since he had them done, though. I have to admit that I have watched him in the past and worried that this might be me when I am his age. But goalies are looked after much better by their clubs now than they were when he was playing and even when I started. Nowadays we can insist on grounds being watered to make them softer. Before, the softest thing we would be offered was a sandpit.

In our hour of specialist training, everything is game-related. One routine involves lying on the ground while one of the others moves to the ball quickly as a striker would do for a rebound. The goalie has to get off the ground even faster and beat him to it. Another has one goalie in goal and other goalies shooting at him. Sometimes we practise the angles; other times we stand side-on to the shooter before turning to deal with the shot. That is good for developing eye co-ordination to the ball when it is moving and is much harder than just facing a shot full on. This exercise can become very competitive between us, but it also gives you a striker's viewpoint when you are shooting at fellow goalies. It is good to learn about the angles from that side. If the goalie takes up a position that makes it impossible for you to score past him, you take that on board for your own positioning.

We do three or four routines like this, all recreating match situations. Sometimes we alter the distance or the rules so that the shooter can do what he wants: shoot, take it in on the goalie or go wide one way or the other.

All the goalies are given equal time on all the routines. There is no extra coaching for me because I am the Number One. But, in any case, you need rest in between goalie stints. Lots of goalies and coaches believe that you have to be knackered when you come off, but I hate doing exercises when I am absolutely shattered and my legs are weak, because you simply develop bad habits such as not diving properly. I don't see any point in practising doing something wrong. With Willow we get quality, not quantity, and for a good confidence boost we always have to end the session with a good save, preferably a 'Worldie' – a world-class save. If we finish with three saves apiece and you do your 'Worldie' on the first one, that's it – finish. There have been times too when I have started a new exercise with two or three great saves straight off and Willow has told me to stop while I am still on a high. Sometimes, when the youth goalies come in and train with us, Willow will pull them out of an exercise if they make a great save. You can see them walking tall, with their confidence way up there.

Nearly every club has a goalkeeping coach now, and they all have their different styles. Peter Bonetti was the England goalie coach when Graham Taylor was manager. His approach was more like that of Alan Hodgkinson, whose sessions for the Under-21 side had so depressed me when I was first called up. Peter believes in working harder and harder all the time. I saw a video he did with Neville Southall and I learned nothing from it at all. Maybe it is because Peter was small for a goalie that he had to do more work, especially on his leg-strength to improve his spring. When he was warming up the three England goalies, he had us running round the goal netting and across the front of the goal, jumping up and touching the crossbar on the way. The daft thing was that he would have to jump high to touch it but the rest of us were all much taller and could just reach up to it with our arms without our feet having to leave the ground. My mistake was in telling some of the other England lads what I thought and in the next training session they started shouting, 'Goalie, you like this one, don't you?' Peter was not very happy.

At Arsenal, we spread the different kinds of training through the week. One day, for example, we will practise taking crosses, and this is the only one where it is difficult to recreate match situations. We do stand people in the area but they can't challenge hard for fear of injury either to them or us. But it is still an important exercise, as coming and taking crosses is one of the most difficult skills for a goalie. When I come for a cross, I have to keep my eyes on the ball all the time. This means that, although I may be aware of other players around me, I never know for sure exactly where or when the challenge will come in. At the moment the ball is knocked into the box, I can't just go straight for it. For a split second, I have to wait and assess where and how fast it is travelling and where the highest point is that I can possibly gather it. I always try to move through the ball as I catch it so that, if anyone hits me, I have some momentum that will knock them away rather than letting myself be knocked over, hurt and made to drop the ball.

The worst balls are those that go straight up and down, as then the goalie has to make a standing jump and that is when we are most vulnerable. You expect to be hit on those so, if you get away with it, that's a bonus.

At set-pieces, opposition players will block goalies and try to hold our arms down. That's why you will see me holding my arms up high well before a corner is taken. It also alerts the referee that I am being fouled. When the ball is in the box, it is down to me to do the shouting and organising. Just 'goalie's ball' or 'runner' should be enough. When the ball's still outside the box, I leave most of the shouting to the back four, as they are usually trying to hold the line and will have a better view of that than me.

As we come towards the end of our session, the rest of the first team arrives and warms up. If the manager wants us, we join them. If not, we can go home although I usually go into the gym and do some plyometric work – that is, jumping and bounding exercises, some-times with weights on my shoulders. With the outfield players, it can be shooting practice, crossing and shooting or a knackering eight v eight game on a short pitch. I might play outfield but usually I go in goal.

Arsène does take into account what we have already done before the other players arrive. He sees us dripping with sweat and lets us off some of the fitness stuff they do. He is very conscious of the importance of not letting players overtrain. Goalies work on their own from 9.45 to 11, while first-team outfield players warm up from about 10.45, then train until about 12.30, sometimes with the goalies joining in. With Graham, we could still be out there after 1 p.m., which made it a long session for the goalies.

The level of training is different for goalies and outfield players. For us, most of the hard work is done in training. In a match, we might become mentally tired because of having to maintain concen-tration, but we are never physically tired. Outfield players, though, will be on the point of exhaustion at the end of a game so they train less in the week. For them, the sessions are geared to ensuring that their energy levels peak for the games.

This is a complete change from years past when everyone was expected to train full-out through the week – although they had fewer games than we do now. If we have a Wednesday game, we only do light stretching and have massages on a Monday. There is a decent training session on the Tuesday, but on the Wednesday there is no training, just a stretching routine at 11 after a short walk. We then have a meal and go to bed to sleep, or at least rest, before the game. Some teams started to warm down after games but doing this back out on the pitch is risky. If fans know that is what you do, some hang around and give the players more stick if they have not played well. That is why some clubs have stopped doing it and we never do it at Arsenal.

We go in on a Thursday after a game because we always train two days before a game. The only time we have a day off is if the game is on a Tuesday, in which case we would have Wednesday off. In a typical week last season, we played Everton on the Saturday, came in on the Sunday, trained Monday and overnighted in a Chelsea

Harbour hotel where we stayed all day on the Tuesday before our game that evening against Barcelona. They let us walk around the harbour, but that was as far as they wanted us to go. So it was a long, mega-boring day before the game. We did have the Wednesday off, though, before coming in again on Thursday and Friday for training. On Friday there is lighter training but still a good session with the focus on team play, as there always is the day before a game.

We practise team patterns, both attacking and defending, with eight v eight or nine v nine games on a small pitch with big goals. We also go through corners, both for and against, and free-kicks – who goes in the wall and who is the blocking man? Size mainly dictates who is in the wall, but we also prefer to have strikers in it because it is better for defenders to be doing the marking in the box. If this is left to strikers, you can bet they will lose their men. These days most teams shoot from free-kicks instead of crossing. This is one of the biggest changes in the game. Even when they opted to shoot in the past, it was just a thump. There was none of this curling and bending of kicks which makes life so difficult for goalies now.

On that particular Friday night last season, it was back to the hotel for an overnight before the game with Chelsea on the Saturday. It was a typical stop-start week with a mixture of frenzied activity and dull spare time where we are really just hanging around waiting for something to happen. These are the most frustrating times for a pro footballer. We have nothing to do and are not allowed to go out and enjoy ourselves anywhere else in case we injure ourselves. Usually I just watch TV, read fishing mags or even take my rods and tie some rigs up. Most of the other lads have their playstations and DVDs to pass the time.

To anyone who has to commute every day for a nine-to-five job, or to those working difficult shifts, this doesn't sound like too much of a hard life and, although it does involve some very intensive physical work, I would not pretend that it is. But, when players complain about the number of games we have to play now, we are not just whinging. Yes, we are perfectly capable physically of playing three games a week – we could play five a week, if we had to – but we would all start to lose the edge in our performances. The Germans have fewer teams in their top league and they have a mid-season break. Look what they have won and compare it with the England team's achievements since 1966. I think there is a connection there.

When I watched goalies when I was younger, I tried to take bits from everybody rather than model myself on one in particular so, if there was anything I could learn from the likes of Nigel Spink that would make me a better goalie, I did. I always watch videos of our games and see what else I could have done about goals that have gone in against me. Concentration is one of the most difficult aspects of a goalie's game. It is hard to stay focused when you have nothing to do for 85 minutes and suddenly have to make an important save. I make a point of watching the ball all the time even when it is up the other end of the field. If play is on the left-hand side, I position myself on the left-hand side of my penalty area, and on the right, if the ball's on the other side. I try to visualise a stake going through the centre of me that is anchored to the middle of the goal and use that to position myself correctly even if the ball never comes anywhere near me. But, if it does, it makes sure I have the angles right.

I have never been one for the whole psychology bit, the type of approach Jim Smith experimented with at QPR, but I do believe in always thinking positive thoughts before and during a game. This can be difficult because performance does affect you. If you have just thrown one in, it can be hard to stay positive but this is where a goalie's mind has to be different from that of any other player. You have to accept that you can make ten fantastic saves but then drop one through your legs and that will be the one everyone remembers. Willow says it is like living on a tightrope. You can be balancing brilliantly but make one mistake and you have fallen on your backside. They say goalkeepers are crazy, but I think they just need to have a much tougher mindset than outfield players. Everyone likes to be complimented but most goalies are still remembered for their errors. Even great goalies like Shilton and Clemence are still trying to live down embarrassing mistakes against Poland and Scotland respectively. As for goalies who are known for their best rather than their worst moments, I can only think of Banks with his Pele save and Jim Montgomery with his double Cup Final save for Sunderland against Leeds. I know I will always be remembered for the Nayim goal.

When I was learning my trade, my idol was David Harvey but only because he played in goal for the team I supported, Leeds. Later, I used to enjoy watching Bruce Grobelaar, which was strange because he was my complete opposite. He was a bit flash and did play for the cameras but I admired the way he came out for crosses. Sometimes he got caught out, but it taught me that you can come out to the edge of the box to take crosses and still play the percentages.

When I first joined the full England squad, I was impressed with the amount of hard training that Peter Shilton put himself through. I was also impressed with his coach Mike Kelly, who was goalkeeping coach for England during Euro 96. After Willow, he was the best I have worked with. One thing I noticed with Shilts, though, was that he would stop training as soon as he felt he was becoming too tired to do good work. I have since learned that he also only did exercises he was good at but that was all a part of the important business of building up confidence. It obviously worked for him, as he was a great international goalie who peaked at the 1990 World Cup. I would say he was the best goalie I have seen play. A lot of people rate Pat Jennings as the best, but he had retired before I could see him play. I never saw Willow play either, but he is always telling me he really was the best-ever goalie. Schmeichel has been a great goalkeeper, and won it all, so you have to admire him but I really did not like his ranting and raving. A couple of the recent Italian international goalies are exceptional too, but I would need to see them week in, week out to compare them with Shilts.

I could not copy Shilts, because he was a totally different shape to me. He was smaller – only just six foot – and stockier. He just seemed bigger because of his strength and how he used his shape. He built up strength with weight training, which has become a very important part of what goalies need to do. Upper body strength is vital in helping us cope with all the challenges we are put under during a game. It helps to be tall as it gives you that extra reach but it is just as important to stand tall, because your size puts opposition players in two minds when you come out for crosses. They are less likely to challenge hard or even at all whereas, if they see a small goalie, they think they can give him a right rattling.

When I was at Posh, I was only about 14 stone; now I am

approaching 16 stone. It was a deliberate gain which came through weight training. It means I have the confidence to catch or punch crosses, knowing that I can usually ride the challenges. Goalkeeping is about knocking people out of the way as well as making saves. The penalty area can be a war zone when there is a corner or free-kick. The worst incident I saw was at QPR when hard man Mark Dennis was playing for us and he was having a right ding-dong with another tough guy, Colin West of Sheffield Wednesday. Wednesday had a corner and the two of them were bumping and boring into each other. Then Colin stamped straight on Mark's foot with his back studs and I knew that must have hurt him big-time. Even Mark, who was as hard as nails, had to go off.

As a goalie, you get used to forwards standing in front of you, and the best way of dealing with them is to keep complaining to the referee. I remember a cup game against Preston when I was out injured and Alex was in goal. He is only a couple of inches shorter than me but is much younger and still a lot lighter. He was being blocked off by their strikers at every set-piece so I told him the next day that he should have held his arms up high every time it happened, both to keep them off and to alert the ref. If the ref's attention is still somewhere else, I told Alex to shout at him. Either way, he would win a few free-kicks and take the pressure off himself and the team.

I always tell young goalies never to listen to any advice except from other goalies. With the odd exception like Ron Saunders, managers don't know anything about goalkeeping and it is hard to take it when one of them starts telling you how to do your job. My prime rule for goalies is always to look after yourself first. Once I know that my game is on song, I can try and help the other players, but not before. Footballers are all the same – if you start telling them how to play, they will tell you to sort your own game out before you start telling anyone else. I am not a goalie who does a lot of shouting anyway. I might let a player know he should have done this or that, but not right after the incident so that all the crowd knows he made a mistake.

Eddie McGoldrick did it to me once, shortly after he came to Arsenal. There was a bit of a mix-up with a through ball which we eventually scrambled clear of our penalty area. After it had gone, he turned and came towards me shouting, 'You should have come for that.' He kept shouting at me until I told him to eff off and that I would sort him out at half-time. He was not exactly a hard man so he made himself scarce when we came off but I found him, grabbed him by the scruff of the neck and told him never to shout at me like that in a match again.

Although he was originally a winger, McGoldrick fancied himself as a sweeper. It looks easy when you watch someone like Baresi in Serie A. He brings the ball out, sprays it about and never seems to be in any trouble. But McGoldrick was a small guy who could not head a ball and, when he was suddenly faced with a massive centre-forward bearing down on him, he could not cope at all. He spent most of his time at Arsenal in the reserves and you had to question his ambition. He was on good money but personally I would never be happy to stay in the reserves just to pick up a wage. I was always surprised at Steve Bull staying at Wolves. He was praised for his loyalty but a player of his ability should have played in the top division. It is a cliché but you do only have one career. I was always determined to reach the top, and now I'm there I have no intention of slipping down the divisions.

One of the ways I use to keep my place as Arsenal and England Number One is to focus all my thoughts on what happened in my last game. If I have made a mistake, I want to make sure I don't do it again. This means not taking any risks until my confidence is right back. It is important to adapt your natural style to your confidence level. Willow and I agree that the benchmark for goalies is a simple one: the great ones make the fewest mistakes which actually lead to goals. I am always very honest with myself about my mistakes but not with the other players. John Lukic gave me a very good piece of advice when we were at Leeds: never admit a mistake in front of your team-mates because it gives them an automatic out. They will pass the blame over to you, even if they had something to do with what went wrong. I tell the other goalies at Arsenal the same thing: never own up but always recognise when you could have done better.

I am not really superstitious although, for a while, I wore a 'lucky' Bob Wilson T-shirt, which then went astray. I do tend to put my right boot and right glove on first but my main preparation now is to withdraw into myself and try to visualise the game, what I have to do in it and how I am going to contribute to the team play. I imagine myself kicking every goal-kick to a specific player or part of the pitch. It is a kind of semi-meditation as I tell myself I have to win, the team has to win. The coaches leave me alone before a game, as they accept that this is the way I need to prepare.

I hate to have anything in my net, so I don't take a goalie's bag or spare gloves. And, if anyone throws anything from the crowd, I have to clear it out. I'm sure this is very Freudian and I dread to think what a shrink would make of it or of my obsession about goalie gloves. For me, they have to be large and padded with furry insides and without any plastic on the outside. They might look clumsy but they are designed to stop the ball, not to tie your laces. They are so personal to me that, every time I have gone with a new maker, I have insisted they make a glove just for me. If there is the slightest scuffing on the gloves, I won't use them again for a match. I am like that with all the kit. If there is a pull in the socks or the shirt, I won't wear them again. The club is happy to go along with that although it might cost them a few bob. After all, if I am worried about the kit, I am not going to play well and that could cost them a lot more in the end.

I would be even happier if no one had ever thought of multi-coloured jerseys for goalies. The first bad one was the red England jersey with socks that looked like a packet of refreshers. When you saw little kids with that kit on, it looked good but it looked daft on a grown-up. The first time I wore it at Wembley, we were lining up during the national anthem and I saw a couple of the opposition players laughing at my kit. I felt *that* big. I had told Umbro I wasn't happy before the game but that was the final straw. We won the game and, when I went upstairs to the players' lounge, I met some of the press. They asked me what I thought of the kit and I said, 'Crap – and you can print that.' So they did and splashed it across the back pages. Umbro later told me that it became their best-selling kit. Well, maybe, but that was hardly the point, if other teams are laughing at the England team because of what they are wearing.

The players are given more say now. At Arsenal, Nike always

show me several kits and I can pick the one I like best. Umbro also know now that I prefer plainer kits. I certainly don't want to give fans an extra reason to have a pop at me.

There is no doubt that the abuse from crowds has become a lot worse in recent seasons. Goalies often bear the brunt of it being so close to the crowd. I remember playing at Oxford, whose fans were notorious at the time. A big fence had been put up and all you could hear was the noise of coins pinging against it as they tried to throw them through the gaps. Not too much poverty there then, presumably. At another game against Middlesbrough at Ayresome Park, just before bonfire night, there were live fireworks coming on, big lumps of stone, all sorts. At least they have clamped down on people bringing fireworks to English games – although not abroad – since those days.

Sometimes I see the fans' faces close-up and the passion is so intense that they look as though they could kill you. They really lose it when a player scores a goal against them. There is unbelievable hatred directed towards him. I have heard all the chants. They seem to think they can shout what they like about you, your wife and your family.

But the best defence is humour. During the warm-up before a game at Southampton, Alex put the ball into the fans behind my goal. This big fat bloke caught it and stuffed it up his jumper. I asked him for it back, he said 'no' and kept it up there. Eventually, some of the home fans had a go at him so he took it out and threw it back. In lifting his jumper, however, he had exposed this huge pot belly so I looked right at him and said, 'Now the other one . . .' Even the Saints fans fell about.

The worst is when you go back for a goal-kick and someone tries their luck with a pie or a pasty. Catering in grounds can't have improved as much as they claim.

Most of the coaches have blacked-out windows now so the fans can't see in but there is still abuse wherever we go. People will be walking down the street doing their shopping and, if they see the Arsenal coach, they will start giving the two-finger salute. We've seen a car with the whole family – mum, dad and two kids – all giving one finger or two or shaking their wrists in the time-honoured fashion for suggesting that we might be self-abuse enthusiasts. I ask you: what sort of family is that, where the mum and dad not only let their kids do it but do it themselves?

The best (or worst, depending on your point of view) example of this happened, ironically for me, at Leeds. We had just come off the motorway and police had stopped traffic at a roundabout to let our coach through. This car stopped with two old ladies – about 70 years old – in the front and, as we went by, they were both sticking two fingers out the window at us.

Away supporters give me a bit of stick if they see me off the pitch but it does not affect me at all. If it is your own fans, it is worse. Luckily, as I am also the England goalie, non-Arsenal fans often see me as being on their side. There is always the odd one who wants to have a go, but the reply is simple – count my medals. If they hang around long enough I might even reel off my most memorable saves, the ones that I would like to be remembered for – instead of the Nayim goal.

These would be the one from Zola when we won the European Cup-Winners Cup and the penalty save against Scotland in Euro 96. The Zola save was probably my best, but the Scottish save was important. In fact, I would pick that Scotland game as the biggest I have played in my career because of all the implications. It wasn't just about reaching the later rounds of Euro 96, there was also all the history between the two countries and the fact that we had not played them for a long time.

Other massive games would include the World Cup qualifier in Italy, the home win against Everton which confirmed the Premiership for us and the Cup-Winners Cup Final against Parma. Technically the biggest game I have played in has to be the Euro 96 semi-final against Germany. But who would pick a game they lost as their greatest? In his book, Wrighty says that any striker who says he does not mind not scoring so long as his side wins is a liar. It is exactly the opposite for me. I always get a buzz out of a good personal performance, but the most important thing for me is that we win. I would always be happier winning 4–3 than drawing 0–0. We need to win games to win trophies and that is the main reason I came into this game.

My other ambition was to play for England and I am not going to give up the 'England's Number One' tag easily. Nigel Martyn has been breathing down my neck for the last couple of seasons but we get along fine. There is mutual respect. If he was spouting his mouth off about me in the press, I would blank him when England get together and it would be difficult on the training pitch. But there is no nastiness with him at all and we help each other, pointing out things one or other of us might not be doing quite right. It is the same deal with Alex at Arsenal, even though it might be against my long-term interests. But when two competing 'keepers fall out, it makes life very difficult and unpleasant for everyone – I have seen it happen at other clubs.

In case you think all that is too good to be true, I will own up that I find it difficult to watch an Arsenal game if I am not playing. In my heart of hearts, I would rather we won 5–4 than 1–0. After all, there is somebody trying to win your place in the side and a part of you does want them to play poorly, so long as it does not mean we lose the game. I still have a soft spot for Leeds but these days I also like to see them letting a few goals in, because Nigel plays for them.

Strangely, Leeds have had an impact on my career ever since I left the club. It was at Elland Road that I picked up one of my nastiest injuries. I went for a low cross and ex-Arsenal striker Lee Chapman, who always liked to leave his foot in, went for it as well. There was no way he was going to get it, but he still went straight through me. I stayed down because he really caught me and when I looked down I could see two red stud marks at the top of my leg and into my groin. Gordon Strachan came up and was screaming at the ref that I was faking it, that I wasn't hurt and was just 'a pansy, a Southern softie'. And me a Rotherham lad, too. The physio was treating it when he spotted all this blood. He looked closer and found that studs had ripped into my balls as well and I needed a couple of stitches in them. When Strachan saw the blood and where it was coming from, he was out of there in a hurry and he did apologise to me later. He would be the first to admit he could be a nasty player on the pitch, physically as well as verbally. Going into managership has not changed him either. Playing at Coventry, I had gone up for a cross, got an elbow and ended up with four stitches in my head. I could hear him going on about me faking it again until one of his players told him, 'Boss, he's cut all over his head.' Again, he soon shut up.

Not all injuries are picked up on the pitch. One time, I was due to meet up for an England squad and was putting my gear into the boot of the car when I turned round and walked straight into a metal ladder that the window cleaner had left sticking out of his van. It sliced down between my nose and eye and over my brow. It nearly blinded me and I needed four stitches just above the eye. I still have the scars but it did not keep me out of the England team. Even more embarrassing was the time I was watching TV, sat with my legs under the coffee table. When I reached forward for a can of coke, without realising the can had been moved further away, I over-stretched and my hamstring pinged. To make things worse, I stupidly told the press how I had done it so they had a field day.

Treating football injuries is still not an exact science, even though there is much more equipment, all geared to getting players back to fitness quicker. Arsenal recently bought a £50,000 machine for heating muscles on the inside – all the others just heat the outside. We have regular MRI scans for bones and muscles to see if there are any tears or other damage but they still can't predict a weakness, only identify it once it has happened.

There was a big story earlier this year about the use of cortisone in treating sports people. A TV programme showed past footballers who are now crippled partly because cortisone injections helped them play through injuries. But much of it was like comparing medical treatment now with what was available during the Second World War. It is true that nearly every footballer over 26 will have had many cortisone injections. I certainly have, because they do help with certain injuries, usually when a long-term injury needs some-thing to calm it down. You never want to miss games so, if the medical people tell you that an injection will help, you have one. It usually does help and you can play. I have never been forced to have one and I trust the people at Arsenal not to give me anything that will harm me.

I had a long-standing problem with one of my hands, being able to put the little finger out wider on one hand than the other. Several times I saved low shots and the finger went into the ground and dislocated. I ended up taping it to the next finger. This went on for ages before the doctor put an injection into the joint and it cleared up straightaway.

I also have that permanent problem with a split tendon in my shoulder, although it did improve after I saw Eileen Drewery. I have been told it will not get better and that, if it finally went, I would have to have an operation. They would take the split tendon away and clean it up and re-attach it. It is a major operation, especially for a goalkeeper of my age. Tennis players often suffer from this kind of injury but can get away with an operation because there is less impact on the shoulder in their game. It is a bit different for goalies.

Although I have missed a few games with injuries, especially last season, I am not as likely to miss games through suspensions which I do not pick up as much as outfield players. I have only been sent off once, when I brought down West Ham striker Trevor Morley when he was clean through. It was a professional foul and I had to go. I have also been booked a few times, mostly for time-wasting although I think they were generally dodgy decisions.

Life is definitely becoming more difficult for goalies. They have introduced a lighter, faster Mitre ball which moves all over the place. If you hit it a certain way, it swerves both ways in flight with the same sort of reverse swing the Pakistani fast bowlers perfected. Outfield players are happy because the ball only swerves when it is hit with power, so it will only affect shots, not passes.

Nike are apparently bringing out a ball which is even faster and swerves more. In fact, all the ball manufacturers are gearing everything to developing faster and lighter balls. There is no doubt that your reactions slow as you get older which means that, if the balls keep developing in this way, it will be difficult for goalies to keep on playing after they are 35 as many of us do now. It will also be increasingly difficult for small 'keepers who struggle anyway with their shorter reach. Already, if the opposition has a small goalie, the first thing coaches say in the team talk is to give him an early clattering.

Personally, I don't mind what ball they use, because I don't want to see it coming my way in any case. When we are in the tunnel before a game, the referees will offer me the ball so that I can have an early touch. I always turn them down, as I would rather not touch the ball all afternoon. Some goalies like to be busy, with loads of saves to make but that is only a good thing if you don't make any mistakes. I would much rather have nothing to do, because I know only too well what will make the headlines in the morning. Not my nine fantastic saves but the soft one I let in.

23

• • • • • •

The Greatest and the Good

Peter Shilton is the greatest goalie I have seen and, coincidentally, it is another former Leicester player who wins my vote as the best striker.

Gary Lineker always seemed to score against me when he played for Everton and he also embarrassed me when he scored for Spurs in that nightmare semi-final. But I can't feel too bad about it because he scored against most goalies. His finishing was phenomenal, but there was a lot more to his game that just that. He was fantastic at judging his runs to beat the offside trap. I always told kids who wanted to be strikers to watch Lineker, not for his strikes on goal but for those runs. He had the intelligence to know when to run and where, that knack of getting in between defenders and finding himself the space. He was a natural finisher, though. I never knew what he was going to do and what made him particularly difficult to read was that he usually shot early. Goalies like to go out and narrow the angles, but great strikers don't wait for them to do that. When goalies haven't had the time to position themselves, that is when most goals are scored.

Tony Cottee has always had that knack, and now it looks as though Kevin Phillips has it as well. Derby's Dean Sturridge is another great finisher and a very under-rated one because he has a variety of finishes. He does not just blast it, he can place or chip it as well.

I have always admired Zola. He used to catch my eye when they first started showing Italian games on TV here. He was one of the first to develop a variety of free-kicks, not just relying on power to beat the wall and the goalie. Seeing him play for Chelsea, everyone can see he is not just a great striker but a brilliant team player, too.

He doesn't spend the game waiting for goal chances to come his way, he is making great runs and working hard when he hasn't got the ball. I love watching him play the game.

Ian Wright has been another great striker and his personality is just an extra bonus for his team. What he is like on his TV show is just how he is off-screen. He is so bubbly, it keeps everyone on their toes. The only trouble is that he is like it at eight in the morning, too. We would be away on a pre-season tour and waking up in bits because we were so tired after playing our first competitive games. We would be looking forward to having a quiet breakfast and then Wrighty would come down, shouting, joking and making as much noise as possible. We would cheerfully have strangled him at times like that, but he was great to have around and to have in your team on the pitch.

I know Tony thought that we relied too much on his goals and geared too much of our team play around him. At one stage, he even worried that we would never win the Premiership with Wrighty in the team. I didn't agree then and I don't agree now. Every team needs a player who scores freely and Wrighty scored so many goals for us. He would have played and scored more for England if he had come into the professional game earlier. That's why I was so disappointed for him when injury kept him out of the last World Cup finals.

On the pitch he would admit he is not the nicest of guys, both towards the players he is up against and also to those on his own side. He can say some nasty things in the heat of the moment but that is just the way he is. As far as we were concerned, the names he called us on the pitch were far outweighed by the goals he scored.

Off the pitch, he was no problem. I never saw a bad side of him before or after the matches. He enjoyed life and was great company. I was pleased to be invited on his *This is Your Life*, which was a very emotional occasion. Wrighty never hides his feelings, good or bad.

Gazza is a similar character. He even gets impatient when we go fishing together. If he hasn't had a bite, he always changes his bait. He complains that I catch more than him, but I tell him that is because he spends so much time tying new knots to his lines. One time, we were fishing from a jetty when he saw a fish rise much further out than we were casting. He was in such a hurry to catch it that he put too much force into his cast and his momentum toppled him head first into the water. Typical Gazza. But I would pay money to watch him play football because, at his peak, he was not just a great player but a great entertainer. He was always up to something.

I remember a time when we played Spurs at White Hart Lane. The two teams were going down the tunnel to the pitch and I felt this tugging from behind. Just as I was about to step on the pitch with 30,000 people watching, Gazza was trying to pull my shorts down. Luckily, they were tied up firmly, otherwise I would have made my entrance with my kecks around my ankles.

At my wedding to Debbie, Gazza asked my brother Colin for the key to our room. He said he just wanted to leave us his present (return Concorde tickets to New York) but Colin didn't trust him and went with him. I am glad he did because I dread to think what Gazza might have done, left alone in a bridal suite.

After his White Hart Lane antics, I bided my time until we played 'Boro a couple of seasons ago. He was on the bench that day and I spotted him signing autographs for a policeman in the tunnel. As I went by, I pulled his shorts right down and did a runner. With Gazza's luck, it is a wonder the copper didn't do him for indecent exposure.

The authorities do seem to have it in for him. I couldn't believe they went after him (and Mark Hughes) for playing in a testimonial while he was suspended last season. If he had pulled out of the game, the press would have slaughtered him for letting the crowd down. But, if the press have it in for him, he has always been popular with the people who actually play the game.

He was brilliant to watch in training for England games. He could do anything, because he had all the skills. Sometimes he would deliberately score with his knees instead of his feet, just for the hell of it. He was different to every player I have ever seen and has been a great player in his own right. He just loves his football and he loved playing for England. Even now, when his pace has gone, he still has great skills and strength.

Off the field, his problems are mainly because he is still naive about people. People are following him everywhere, determined to stitch him up. In his position, he needs to be more aware and more cagey but it is just not in his nature.

Last season, I met him at a party in London after he played at Wimbledon. The press were there and I knew they were after a Gazza story. I spotted a photographer talking to a waiter and the next thing he was bringing over a tray full of pints of beer. Gazza had his back to all this but would probably not have clocked it anyway. I leaned over and warned him, 'Whatever you do, don't turn round.' When the waiter started to offer us the beer, I told him to take it straight back. The press were just waiting for Gazza to turn round and grab a beer so that they could catch him with all those pints in front of him. I caught the snapper's eye and told him to back off. But they waited for us outside and still got their photos of Gazza, supposedly drunk again.

David Beckham is begining to get the same treatment from the press, who seem to want to knock down our greatest players. I thought the way Becks played the season after the World Cup was magnificent. Despite all the flak from the press and the abuse from the crowds, he had his best-ever season and was a major reason why Man Utd won the Treble. I have never seen anyone strike a ball the way he does. Watching him in training, he doesn't just put swerve on a free-kick but top spin as well so that it comes down quickly after it has gone over the defensive wall. He practises free-kicks all the time at England training but, as the coaches can't find four people willing to stand in a wall and have a ball battered at them all afternoon, they use steel walls on wheels. He does not need goalies to practise against because he knows when he hits it whether it would beat one or not. He knows all the right areas to hit. If it goes in that top corner with enough pace on it, no goalie is going to save it.

One strange quirk Becks has is that he always wears a brand-new pair of boots every game. Adidas do a mould of your feet, so each pair should fit exactly right from the start and you should not need to wear them in. But most players still like to get used to a pair of boots and it is just Becks who only feels right with a new pair on every time. Anyway, on his money, he could always pay someone to wear them in for him if he wanted to.

I went to Becks and Victoria's wedding but I would not say he is a close friend. I have seen more of Gazza and Incey over the years, but we all live a long way apart and there is not much time to meet up in between games for some fishing or snooker any more.

Incey became a close friend at Euro 96 when we had that marathon snooker competition. We share similar tastes – his two sons even have the same names as my two oldest children: Daniel and Thomas – and the same approach to life. He always remembers where he has come from and he does not treat people badly just because he is now a star. In fact, despite the aggressive way he looks on the pitch, off it he is naturally a very friendly person. At England get-togethers, it is always open house in his room. In fact, it was nicknamed the 'Queen Vic' at Euro 96 because he had it all set up in there: music system, playstation, drinks, the lot. And he is a great player because he is so competitive. When he was left out of the England set-up, he didn't complain. He just took it, kept putting in performances for his club and forced his way back into the reckoning.

Some players moving late in their careers from a huge club like Liverpool to somewhere not quite as big like Middlesbrough would have relaxed and taken their foot off the pedal but not Incey. He has not altered his game at all and is playing just as well and hard as ever. Every time we play against each other, he always says he is going to score against me and that he will make sure I never hear the end of it when he does. But, although he has had a couple of chances, I have managed to keep him out so far. Every time he has had a shot and missed, I have fired a little smile at him and he has had to stop himself laughing, too, in case the fans took it the wrong way.

In last season's game at the Riverside, I had to come off at half-time with a neck injury, so I was in the changing-room when I heard a huge roar in the first minute of the second half. I was upset because I knew Boro must have scored but then it came on the Tannoy that it was Incey and I burst out laughing. I shouldn't have but I couldn't help it because I knew what he would be thinking. On our coach on the way back, I sent him a text message on the mobile. It just read 'UNLUCKY'. Two hours later, I received a message back telling me what an effing whatsit I was and suggesting that I had only gone off because I knew he was going to score. As if, Incey.

But the footballer's life makes it difficult to find and keep close friends. Although I have been with Arsenal a long time, before that I was moving clubs and houses every couple of years and leaving friends behind every time. But it is also in my nature not to let friends become too close. I prefer to be friendly with lots of people rather than best mates with just a couple.

Sometimes I wonder what happened to Daryl Hawley, who was one of my best friends at Kimberworth School. He was the most talented outfield player the school had produced for years and was the one you would have put your house on making it to the top in the game. Instead, I think he just discovered what girls and pubs were for and started enjoying them more than his training. It seems a shame now, when I think what he could have achieved.

Yet I know I would not have achieved so much without the support of Debbie, my best friend as well as my wife.

24

• • • • • •

A New Start

Sandra and I had married and had our two boys while we were still very young and, at the time, neither of us had any idea of just how successful a career I was to have and the impact it would have on our lives.

Being married to any professional footballer has special difficulties because of the strange hours we keep, the travelling we do and the repeated moving of house and home as we transfer from club to club. Add to that the extra pressures of celebrity that come to those who play for the top clubs and their country, and it is no wonder that some marriages don't survive the journey. Sadly, ours was one that didn't.

As my career took off, Sandra did not enjoy life in the media spotlight. There were problems between us for some years and we were effectively estranged for about a year before I finally left. When there are children involved, this decision is all the more difficult, but I decided that it was doing the boys no good to be growing up in the middle of it all. They were only seven and eight then, but still old enough to be aware of the bad atmosphere at home. When the situation did not improve even after I moved to Arsenal and we had a new home and the chance of a new start, it was the beginning of the end.

It was at that stage when Sandra and I were living together – but apart – that I met Debbie Rodgers.

Having been persuaded by a friend to do some promotional work, Debbie had enjoyed it so much she had set up her own promotions agency – Compliments. She ran it from home, using girls she had met when she had been working for other firms. After a sticky start, she had won impressive contracts, including United Distillers and Park Lane Tobacco, by coming up with some creative ideas for themed promotions.

She tells me now that she was behaving like a typical Capricorn, who are supposed to be very career-minded. She had a few relationships and even lived with a boyfriend for four years but she was certainly not on the look-out for Mr Right or particularly anxious to settle down with anyone permanently. Then Fate stepped in – despite my best efforts to mess things up.

Another agency approached Debbie to help out supervising their promotional girls working at Arsenal. She had become bored with being stuck at home just administrating and not meeting many people, so she jumped at the chance. She was not interested in football at all, although she had pretended to be a Chelsea fan sometimes just to wind up her brother who happened to be a Gooner. So she was not impressed by or particularly interested in the Arsenal players she saw around the place. She was much happier, she told me later, gossiping with the girls she was there to supervise. But, after a while, she got to know some of us and she does remember noticing that I was very polite – better than nothing, I suppose, but hardly an overwhelming sign of love at first sight.

The last thing she fancied doing, then, was going to a pre-Christmas party where footballers had been invited but one of her close friends talked her into it. She was none too impressed with some of the chat-up lines the lads tried on her and was sliding off early when she bumped into me. We talked for an hour and just clicked but she knew I was married so, when I asked for her number, she refused to tell me. I hinted that my marriage was not a happy one, which was certainly true at that time, but she still would not cough it up. As far as she was concerned, her number was in Yellow Pages under 'Compliments' and, if I was really that interested, I would find it.

I didn't think of that, of course, so the next time I bumped into her at the club, I asked for her number again. She still refused but I could see she was wavering and her friend finally persuaded her to tell me. She wrote it down but then I went and lost the piece of paper. It was really embarrassing. I was going to look a complete idiot if I told her

I had lost it but, if I didn't, I was never going to get anywhere with her. It took some bottle but finally I owned up. She told me to forget it as it was obviously not meant to be, but I persisted and, in the end, she gave me the number again.

We talked to each other on the phone regularly for the next six months. During the same period, things were coming to a head at home and, in the end, I left and moved in with Debbie at her flat. But I made it clear that I would have left anyway and it was not a case of Debbie having broken up a marriage. In fact, because I was just coming out of one failed marriage, I was very uncertain about going into a new relationship and making it a permanent one. But, although it was a big move for both of us to make, we got on together so well straightaway that I think we both knew that it would end in marriage.

The press quickly got wind of what was happening and we were under siege. They were determined to have photographs of the two of us together so they camped outside the flat for two weeks. I remember one lot pointing two enormous telephoto lenses out of the back window of a van. As well as two cars, they even had a motorbike in the back on which to chase us in case we went out in the car. They also asked our next-door neighbour if they could come into her garden because they had seen a badger on the railway embankment and wanted to take its picture. Fortunately, she saw through that scam and told them to get lost. We even had the *News of the World* ringing up saying they were running stories in the following day's edition claiming all kinds of scurrilous rubbish.

Debbie was taking the calls and was becoming very worried about what they might print, but I kept telling her that they were all lying and simply trying to con her into talking to them. They even sent her flowers to try and persuade her to talk but I just checked every stem to make sure there was no hidden microphone. It was the worst press hassle I had ever had and, of course, Debbie had never experienced anything like it before. She began to believe they were everywhere – next door, on the roof, all over the place. One of her neighbours kindly did all the shopping for us so she did not have to run the gauntlet of the hacks and snappers. In the end, they sent a message through that, if she would pose once for a photo, they would go away and leave us alone. She didn't want to go out and just pose, so instead she went to the car and drove to the local chippie – very salacious behaviour, that. Anyway, she let them take their photos and, to be fair, it did all calm down after that.

It never stops altogether, though. One of the roofers we had working at our home this year was offered £1,000 cash to let a photographer take photos of the work we were having done. Luckily, the one they tapped was the boss and he said he would check with us first. The guy offering the bribe shot off pretty sharpish then.

Debbie is used to this kind of thing now but, when it first happened, it was difficult for her and for her family. Her parents were being approached by the press and, although they were understandably not totally happy about me because I was still married, they stuck by me and their daughter and did not say anything critical to the media.

Debbie's parents had met in Oxfordshire, where her American father, Robbie, was stationed with the US Air Force. Instead of her mother, Georgina, doing what most GI brides did and going back with him to the States, Robbie decided to stay with her in the UK and became a property developer. Debbie's mum, always very lively and extrovert, had found a good foil in her dad, who is calm and thoughtful. They had four children, two of each, with Debbie the youngest.

Debbie was born in Kensington and lived in different parts of North London when she was growing up. She did OK at school but she remembers that she was just impatient to grow up and get on with her life. She has always been ambitious. She went on to sixth-form college and, while she was there, decided she would become a fashion buyer. She went to work for Fenwick's in Brent Cross and worked her way up, but left after a couple of years because there were just too many people ahead of her, head buyers who were young and not about to leave.

It was the same story when she switched to the Halifax Building Society so she left again and toyed with the idea of taking a year off and going to America, staying with her dad's family and studying again. But, when it came to it, she admits she wasn't brave enough to leave her parents for a country she had only been to once and to stay with family she hardly knew.

Instead she stayed in London and ending up starting Compliments. As far as I am concerned, it was the best decision she ever made.

When we were first together, I used to help her out with the business. She had no permanent staff because the promotions business is all peaks and troughs. Its busiest times coincided with trade fairs and motor shows and then it was all hands to the pumps. I would help her stuff endless presentation packs and I can remember the pair of us counting out about 2,000 knives, forks and spoons for one particular job. I would also help out delivering packs to shops. Sometimes the managers would deliberately keep Debbie waiting and be positively unfriendly. It was as if she was a rep trying to sell them something rather than helping them sell their stock. When I went in her place, they used to double-take when they saw me and their attitude suddenly changed. No one was rude to me. Even if they didn't recognise me, I was 6ft 4in and that always prompts a little politeness.

I had been living in a large house in Waltham Abbey, so moving to a two-bedroom flat in Kensal Green which backed on to a railway line was quite a culture shock. Debbie owned the flat and had made it very trendy so I soon adjusted, even though I never quite got used to the way the indoor plants shook every time a train went by. It was more central than anywhere I had lived in London before and nowhere was more than a fiver's taxi ride. We were past the disco and clubbing stage, but we went out to restaurants and friends' places and generally had a good time.

We lived there for about two years and then moved to Chorley-wood in 1995. It was a decent house but quite rundown so, with the help of Debbie's dad, it was totally gutted and redeveloped. We were still living there when I played in Euro 96 and that was when we realised its downside – the garden was overlooked. With all the publicity surrounding Euro 96, we found that people started turning up at the front door. We found we could never relax so, 18 months on, we sold it and bought our current home, originally a farmhouse, in Hertfordshire.

I had invited my parents down to London for Euro 96 and that was as a direct result of my getting together with Debbie. She was very close to her parents, and I got on very well with them, too. Her mother's real name was Dorothy, but Robbie always called her Georgina because he preferred that name and I was the only other person allowed to call her that, too. With that background, Debbie was appalled when she found I was barely speaking to my parents. They and my first wife, Sandra, had not got on at all and I was piggy in the middle. I had taken the easy way out and kept them at arm's length, but it meant there was a definite rift between us. Debbie told me that I had to sort things out and repair the relationship. I called them and told them I was leaving Sandra and later I introduced them to Debbie. They got on very well from the start and, since then, I have seen a lot more of Mum and Dad and we speak regularly on the phone.

Before, it had been difficult for them back home in Rotherham. Their friends would always be asking after me and often they did not know what I was doing at all. Everyone was assuming, wrongly, that I was sending them tickets for games when Arsenal played up North. Fed up with having to pretend they had seen me when they hadn't, they decided one day when Arsenal were playing Leeds that they would avoid their local pub. Instead they drove five miles in the opposite direction and stopped at another pub at random. They saw disco lights upstairs and a coach outside and realised there must be some kind of a 'do' on. But the bar downstairs was empty, and they had just bought a couple of drinks when the party upstairs moved down. It was all the people from their own local who were over for a fishing club party. Straightaway it was, 'Rog . . . Pam . . . been to the game?' They didn't try that one again and it was good for all of us when we became close again.

My divorce came through in October 1995 but it was almost another three years before Debbie and I married. We did not think there was any need to rush into it but, sadly and out of the blue, Debbie's mum was diagnosed with bowel cancer. After a major operation followed by other treatments, we lost her within three months of the cancer being diagnosed. It was a terrible shock and devastating for all of us, but obviously most of all for Robbie, Debbie, her sister Karen and brothers Robert and Richard. I had to draw on all my resources to support Debbie through this difficult time. And it was hard for me, too, because I had lost a very special friend.

Ever since Debbie had first taken me home to meet her parents, her mum had been very good to me. We immediately struck up a good rapport with plenty of gentle mickey-taking but many was the time I would get back home to find her doing some painting or gardening to help us out. She was a great lady. The one comfort for the two of us was that she passed away knowing we were engaged to be married.

In April 1997, I had realised the time was right to ask Debbie to marry me. I had found out what kind of engagement ring she would like – a heart-shaped diamond – and 'borrowed' one of her other rings so that the jeweller would know the right size. Her parents were going away for the weekend but, before her dad left our house, I took my chance. After we had said goodbye at the door, I made an excuse to run after him up the drive. Through his car window, I asked him for his permission to marry his daughter – which he was happy to give. (In fact, from that moment, Debbie's mum always introduced me as their son-in-law.)

The following week, Debbie and I went out for a meal. While she was getting ready, I nipped out into the garden and put candles around our 'lovers' nest', a sheltered alcove with a bench inside just big enough for two and with a dovecote on top. After the meal, I made sure I went into the house first so that I could pick up the ring. Then I let the dogs out into the garden, so that I had a reason to go out there and I rushed around lighting all the candles. Then I went back in and suggested we went for a walk with the dogs because it was such a nice night. Debbie said it was far too cold and I had to work hard to persuade her. She said afterwards that she couldn't understand why I wanted to go out on such a chilly night, and only agreed when I said I wanted to show her something the dogs had done.

Even when she saw the candles, she didn't twig. 'Who did all that?' she asked. 'Who do you think?' I said. And I led her into the lovers' nest, sat her down on the bench, got down on one knee, and asked her to marry me. Even though we had talked about the ring, she was still surprised by all this but happily for me it didn't stop her saying 'yes'.

But, as anyone who has ever organised a wedding knows, that was the easy part. We now had to decide where to marry and who to invite. We looked at dozens of places, searching for somewhere that we both liked and also for somewhere secure, because we had decided to allow *OK!* magazine exclusive rights to the wedding. Some people say they can't understand why any couple would do something like that but, for us at least, there was a very good reason.

Our friends in the press warned us that, if we didn't, we had no chance of keeping all of them out. The ceremony would be turned into a circus with photographers all battling each other for the best vantage-points. Our best bet, they told us, was to let one paper or magazine have the exclusive rights and, with them, the responsibility for all the security on the day. It would, of course, be as much in their interests as ours to keep all the other media out. Once we decided this was a good idea, we thought we preferred a glossy magazine rather than a tabloid so it came down to a straight choice between *OK!* and *Hello*. The fee covered the cost of the wedding but the money was not the point; we wanted the day to run smoothly and this seemed the best way of making sure it did.

We fixed a date: 15 July 1998. This was the week *after* the World Cup Final, just in case . . . We had more faith in England than its captain clearly did – Alan Shearer had booked his holiday for a couple of weeks earlier. It would normally have been my first day back at Arsenal for pre-season training, but I had special dispensation to start later because I had played in the World Cup.

We had been stuck over a venue for some time when Debbie remembered Castle Ashby in Northamptonshire from a Ford car promotion she had worked on years before. At first I thought: Northampton – no way. Then I realised that, off Junction 14 on the M1, the castle would actually be quite convenient because there would be almost as many guests coming down from the north as from the south.

I was sold on it the moment we turned into the drive. There is a lodge and then all you see is a mile-long, dead-straight road leading to the castle at the bottom. As we drove along, the castle just loomed larger and larger and looked more and more impressive. Its banqueting space was not that large, though, which meant we were limited as to numbers and some family on both sides were disappointed. We decided to invite just close family and close friends – in all, about 120.

Bob Wilson agreed to be my Best Man and I stayed with him the night before. The only unauthorised photograph that was taken the whole day was of the pair of us arriving at the castle. Since we had not changed into our wedding togs, it was a photo they could have taken any time. They still used it, though, because it was the only one they had of either me or Debbie.

While we were changing, we heard a helicopter hovering overhead. It was the press trying to get shots of the guests in the courtyard, where drinks were being served. *OK!*'s security called the police and the next thing there was a police chopper guiding the press one away. It is apparently against the law for helicopters to hover over a private residence without permission. The castle had its own church in the grounds and the press thought that was where we would be married, not appreciating that it was a non-starter as I had been married before. Security moved in to clear them away, anyway, and found photographers hidden in bushes and up trees.

Debbie's day had an unusual start. She had stayed at home the night before with the bridesmaids (her best friend, Debbie, and two nieces Natalie and Lora) and, in the morning, had to feed our sheep and chickens before setting off for the castle. This was *before* she changed into her wedding dress, mind. I don't think the wellies would have set it off properly. For some reason, she didn't realise they would be able to have breakfast at the castle, so she stopped at a bakery on the way to stock up on buns and cakes. Staff at the castle were amazed when they turned up with enough food for a family picnic.

After that, everything went just about perfectly on the day. There were one or two gripes about the photographers because they were doing celebrity shots as a priority rather than the usual family groups. But we were very happy with everything that was done by *OK!* and part of the deal was that every guest received a selection of photographs afterwards. As the main photographer was Terry O'Neill, this was a good deal for everyone.

Most of the guests stayed over at the castle and we had the State suite. It was magnificent, with a four-poster and huge fireplace in a set of rooms full of antiques and paintings. It almost made us feel as though we should have spent our whole honeymoon in there. *OK!* wanted to buy rights to our honeymoon, too, but we just thought that was going too far. The following day, we had a quick meeting with the magazine before flying off to Bermuda where we had no hassle from the press at all.

When we flew back, we arrived at Heathrow at 6 a.m. and I was at Arsenal for training by 10 a.m. The honeymoon was well and truly over.

Which is more than can be said for the work we were and still are having done at our home. We seemed to have been living with the builders as long as we had lived with each other but it should be worth it in the end – hopefully this year.

Ours is a sixteenth-century house, which was originally part of a small farm which grew larger over the centuries, and has had a colourful history. A fighter pilot is supposed to have crashed his plane into the paddock during the last war; the actor James Mason was a previous owner; and local gossip has it that Princess Alexandra was a regular house guest.

We had found it completely by accident. We were in an Indian restaurant in the area when two guys came up and started to talk to me about football. Debbie was bored and opened the local rag where she saw an advert for this house. We went there the next day and, as soon as we saw the gates, the drive and house, we wanted it. It needed a lot of work but the price was reasonable so, in April 1997, we moved in. All the place lacked was a fishpond so I had one dug. It's a big one so I had to pipe the water in to fill it (I made sure I avoided seeing the next water bill as we are metered). Then I stocked it with a dozen common carp, a few eels and perch and a couple of roach. There are now thousands of little carp on which the other fish will start feeding. It is developing its own eco-system, which is exactly what I wanted. We also have five Jacob's sheep, which look more like goats and are sheared for me once a year by a local farmer, and four chickens, which lay two or three eggs a day. The sheep are fantastic lawn-mowers, which is why I took them on. They keep the grass nice and tidy.

It is so quiet where we live that the main traffic down our lane is a succession of horse-riders. Tempted by the sight of them, Debbie and I decided to have riding lessons at a local school. I told them I was 6ft 4in and 15 stone so I needed a big horse. But, when they brought this massive horse out of the stables, I thought I might have made a serious mistake. But I still climbed into the saddle and, while we were walking around the stable, everything was fine. Then we walked by a hedge with a road on the other side. A car went by and the horse bolted – just for a few seconds but it was enough to feel all that power. It was frightening but I still enjoyed it. My only problem is that I appear to be allergic to horse dust. I started to sneeze and my eyes puffed up so I might have to wear gloves if I want to carry on riding.

At least Arsenal does not have a problem with players horse-riding. The only activities I know the club bans players from doing are skiing and motorbiking. Mind you, they might think again about horse-riding if they knew our dogs: Charlie, Maxie and Sadie, all rescue dogs (or bitches, to be precise) from the RSPCA, one of the charities I support. They all go absolutely mad when the horses go down our lane.

The latest addition to our menagerie is an African grey parrot called Rosie. She was my surprise birthday present from Debbie two years ago. Debbie had to keep her hidden in the house overnight but I don't know how she kept her quiet, unless she stayed up all night with her hand over her beak. This is not a quiet parrot. African greys are superb mimics and she quickly had Debbie, me, the dogs, the phone ring, and even the washing machine off to a T.

And Rosie has lasted a lot longer than a feathery present from Chris Evans.

I have been on *TFI Friday* several times but one time when I thought I was just going on to talk about football Chris kept asking me where Debbie and the dogs were. I was making some excuse when they all walked on to the set. Because the show went out on or near St Valentine's Day, and Chris knew we had a farm, he bought us two white doves to take home. He promised us that a proper dovecote would be sent on afterwards. But a week passed with no sign of a dovecote. We put the pair in one of the rooms in our adjoining cottage, which we are also having renovated. We fed and watered them, and they repaid us by crapping absolutely everywhere. I went to the pet shop and explained our problem. They were reassuring. Once the doves have been in there three or four days, they said, I could just open the window. They would fly out but come back later because they would know that was where their food would be. Wrong. When I opened the window they flew out and never came back.

The dovecote came the next day and I put it up just in case but they had gone for good. They had flown back to the place where Chris's people had bought them, but that was a blessing in disguise. I have found out since that they breed so fast, you have to keep taking the eggs out or they overrun you. It wouldn't exactly have been a scene out of Hitchcock's *The Birds*, but they would have made a terrible mess of the place.

But, however much wildlife we were going to surround ourselves with, there was never any chance of it being any kind of a substitute family. We were both keen to start a real one of those together so we were delighted to learn in July 1999 that Debbie was pregnant. We kept quiet about it until she reached three months and then we told our family and close friends. In fact, the day before we had agreed to spill the beans, my mum phoned me and was saying, 'Isn't it about time you had a baby?' I had to lie through my teeth and tell her we were still trying.

The next day, I was playing for England against Belgium at Sunderland's Stadium of Light. In the players' lounge after the game, I met Mum and just dropped into the conversation, 'By the way, Debbie's pregnant.' She was so delighted, she went all red and goosepimply.

We chose not to find out whether it was a boy or a girl in advance, so that it was a surprise when, on 24 April 2000, Debbie gave birth to a baby girl, Georgina Megan. I would like to have more but, for the moment, Georgina will bring more than enough change into our lives.

My life had already changed – and for the better – from the moment Debbie and I got together. She has just been so good for me. She was so organised in her own life, owning her own home and running her own business, that it seemed to shift me into a higher gear. I think that at that stage in my life and my career I needed an extra push and she delivered it.

I don't believe it was any coincidence that my career really took off so soon after we met and it was no one-off boost, either. It has been moving in the right direction ever since to the stage that we are now both looking forward and planning what happens after my playing days are over.

She did not take over as my manager until after Euro 96 but it was because she was dealing so efficiently with what my agent at the time was sending through that we made that decision in the first place. She eventually wound up her own promotions agency because she could not do both. Willow and I always say that the difference between a good goalie and a great goalie is tiny but it is that little bit extra, that added edge that counts. And Debbie has been that little bit extra for me in my life.

I am a Virgo, so it is in my nature to be organised myself, but I simply don't have the time to deal with everything at home and in my career. I am away so much that Debbie has had to take control of important areas like the finances, running the house and dealing with the various building contractors. She has taken it all on board and handled it brilliantly. I am very easygoing but I do have a few hard and fast likes and dislikes and Debbie has learned to cope with them as well. For a start, she knows I will turn down most jobs, however lucrative, if they mean I will miss my Sunday lunch. I just love a roast so I hate it when I have to play on a Monday because I know a roast is too heavy a meal for the day before a game. I have become interested in wine and keep a small cellar of good bottles at home, and now I also enjoy a cigar or two. I have never smoked cigarettes but I saw how much Debbie's dad, Robbie, enjoyed his cigars so I thought I would try one. Now I keep a selection of Davidoffs, Monte Cristos and a few others. I even have my own humidor, although I only smoke in the games room at home. I usually have a cigar when I go fishing but I don't smoke in public because I think it is the wrong image for me to present.

How I look has always been important to me. I have already admitted how I have to have a new goalie jersey or socks if there is the tiniest pull in them. It is the same with my normal clothes: if I spot a little crease in my jacket on my way out of the door, I will stop, take it off and iron it out myself.

I like to buy from all different designers and, although most of the time I am happiest to be casual, wearing trainers, an old (but clean) pair of jeans and T-shirt, when I am going somewhere smart in the evening I really go for it. I love the traditional English gentleman look with smart cuff links, highly-polished shoes, even a money-clip. I was delighted to win an *Elle* style award in 1998. It was presented by Sophie Dahl and, since the lads didn't give me too much stick about it, I reckon I must have deserved it.

25

......

Safe Hands, MBE

The day after Pol Pot died in April 1998, the story was the front-page lead in every newspaper except the *Sun* which, instead, led on my car crash in a service station off the M1.

Well, obviously. A crash in which no one was injured, let alone killed, was clearly more newsworthy than the death of the man blamed for the killing fields of Cambodia. After all, the crash involved a 'celebrity'. It is one of the things I have had to get used to – the change from being a snotty-nosed kid kicking a ball about in Rotherham to having the most minor events in my life reported in the papers. Although only the *Sun* rated it up there in importance with Pol Pot's demise, most of the papers ran the story of my crash somewhere in their pages.

I have to admit it was a crash with its funny side. I was on my way to the Birmingham NEC for the launch of the new England Umbro kit when I pulled into a busy service area. There were cars going in all directions as I looked for the sign to the petrol station. As I drove my soft-top Jaguar XK8 towards it, a car was suddenly across my path and there was an almighty crunch as the two cars met. The airbags activated and there was so much dust from them that I thought it was smoke and jumped straight out of the car in case it was on fire. I went to check on the other driver and, when she saw who she had hit, she was horrified. I think she could already see the headlines because, of all things, she was a journalism student on work experience at a motoring magazine (*Top Gear*) and this was the first time she had been given a car – a brand-new Peugeot 306 – to test.

There was no chance of keeping it quiet, either. There were too many people about who had seen what had happened and recognised me. As luck would have it, there was even a press photographer on the scene. So it was a classic news decision for Fleet Street to make:

the death of foreign dictator held responsible for genocide of his own people?

or

a car park shunt with no casualties but involving a sports celebrity and a car magazine's greenhorn writer who – even better – was a woman off on her first test-drive?

I can't complain about the tone of the stories they ran because they used quotes from the other driver about how I had been polite and understanding despite our collision. The truth was that it was as much my fault as hers, as the knock-for-knock insurance settlement reflected. But it made a better story the way they told it. But there was a lot more damage to my car than to hers and, although the garage fixed it up, I sold it soon afterwards. And I reckon I lost something like £10,000 on the deal. Because the crash had been given so much publicity, everyone knew my car had been in a big smash and therefore would not touch it unless I brought the price right down.

It was not the biggest or most expensive smash I've had, though. That came after we played Wimbledon at Selhurst Park in April 2000. We had come back by coach to our training ground where we had all left our cars. It had just started raining and the road was already very wet when I turned my Aston Martin DB7 out of the car park, straightened up and began to accelerate away. I must have pushed it a bit too hard as, when I went into a gentle bend about 60 yards along the road, I felt the back end swing out. I tried to correct it but only succeeded in turning the car sideways. I hit the kerb and the car flipped right over.

It was a scary moment. It had happened so fast – one moment I was in control, the next I was helpless. Even though there must have been a lot of noise from the engine and the stereo, it seemed as though my world went quiet for a few seconds as the car took off and I knew I was in serious trouble.

Fortunately it cleared a ditch and had a soft landing in a clump of small trees and bushes. But the car was on its soft-top roof and I was trapped inside. I tried forcing my way into one small gap but I could only get my legs through. The rest of my body stuck, so I had to wriggle back inside.

All this time the horn was blaring and the car was full of dust from the airbags. I started to panic as I was worried about the car blowing up. I tried to smash one of the windows with my elbow, and then I heard Lee Dixon shouting. He had been driving behind me and had stopped when he saw my car go off the road. There was too much noise for him to hear what I was shouting back but, as he pulled at the driver's door, I pushed it from the inside. Because they don't have frames, the force of this twin assault shattered all the windows as well as opening the door. The glass was flying everywhere as I forced my way out. As I put my feet down on what I thought was the ground, my legs went knee-deep into branches and thorns. I was treading where the bushes and trees had been crushed by the car and they gave me the worst injuries of the accident as my legs were badly scratched.

When the story came out in the papers, I was quoted as saying – referring to Lee's efforts – that the back four had dug me out of trouble once again. Good quote – except I never said it. The papers missed the best quote. I had gone back to the training ground to be checked and cleaned up by the club physio. The police had also come along to ask me what had happened, and then Arsène walked in. The first thing he said was, 'You see, David, that's why we don't let you have a drink on the coach.'

I hadn't had a drink for days and, although I was playing INXS on the stereo, I wasn't speeding, either, so the police had no problems with it. They had got there pretty quickly but the press were slower off the mark. The first photographer arrived as the car was being taken away to the garage and he could only grab a shot of it on the back of the pick-up. I had only had the car about 15 months and the repair bill was £50,000. The press staked out the garage but the car was kept under wraps and out of sight. There were more reporters hanging about in the rain outside my house and Lee's as well. I am still surprised at the lengths they will go to for a story.

Although it was Euro 96 that really propelled me into this strange celebrity world, I had already had a taste after those penalty saves against Sampdoria in the Cup-Winners Cup. They had been shown live on TV and, as a result, I was invited on to Sir David Frost's late-night TV show. I had done a few TV slots before but this was my first major interview on a programme with a big audience.

I would have been nervous anyway, but what made it worse was that it was live and that, when I was introduced, I knew I would have to walk from the back of the studio down a flight of steps to the studio floor. My insides were in an uproar and I kept asking myself what I had let myself in for, but I managed to negotiate the steps without falling over and to survive the interview without making too much of a fool of myself. I even quite enjoyed it in the end, but it was all a bit of a blur. All I can remember now is that Boy George was one of the other guests along with someone from *Private Eye*, and that things got a bit heated when George started on about gay rights and gay MPs.

After that experience, I started doing a few more TV shows but it was after Euro 96 that it all took off. I was asked on all the chat shows and I enjoyed doing them.

Then we met David Frost again at a movie premiere and he invited us to his summer garden party in Chelsea. It was a surreal experience: there were all these famous people there but, because it was just after Euro 96, most of them were queuing up for my autograph. At one stage, I had Bob Hoskins telling me to lean on his back to write one and I'm saying, 'I can't do that, you're my hero.'

My all-time hero is Michael Caine and I met him there, too. Sometimes your heroes are disappointing in real life, but not him. He is exactly as you see him on TV or film – a friendly, witty, funny man and completely natural.

We have also been to David's country house for Sunday lunches. Other guests are a mix of politicians, rock stars, showbiz celebrities and financiers but, after lunch, everybody joins in a five-a-side game – 'kids v dads' – in the garden. David is a big football fan and apparently was a decent goalie in his youth. A big lunch is hardly the ideal preparation and we have to play in the clothes we have turned up in but it is another surreal experience I could never have imagined having when I was diving into those canals back in Rotherham. Not too many people ever have the chance to tackle a cabinet minister or ankle-tap Rory Bremner. Princess Diana had been godmother to one of David's sons, George, who is a regular team-mate of mine in those five-a-sides. She was obviously irreplaceable, but David thought George would still appreciate having another godparent and I was honoured when he chose me. Although I have met Prince Charles, it is one of my few regrets that I never had the chance to meet Diana. I had a lot of admiration for her, and both Debbie and I took flowers to Kensington Palace when she died.

At first, I was nervous meeting famous people, feeling a million miles from their lives, but now I am fine about it. I soon realised that no one is expecting a massively intellectual conversation and, if I just concentrate on being myself, that is all that is expected. It has helped that I have Debbie with me now as she copes extremely well with this lifestyle. She has been very independent in her own life so she is confident in herself and has no hang-ups about most of the attention being focused on me rather than her.

But, although I am getting used to this taste of the lives of the rich and famous, there was no chance of my being at all blasé when I was summoned to Buckingham Palace to receive an MBE for services to football. This was the biggest thrill in my life, bar none. It has to rank ahead of any of the trophies I have won, World Cups I have played in or saves I have made. It was made even more special when I learned that it was the Prime Minister of the time, John Major, who had recommended me for the honour.

As far as I was concerned, it came right out of the blue as part of the New Year's Honours List for 1997. I was officially informed about a month beforehand but it was made very clear that I was not to tell anyone. Debbie knew because, as my manager, she opens all my mail, but I had to keep it from all my other family and friends. This was the hardest part but I was told this story of someone who had their award taken away because he threw a party to celebrate before it was announced. I don't know whether it is true but it certainly put the frighteners on me. They always tell the press the day before the awards are officially announced so that they can put it in the following day's papers, but I didn't know that so, when the journalists rang me up for my reaction, I refused to say anything. In fact, I kept quiet about it until I saw it on Teletext.

The day itself was so frightening, easily the most nerve-racking experience of my life. I had the top hat and the rest of the outfit but I just didn't know what to expect. Debbie was with me but the first thing that happens when you arrive at Buckingham Palace is that friends and family are sent in one direction while award recipients are taken to a separate room. There we were given the protocol of what to do during the ceremony. We were told to join our queue, walk forward, turn to one side, walk straight forward to the Queen, shake her hand (but not too hard), then walk backwards, never turning your back on her. Sounds fairly simple now but, at the time, all I could think of was that I was going to get it all wrong in front of her.

After our instruction, we were led down the back corridors of the Palace and through a door into a massive ballroom which was full of guests. At the back was a large orchestra, all the guards . . . and the Queen. When I went up to receive my MBE, she said, 'You're the footballer, aren't you?' Arsenal had played the night before and she was obviously well-briefed because she mentioned it. We must have lost because I can remember saying, 'Just don't ask me the result.' She had a chuckle at that and there is a photograph of us both laughing.

There is a video made of the day and there is also a commemorative book you can buy. Palace merchandising is almost as sharp as Man Utd's.

When Tony Adams was later awarded his MBE, he asked me what the day was like and I said that it was very frightening and he thought I was winding him up. He couldn't believe it had made me that nervous. After his day at the Palace, he admitted that I was right. He had never been so nervous in his life either.

I can remember walking down the corridors after it was all over and punching the air in triumph because I had got through it without making a mistake. It was even better than saving a penalty.

I have met the Queen on other occasions since and it is always a thrill.

One time, Debbie and I were invited to the Royal Box at a Cartier-sponsored polo match. We'd had an escort from our marquee and I can remember all the photographers effing and blinding because the security men were stopping them taking the pictures they wanted, the first ones of us after our wedding and honeymoon.

In the box we met the Argentinian ambassador and the actor, Dan Ackroyd, but the Queen was watching the match from a gantry above. We were wondering what happened next when a member of her staff asked us if we would like to have tea. We refused, thinking we would rather go back to our marquee. But he said, 'No, tea with the Queen.' We changed our minds rather quickly and were taken round the back of the box where it was being served and the Queen was there, chatting away to everyone.

Sometimes it is hard to believe that this all started with me kicking a ball about in a park in Rotherham.

26

......

Looking Ahead

Anyone who says he has planned his career in football is either kidding himself or telling porkies. The simple fact is that planning your career in this game is a waste of time because there are too many factors beyond a player's control: injuries, form, changes of club and country managers, to name just a few. But I have to admit that, if I had planned my own career, I could not have made a better job of it. There have been many more ups than downs and apart – maybe – from failing to making it to the top with my first club, Leeds, there is nothing about it that I would have changed.

Instead of the roller-coaster career that some high-profile players have gone through, mine has been one of steady improvement. All the time I have been moving to better clubs, playing for better teams with better players in better leagues and, let's be honest, for a lot better money.

In some ways, though, my life in the game has turned full circle. When I started, I played simply because I loved playing; then it became my work because that is how I earned money for my family; now, with the end of my playing career in sight, I am starting to realise how much I still enjoy it. To be fair, I have never turned up for training at any of my clubs and wished for a moment I was doing something else for a living.

Debbie believes I will play till I am 40. I don't. At this level, standards are too high and I don't want to go down the leagues. I think I might have had enough by the time I do finish and that I won't miss playing too much. I hope so, anyway, because there is nothing much I can do about it if I do. I will keep myself fit and still play in testimonials and celebrity games – but probably as a striker just so I can give some other poor goalie a clattering. But I am sure the buzz of playing for real will be irreplaceable. It will be hard to find anything to match the high I feel after every game, which makes it difficult for me to sleep that night.

Alan Hansen quit the game early because he admitted that, by the end, he couldn't stand the pressure of playing. He was so nervous and knotted up before games that it was a relief to be out of it and he says he doesn't miss it at all. Strangely, it will probably be those nerves that I will miss most.

But, just as in the rest of my career, it won't be my decision alone which influences when that final moment comes. This season (2000–01) is, as well as being my testimonial year at Arsenal, also the last year of my contract so I will not be moving anywhere before it is over. Now that the taxman has made clubs limit testimonials to players who stay for at least ten years, there will be fewer and fewer of them, so I want to make the most of mine. Ideally, I would like an England XI to be Arsenal's opponents for my game. I remember playing for one against Liverpool in front of a big crowd for Hansen's testimonial but I suspect it would be difficult now to get the FA to agree to this in the middle of a busy season. And I am determined that the game will not be played in the close season. Tony Adams scheduled his game for a week after the pre-season Makita tournament and, although he had hundreds of fans sending him their ticket money in the post because they were away on holiday, it didn't make up for a very disappointing crowd of 12,000.

By the end of this season, I will be coming up to 38 so it might be a good idea to finish then. Then again, it might not. At the moment, I would like to have a contract for another year after this one but Arsène Wenger will have a major say in what I finally decide. He has made it clear that he is grooming Alex to take over from me sooner rather than later. Although he still has problems with big match nerves, Alex is an excellent goalie, but if I find I am number two at the end of this season, then it will obviously be time to move on or to move out altogether. It is a hard decision to get right. I believe Peter Schmeichel quit Man Utd too early. I am sure he would have had another couple of years at the top level. One thing I am unlikely to do is an Alan Shearer or a John Collins – that is, retire from international football before I do from the club game.

I might feel differently after I have reflected on Euro 2000 but I doubt it. For a start, I find that playing in the Premiership is more draining than international football rather than the other way round. Those players who have retired from international football perhaps felt they could not continue to raise their game from club to international standard but, so far, that has not happened to me. There were a few rumours, particularly after Euro 96, of a top European club coming in for me but nothing came of them. It may be too late for me now, but I have always thought it would be good to live and play abroad for a couple of years. The USA is still a possibility as the pressures would not be as great as they are in Europe, and Debbie and I would not need to learn a new language.

Manu Petit told me he'd had lots of offers from Italian clubs before coming to Arsenal, but just did not want the kind of life top players have in that football-mad country. They train afternoons as well as mornings and spend half the week staying in hotels away from their families. Arsène would love it but Manu said he chose to come to England because he knew the lifestyle would be more relaxed for him. It was a surprise when, with Marc, he agreed to join Barcelona at the beginning of 2000/01.

Not that it is always that relaxed here. If we have a Wednesday night game away at, say, Liverpool, I leave home Tuesday morning and will not be back until very late on Wednesday night and I might be staying away at a London hotel on Friday night, too, for a derby game.

But, if playing is increasingly taking over players' lives, imagine what it is like for managers and coaches. I am with Hansen on this one, as I really don't fancy being a manager. For a start, I am not a great watcher of games. It would drive me batty if I had to watch the number of videos that Arsène and Pat Rice sit through. I can't even watch a full game on Sky, never mind watching videos of players I might want to buy or who are in teams my club is due to play. But the pair of them do it all the time, which is one of the reasons Arsène is such a good manager and Pat is a well-respected coach. But I can't imagine ever wanting to put myself through it.

On the other hand, just doing some goalkeeping coaching does have some appeal to me. In fact, Bob Wilson's situation would be ideal: some TV work mixed with some coaching.

I am definitely not after Ray Clemence's job as full-time England goalkeeping coach, though. He has to watch game after game to monitor different goalkeepers of all ages. Frankly, I just don't think I would have the patience.

It would be the same with management, although I have to admit I did enjoy the little taste of it I had the season before last, courtesy of Sky TV. It was part of a series called 'Guiding Stars', which took well-known personalities with a particular skill and challenged them to pass it on to a group of amateurs. The sporting programmes were presented by Lawrence Dallaglio, then captain of the England rugby team, who was made temporary manager of a woman's rugby team, while I became manager of Chiltern FC, a pub team playing football in the Chesham Sunday League. The team reached its own cup final for the first time in its history and I found the whole experience very rewarding even though I had a few second thoughts during our training sessions in the wind and rain of a typical English winter.

I enjoyed working on the programme but I still believe that managing a professional club is not for me. The expectations and the pressures would be so much greater and the job is just so time-consuming. There are other things I want to do with my life when I stop playing, like more fishing, more travelling and more TV work.

Now I try to go fishing at least once a week but, as the games pile up during the season, it becomes more and more difficult, especially with all the hotel overnights as well. I would love to go on long fishing trips to France, which is where the biggest carp can be caught. The record carp here is 56 pounds; in France, they can catch 70 pounders. I know this because, to Debbie's horror, I subscribe to just about every fishing magazine there is, including *The Crafty Carper* and *Carp Talk*.

But, if you think that's sad, you should know that Chris Tarrant is, if anything, even more fanatical about fishing than I am. For a while, every time we met we would talk about going fishing together and eventually we arranged to go to my local lake at Croxley, which is a beautiful spot and very quiet, with few members.

I turned up as usual in my Range Rover and I couldn't believe it when I saw that Chris had driven his S-class Mercedes right up to the water's edge. He was stood there in all the gear, right down to the traditional fishing hat with old flies stuck in it and a pair of dodgy wellies.

I have got to know the owners of the fishery very well but it did not go unnoticed that it was only when I had Chris along that they suddenly produced a tray of tasty sarnies and a bottle of wine to keep us going while we fished. I have never let them forget it, either, but at least I was the only one to catch a fish that first time.

Chris has been fishing longer than me and has done the lot – carp, trouting and coarse fishing. He has fished abroad, too, in places like Canada. I have not really fished abroad except on a trip to Florida with *Wish You Were Here . . . ?* and a holiday to Tobago, where I tried deep-sea fishing. I did not really enjoy that because we were using big thick lines and thick rods and I couldn't 'feel' the fish.

I would also like to see more of the world. Fans might think I have travelled all over the world already and been paid for it into the bargain. But all that the players generally see is the hotel and ground. We are taken to the games, and the management are not keen to let us out and about on our own for security reasons.

It has not been first class all the way, either. Most of the time the club or England charter planes and try to fit in as many seats as possible so there is not much leg-room for big fellas like goalies and central defenders. We end up with our knees around our ears. Even when we fly scheduled, it is usually business class for us while the manager, directors and other staff travel first class. At least, if there are fans on board, they are not allowed to mingle with the players. That could lead to some dodgy situations on the flight home as, if you have been beaten, someone could decide to come up and have a go.

But I am not complaining. After all, we are travelling to do a job and not to sightsee and there have been a few memorable moments such as when the Concorde pilot flew over the pyramids on the way back from my first international in Saudi Arabia and when we were allowed to kick a ball about in the Forbidden City. When I have stopped playing, there will be time to see more of the world beyond the football stadium.

I am also keen to do more TV work. I am not suggesting I front something like Wrighty's show, because I know I couldn't handle that but I do see myself doing a more relaxed kind of chat show, probably with a sports angle. One suggestion from David Frost was for a show which sees me doing the interview while playing the sports star at his or her sport. I am lucky enough to be able to play quite a few sports – golf, tennis etc – to a good standard so I think it would work. David wanted to sign me up to do this for one of his production companies a couple of years ago but I have put him off until I finish playing. This was not just because I would not have the time to do it now but also that people are quick to get on your back if you have other interests. They point to them if you don't play well as happened with Wrighty when he went to Celtic.

But there is a difficult balancing act here. It is while you are playing that you have the highest profile and these offers are made. I know there is a danger that the phone will stop ringing when I stop playing so it is important to have some plans in place to keep my profile high enough even when I stop.

I have had quite a lot of TV experience now. One of my first programmes was *Parallel Nine*, a children's show on Saturday mornings, and I have worked for the Disney and Nickelodeon channels as well. One of my biggest thrills, though, was a fishing video I presented with a long-time friend of mine, Andy Little. It was called 'Gravelpit Carping with Andy Little featuring David Seaman'. This was back in 1990 and I really thought I had hit the big time. It was an instruction video with Andy teaching me, although I already knew a fair bit by then. During the filming, I even caught a 22 pound fish – my personal best at the time. It was a decent video and it sold quite well but I have since gone on to programmes with slightly larger audiences. It has all helped me become used to being in front of the camera. The nerves have gone and I now feel quite comfortable with it.

Except this one time in 1999 when I found myself worrying that my reputation in the fishing world was about to be destroyed because of a daft TV programme. It all began when Debbie was approached by Noel Edmonds's production team and asked if she would help them set me up for a 'Gotcha'. She agreed on condition they came up with something to do with fishing, to make it easier to get me interested. They faxed through details of a 'programme' they wanted me to appear on called 'Catch of the Day'. In this, celebrities went fishing and what they caught was cooked and served up as a meal at the end of the show. I thought it was a joke at first but Bruno Brookes, who does Sky's fishing programme, was presenting it and Debbie told me it was a good 'fee' so, in the end, I agreed to do it.

After training with Arsenal, I drove along with Debbie to meet the film crew. I put all my fishing gear on and went down to the lake but there they said they had already caught a suitable fish in the morning. They lifted a net out of the water and in it was a huge pike – a full 29 pounds. Immediately I was worried because they had killed this fish and everyone watching was going to think I had a part in it, especially as the crew wanted to fake some shots to make it look as though I had caught it. I had one of the crew hanging on to the end of my line so that it would appear the fish was pulling it. I thought they were only shooting me but one of the cameras had a wide shot with both of us in the frame.

I felt stupid, but I was committed to doing the programme so I felt I had to play along. But I did take Bruno aside and warn him that people would go mad if they thought we had caught a fish of that size just to eat it. He did not seem bothered, though, and told me not to worry. Then, as we arrived at the pub where the fish was going to be cooked and served, I recognised Noel Edmonds's Jag outside. I was pretty certain it was his as it was a new XJR – the same as one I had seen him getting into at the BBC. But it was empty, so I could not be 100 per cent sure, even though I had also recognised the make-up girl from the last time I had been a guest on Noel's show.

In the pub, the man supposedly from the fishery told me how proud they were that I had come fishing there and that they had heard I had caught their most famous pike, 'Mike'. I turned to Bruno again and said, 'You've killed their top pike.' He looked horrified but, before we could talk any more, this little girl was brought on to read a poem about 'Mike the Pike'. It was all about celebrities catching him and having photos taken before releasing him back to his home.

I was thinking, hoping, that this had to be a wind-up but nothing was given away and I was not certain enough to call a halt. It would have been just too embarrassing to do that and then find out it was for real after all. It was only when the pike was brought on by the chef and I recognised Noel behind the disguise that I knew for sure.

Noel raised the silver dome from the plate and, sure enough, instead of 'Mike', there was my Gotcha.

Although I had half-guessed – mainly because the fish had been so big – it made a good Gotcha. Just in case anybody out there is still worried about the fish, I can assure you that 'Mike' had actually been bought from Billingsgate fish market that same morning.

But – Gotchas apart – I enjoy being on TV. I would be happy to be a football pundit but just would not want to be doing it all the time like Andy Gray or Alan Hansen as it would start cutting across everything else I wanted to do. But, in case they never ask me, here are a few points I would like to make about the game, especially the referees, the rules and the impact of foreign players:

Firstly, referees must go professional and the sooner the better. There was a stage a few years back when they started coming to clubs, taking part in training sessions, talking to players, explaining new laws. But referees have other jobs and calls on their time so it was no surprise to us when this soon fizzled out. But they should be doing more of that with clubs and players, not less. I would like to see them referee our practice games. That way, while we were learning more about the game's rules from them, they would pick up a better understanding of why certain tackles are made and make a better job of spotting the difference between the malicious and the accidental.

For the first half of last season, red cards were being given out for silly things, and all it meant was that top-class players were in the stands instead of on the pitch. Nobody wants that, not the clubs who pay their wages, not the fans who pay to watch their best team and certainly not the players. But players have a responsibility, too, and not just to avoid making dangerous tackles. Most players accept opponents not being sent off if the second yellow card is for something silly like a handball, so refs should be allowed to use their discretion. But we have all seen some players taking dives, faking injuries or waving imaginary cards to intimidate the ref into a sending off. That is nothing more or less than cheating.

Only three things in football are guaranteed to make me angry: cheating, elbowing and players spitting at other players. There have been many good things about the top foreign players coming into our game but there is no doubt that they have also brought an increase in all three.

Spitting is the lowest of the low. I am not sure if I could control myself if someone spat in my face. I think I would hit them and walk straight off down the tunnel. Although he had been provoked, there was no excuse for Patrick Vieira spitting at Neil Ruddock in our game against West Ham last season. Ruddock did well to hold himself back and not react. I like Patrick and he is a great player but I would have decked him if he had done that to me.

Frank Rijkaard was a great player for Holland and became the national coach, but I will always remember him most for spitting at a German player in an international.

The worst case of elbowing last season was in fact from an English player, Wimbledon's Ben Thatcher in a game against Sunderland. He could have broken Nicky Summerbee's neck and you could see from the look on his face that it was deliberate. It was the same when John Fashanu caught Gary Mabbutt a few seasons back – totally unnecessary. I agree with video evidence being used for this kind of incident if it has been missed by the ref, and I still thought Thatcher was let off fairly lightly. I am sure that if he had been a higher profile player with a bigger club, the punishment would have been greater.

The FA certainly likes to make examples of big-name players, which is completely unfair. The punishment should be the same for the same offence, not loaded because you are supposedly a bigger role model.

Punishments on the field also vary too much, but that is because there is such a big difference between referees. This applies just as much abroad as here. With most Italian and French referees, virtually no contact is allowed but then we will have one who lets everything go. I think it is a better game when it is allowed to flow, but referees do have a thankless task because they are hammered by their assessor if they haven't given all the free-kicks. I can't see why they can't use the advantage rule, as they do in rugby. There the game can run on for a couple of minutes before being pulled back for a foul if, at the end of it, there is no advantage.

Now that they use the same pool of refs for all Premiership games, we know what to expect when we see which one we have for each game. Some, like Graham Poll, we can talk back to and have a laugh with. We can even swear and not be pulled up for it. Players never complain if referees swear at them as it is only industrial language, after all. But some referees won't allow any swearing from players, even at each other.

We all want consistency, and that is why refs should turn professional. If there was a professional body then surely they would be able to talk to managers and players and establish more common ground. As it is, we find ourselves having games reffed by Uriah Rennie, who is bordering on being over-aggressive on the pitch himself. His physique and whole attitude are intimidating, and he seems to push himself into situations and make them worse rather than better. At the same time, he can miss the most obvious incidents like Matt Elliott's elbowing of Michael Owen last season.

As I said, I am in favour of video evidence but I don't believe in stopping a game to look at replays. I was, though, pleased to hear that they are developing the technology to prove when the whole of the ball has crossed the line for a goal. We must do something to stop ridiculous situations like Mark Hughes's 'goal' for Southampton last season which hit the boards at the back of the net and came straight out. Everyone knew it was a goal except for the ref, who waved play on.

Other than that, the only rule change I would like to see is one outlawing offsides right up by the centre line. They should draw a line halfway between the centre and the penalty area with players only being flagged offside on the penalty area side of it. Tony Adams would probably disagree, but nothing is more frustrating than seeing someone just inside the opposition's half being flagged.

In fairness, that does not happen as much as it used to in the English game. I believe we have the most exciting league in the world here, now. When I was starting in the game, the trend was for all the top players to play in Italy; now the Premiership is attracting them. It has given fans a chance to see players they would only ever have seen on the TV before but there is a downside. Just as happened in Italy, our own players are starting to be squeezed out. Today, 18- and 19-year-olds, who would once have been coming through early to the first team, are finding their way blocked not just by 11 players but by squads of 18 or 20 top players, most of them foreign internationals.

There are moves afoot to put a limit on the number of overseas players playing for a club's first team. I am not sure this restriction would ever be allowed under European law, but I would certainly not want to see English clubs regularly putting out teams with seven or more foreigners. Chelsea do that all the time and Arsenal were guilty of it in many games last season. If quotas are ruled out, I would like to think our game will find its own balance in the end, as I am sure fans will want to see more young British players in their sides once the novelty of having foreign players has worn off.

Football tends to move in cycles, and it will be interesting to see if the trend for squad rotation is also reversed. There is a lot to be said for keeping a settled side, although I appreciate the problem of keeping players fit and sharp when there are so many high-pressure games coming along so fast.

Although all the money coming into the game has been good for the players, it has meant the cost of watching football has gone up dramatically. It was, though, sold too cheaply in the past and that was reflected in the kind of tatty, run-down stadia in which even the top clubs played. There are some superb new stadia being developed now and it is just ironic that the design of some of these now appears to be causing problems with the pitches. Until recently, the standard of pitches had improved immensely from when I first started playing. At that time, even some First Division pitches were little more than mudheaps in the middle of winter. That all changed in the 1990s, but now places like Old Trafford are having trouble again because the new stands are literally overshadowing the pitches. But the techniques of producing good pitches have come on so much that I am sure they will find a way of compensating for the lack of sunlight.

It is not just the facilities at the grounds that have improved. Clubs are now investing in state-of-the art training centres. Midway through last season, Arsenal opened our new one on a 150-acre site at Colney. It is next door to where we used to train but there is no comparison. We now have our own swimming pool with a floor that can be raised to alter the water-depth, so that players with leg injuries can run through it. There are also underwater cameras so the physios can monitor those injuries. There are Jacuzzis, too, and the place even has a full-time chef and a squad of waitresses.

When Nigel, Lee, Tony, Martin and myself first went there, we looked at the youth team players getting changed in these plush surroundings and thought back to the draughty old huts we used to change in and we felt even older than usual. But it was good to be back together with the younger players. Something of a gap had developed between us and them since the changing-rooms at the previous training centre burned down about four years ago. Until the new centre was ready, we were changing at a hotel before being taken by coach straight to the training ground, where the youth players would be changing in Portakabins. As we rarely trained together, we hardly ever saw them. Yet I remember when I was a youth player how exciting it was to mix with the first team. It was also the way we learned how to conduct ourselves as senior pros.

Youth players don't have quite such a hard a time of it off the pitch as they did when I started out. For a start, there is no question of them having to clean our boots or the dressing-room toilets. However, just to even things up a little bit, there is a traditional Arsenal get-together around Christmas which I suspect the senior players look forward to a lot more than most of the youngsters.

This is when all the new apprentices have to sing in front of their mates and everybody else, including first-team players and coaches. They have to choose a carol, get up on a box and belt it out. If they can't get us singing along, there is a price to pay. When Wrighty was there, he would line up buckets of freezing cold water and let them have one if they got the thumbs-down from us. The best moment was when a lad with a Chris Eubank-style lisp announced what he was going to sing. One of his mates must have stitched him up because he let out that it was to be 'Thilent Night' and he had barely got through the first verse before we were all falling about and Wrighty had given him both buckets.

With apprentices not coming into the first team as early as they used to, because we have such a large and experienced first-team squad, it is difficult to know just how good the young players are at Arsenal at the moment. Jermaine Pennant, who came from Notts County, did come on the first-team tour before last season and he looked a decent player, as a winger or striker. But he is only 18 and it could be another two years before he breaks into the first team. He will probably be loaned out first so that he can pick up some first-team experience that way.

Because all the goalies do train together, I have seen a fair bit of the young ones and I predict a good future for Stuart Taylor. He is very tall but is still on the skinny side, as I was at his age. He is already an Under-19 international and he could go all the way. Behind him, Graham Stack has a good chance of making it as well.

Watching them brings home to me just how far I have come and what I have learned along the way. The first thing is that you can learn from everything that happens to you – good and bad. It seemed like the end of the world when Leeds let me go but I still went on to play for England and to win cups and championships in England and Europe. I learned about dealing with disappointment and moving on. Who knows what would have happened if I had stayed in Leeds reserves for another couple of years instead of playing in Peterborough's first team? I learned that to make it to the top and stay there means staying focused on the job in hand. At that stage, this meant playing for Posh and not worrying about what might have been at Leeds.

When Debbie switched from running her agency to working as my manager (well, we thought we might as well keep the ten per cent in the family), the biggest change for her was that she was no longer spending her time looking for business but turning it away instead. I still do work for my favourite charities but increasingly we have to turn other offers of work down. With all the extra games, there simply is not the time any more and playing must always come first.

But, the closer I am coming to the end of my career, the more I realise I will have to focus just as hard on my life after playing. What I may do is take a year off when I retire and do all the things I have had to put to one side while Arsenal and England have taken up so much of my time. I could also use that time to take stock and decide exactly what to do with the rest of my life. I might find something totally different from football, like buying and running my own fishing complex. Or I might develop my TV work. Or do some coaching. Or I might do a little of everything.

One thing is certain. With Debbie and Georgina, my future will still be in Safe Hands.

PLAYING RECORD AND ROLL OF HONOUR
To End of 1999–2000 Season

Full England caps: 59
B internationals: 6
Under-21s: 10

First-Team Appearances

Club	Peterborough	Birmingham	QPR	Arsenal	Total
League	91	75	141	336	643
FA Cup	5	5	17	43	70
League Cup	10	4	13	32	59
European Cups	--	--	--	41	41
Charity Shield	--	--	--	3	3
Others	--	--	4	2	6
Total	106	84	175	457	822

Club Honours

Birmingham
    1984–5 Promotion from old Divison Two

Arsenal
    1990–1 Division One Championship
    1992–3 FA Cup
    1992–3 League Cup
    1993–4 European Cup-Winners Cup
    1997–8 Premiership winner
    1997–8 FA Cup
    1998 Charity Shield winner

Other Personal Honours Include:

1994–5 Arsenal Player of the Year (Supporters Club)

1994–5 Arsenal Player of the Season (Junior Gunners)

1996 Euro 96 Player of the Tournament (Philips)

1996 Best Sporting Achievement (Capital Radio – for Euro 96)

1996 Radar Abbey National People of the Year Award (for Euro 96)

1996 Yorkshire Sporting Achievement Award (for Euro 96)

1996–7 England Player of the Year (Green Flag)

1997 MBE

1997 Special Directors' award for record number of appearances as goalkeeper for the club

1998 Goalkeeper of the Year (*The Footies* – BSkyB/Soccer Stars)

1998 Best-dressed Sportsman (*Elle* Magazine Style Award)